ANNE GRUNEBERG • JEAN LACROIX

with the collaboration of
ROSALIE GOMES • VIVIENNE VERMES

Translations by KAREN DUBOIS, JOHN THOMSON

Illustrations : LA MOUCHE, XAVIER DE SIERRA, ZAÜ

Cover design : ZAÜ ET GAËL

Design concept : CLAUDINE COMBALIER

And many thanks to Jean Gruneberg for all his help.

CLE International
79, avenue Denfert-Rochereau
75014 Paris

 ISBN 2.19.033602.3

WELCOME TO VOIE EXPRESS !

Maybe you have never learned French, and feel that now is the time to start. Maybe you learned French years ago, and want to brush up. Maybe you're also interested in finding out about France and the French, and, if you're going to the country, you'll also want to find your way around its customs and culture. Maybe you're going to work with the French, and need the basis of a business vocabulary. Maybe you're just a traveller who likes to talk. . . . Whoever you are, the authors of Voie Express wish you a warm welcome: in French — BIENVENUE!

They have carefully thought out a complete, step-by-step guide to the French language.

What you will find in Voie Express

- *THE BOOK contains dialogues, vocabulary lists, exercises, games, articles about France, a short story, a tourist guide and a 1,500-word glossary.*
- *FOUR CASSETTES totalling six hours, with dialogues, exercises and games.*
- *A BOOKLET with a complete transcript of what's on the cassettes, translations of the dialogues, and a grammar guide.*

Now you know the basic structure, it's up to you to use Voie Express as you wish. Depending on your time, and your preferences, you can tailor Voie Express to fit your own specific needs.

... For the serious student

Follow the Voie Express method step-by-step. Each lesson begins with a dialogue CONTACTS. Listen to simple, practical French in everyday situations, practise your comprehension, and acquire vocabulary.

All the dialogues are on cassette, with a selection of important phrases highlighted at the end of each dialogue. Listen for the sound signal, stop the tape, repeat, and practise your pronunciation and intonation.

Important words and expressions used in the dialogues, as well as other related vocabulary items, can be found under the headings WORDS and HOW TO SAY IT. Learn them all, and you'll go a long way !

REMEMBER gives you a guide to some grammatical points, and some pitfalls not to fall into! And . . .

. . . For those who want to speak fluently

ORAL PRACTICE gives you a chance to concentrate on the spoken language, with a series of structured exercises on cassette (again with sound signals for you to stop the tape and speak). Grammar buffs will find explanations of all the structures in the grammar guide in the booklet.

. . . For those who like things in writing

At the end of each unit you will find WRITTEN PRACTICE, a series of exercises on all the French you have acquired in the preceding five lessons.

. . . For those who like competition

even against themselves!
You can count up your scores at the end of each unit in the section *TEST YOURSELF.*

If you have done all of the above, you might be ready for a bit of fun (in French, of course !) So . . .

. . . For the more frivolous

You will find, in each unit: Short, humorous accounts of all that's good and bad in France, and what awaits the unsuspecting traveller. A selection of famous French songs, with their translations. Listening games, as well as word puzzles, quizzes and crosswords to fill in on the page. A brief guide to French slang, so you can communicate at street level, even if you haven't grasped how to say it the straight way. A short suspense story, in four episodes. Who is Martin Daniel, or is it Daniel Martin? You will start by reading in English and end up reading French without even noticing how it happened!

... And, for the practical traveller

At the end of the book, *PRACTICAL INFORMATION* *tells you where to go, what to do, and how to get around. Useful addresses of hotels, restaurants and museums, as well as prices, maps and travel tips for when you first arrive in France.*
. . . And, of course, a 1,500-word glossary.

So, whether you've been bitten by the language bug and want to really go for French in the fast lane, or whether you want to take it easy and learn by listening and having fun, you'll find there's something for you in VOIE EXPRESS.

In any case, you're on the right track, or, as they say in French: Vous êtes sur la bonne voie!

The Authors

UNIT 1

HOW TO INTRODUCE YOURSELF

1.1 CONTACTS

[• •] *Listen*

UN CONGRÈS INTERNATIONAL

À Paris, dans le palais des expositions du CNIT situé dans le quartier de la Défense

L'organisateur : — *Mesdames, Messieurs, en tant qu'organisateur du 19e Congrès International des Techniques Nouvelles, je vous souhaite la bienvenue à Paris. Maintenant, je voudrais demander aux différents intervenants de se présenter.*

— *Je me présente : Nakoto Nakajima.*
Je suis japonais.
Je suis ingénieur électronicien.
Je travaille chez Pioneer, nos bureaux sont à Tokyo.

— *Je me présente : John Smith.*
Je suis anglais.
Je dirige le service après-vente chez I.B.M. à Londres.

— *Hans Fischer.*
Je suis allemand.
Je suis responsable des études techniques.
Je travaille chez Grundig, à l'usine de Stuttgart.

— *Je m'appelle Hélène Dufour.*
Je suis française.
Je suis informaticienne.
Je travaille au Musée de la Villette à Paris.

— *Mon nom est Jane Thomas.*
Je suis américaine, je viens du Texas.
Je travaille chez Hewlett Packard, à Seattle.
Je m'occupe du service commercial.

— *Je suis Omar Diop.*
Je viens du Sénégal.
Je suis agronome.
Je travaille au ministère de l'Agriculture.

L'organisateur : — *Maintenant vous connaissez les noms et fonctions des différents intervenants ; la séance est ouverte.*
Voici l'exposé de M. Nakajima.

[• •] Listen and repeat
(You may look at the translation on page 1 in the booklet.)

1. C.N.I.T. (Centre National des Industries et des Techniques)
2. Vue du quartier de la Défense, à l'ouest de Paris

1.1 WORDS

congrès (M) — conference, congress
palais (M) — exhibition centre
exposition (F) — exhibition
quartier (M) — district or area of a city
organisateur (M) — coordinator, organiser
ingénieur (M) — engineer
bureau (M) — office
service après-vente (M) — after-sales service
informaticien(ne) — data processor
musée (M) — museum
responsable (M) — person in charge
étude (F) — study, research project
usine (F) — factory
nom (M) — surname
service commercial (M) — sales department
agronome (M ou F) — agronomist
ministère (M) — ministry
fonction (F) — job, professional function
séance (F) — session
exposé (M) — lecture, paper

M *la France* — France **(1)**
l'Angleterre — England
F *la Grande-Bretagne* — Great Britain
l'Allemagne — Germany
l'Espagne — Spain
l'Italie — Italy
M *la Belgique* — Belgium
M *le Sénégal* — Senegal
M *le Japon* — Japan
M *le Canada* — Canada
P *les États-Unis* — the United States
siège social (M) — company headquarters
banque (F) — bank
directeur (trice) — director, manager

assistant(e) — assistant
comptable (M ou F) — accountant
secrétaire (M ou F) — secretary
service (M) — department

se présenter — to introduce oneself
être — to be
travailler — to work
diriger — to manage, to direct
s'appeler — to be called
venir (de) — to come (from)
s'occuper (de) — to look after, to be in charge of
connaître — to know, to be acquainted with

international(e) — international
nouveau (nouvelle) — new
japonais(e) — Japanese **(2)**
anglais(e) — English
français(e) — French
allemand(e) — German
américain(e) — American

---

espagnol(e) — Spanish
italien(ne) — Italian
canadien(ne) — Canadian
mexicain(e) — Mexican
belge — Belgian
sénégalais — Senegalese

HOW TO SAY IT

1. INTRODUCING YOURSELF

Je me présente : John Smith — Let me introduce myself, I'm John Smith
Je suis John Smith — I am John Smith
Je m'appelle John Smith — My name is John Smith
Mon nom est John Smith — My name is John Smith ***(3)***

2. SAYING WHERE YOU'RE FROM

(your nationality)
Je suis japonais — I am Japanese
Je viens du Japon — I come from Japan

3. GIVING YOUR OCCUPATION

Je suis ingénieur électronicien — I am an electrical engineer ***(4)***
Je dirige le service des achats
Je suis responsable du service des achats — I'm in charge of the purchasing department
Je m'occupe du service des achats
Je travaille au musée de la Villette — I work at the Villette Museum
Je suis de la société Grundig — I'm from Grundig

4. WELCOMING

Je vous souhaite la bienvenue — I'd like to welcome you
Bienvenu(e) à Paris — Welcome to Paris

REMEMBER... REMEMBER... REMEMBER... REMEMBER... REMEMBER

(1) *In French the names of countries are preceded by the definite article. See grammar page 40.* — ***(2)*** *In French the adjectives of nationality are always written with a small letter.* — ***(3)*** *« Nom » refers to your surname, « prénom » to your first name.* — ***(4)*** *A profession is given without the definite article : je suis ingénieur.*

1.1 ORAL PRACTICE

1. GRAMMAR : SEE PAGE 41

GIVING YOUR NATIONALITY : MASCULINE FORMS

Listen :

(France)
— Je suis français.
(Angleterre)
— Je suis anglais.

NOW, GIVE YOUR NATIONALITY, IMAGINING YOU ARE FROM THE FOLLOWING COUNTRIES :

(France) — (Angleterre) — (Allemagne) — (États-Unis) — (Japon) — (Sénégal) — (Espagne) — (Canada)

2. GRAMMAR : SEE PAGE 41

NATIONALITIES : FEMININE FORMS

Listen :

(américain)
— Elle est américaine.
(anglais)
— Elle est anglaise.

NOW, CHANGE THE MASCULINE FORMS OF THE NATIONALITIES INTO THE FEMININE FORMS :

(américain) — (anglais) — (belge) — (italien) — (allemand) — (français) — (japonais) — (espagnol) — (canadien)

3. GRAMMAR : SEE PAGE 41

STATING NATIONALITY

Listen :

(japonais) : (je)
— Je suis japonais.
(il)
— Il est japonais.
(elle)
— Elle est japonaise.

NOW, GIVE THE CORRECT FORM OF THE FOLLOWING NATIONALITIES, ACCORDING TO THE PRONOUN, CHANGING THE VERB AS NECESSARY :

(japonais) : (je), (il), (elle) — (américaine) : (je), (il) — (allemand) : (elle), (je) — (français) : (il)

4. GRAMMAR : SEE PAGE 46

VERB PRACTICE : THE VERB « ÊTRE »

Listen :

(je)
— Je suis ingénieur.
(il)
— Il est ingénieur.

NOW, GIVE THE CORRECT FORM OF THE VERB « ÊTRE », ACCORDING TO THE SUBJECT :

(je) — (il) — (Françoise) — (nous) — (vous) — (Béatrice et Anne) — (tu) — (elle) — (Pierre et Jean)

5. GRAMMAR : SEE PAGE 41

PROFESSIONS : MASCULINE AND FEMININE FORMS :

Listen :

(Pierre — informaticien)
— Pierre est informaticien.
(Hélène)
— Hélène est informaticienne.

NOW, CHANGE THE FOLLOWING SENTENCES USING THE NAMES AND PROFESSIONS GIVEN. REMEMBER TO USE THE MASCULINE OR FEMININE FORM OF THE PROFESSION, ACCORDING TO EACH PERSON'S NAME :

(Pierre-informaticien), (Hélène) — (Brigitte-directrice), (Jean-Pierre) — (Philippe-comptable), (Corinne) — (Marc-assistant), (Béatrice)

6. GRAMMAR : SEE PAGE 46

GIVING YOUR NAME, JOB AND PLACE OF WORK :

Listen :

(Jacques Blanc)
— Je m'appelle Jacques Blanc.
(ingénieur)
— Je suis ingénieur.
(chez Grundig)
— Je travaille chez Grundig.

NOW, IMAGINE YOU ARE EACH OF THE FOLLOWING PEOPLE AND GIVE YOUR NAME, JOB AND PLACE OF WORK :

(Jacques Blanc) (ingénieur) (chez Grundig) — (Catherine Clément) (agronome) (au ministère) — (Philippe Pouchain) (informaticien) (chez Renault) — (Didier Calamec) (directeur commercial) (chez Danone)

A SIMPLE "BONJOUR"

'ou are at a café in Montparnasse. 'erhaps you are waiting for a French riend you have met a couple of imes, and you like each other. Maybe 's love at first sight, maybe it's just warm camaraderie. Your friend arives, sauntering happily down the oulevard. Now what do you do?

ı England it would be a friendly Hello", in the States a welcoming Hi". In France, there are the delightıl and near-obligatory kisses on either ide of the face. A lovely custom — ut one that leaves room for a multude of complications. How many isses do you give? One? It's just not done". Two? Yes, often... but, h dear, does it reveal a meanness f spirit? Three? Why not? But then there's that awful hesitation as to whether or not to indulge in a fourth. Four? Yes, but aren't we overdoing things just a little bit?

THE HANDSHAKE *You're about to go into a business meeting with some French colleagues. Ah, here, at least, you can get away from the traumas of the informal greeting. Sorry, no. It just won't do to smile and say: "Bonjour. Très heureux de faire votre connaissance." You must go through the handshaking ceremony. And it's not just at the first meeting. Walk into any French company and you'll see work colleagues doing the rounds, faithfully shaking hands first thing in the morning (and, incidentally, at the end of the day). On a Monday morning, your arm vibrates, your fingers go numb and your head spins as all your French friends say "Hello" in their own particular way.*

"A VOTRE SANTÉ!" *Does it all seem suddenly very complicated? Do not despair, it's all just a bit of fun, really. Head down to the nearest bistro and drown your sorrows. A guarantee: after a good bottle of Beaujolais, all the French you never knew will suddenly come rushing back to you. (And one last word of consolation: the way of saying "Cheers!" in French is very simple. It's only "A votre santé" or one word "Santé!"* □

Listen ***J'ai rendez-vous avec vous***

Georges Brassens

Mon Seigneur l'astre solaire,
Comme je ne l'admire pas beaucoup,
M'enlève son feu, oui mais de son feu,
Moi je m'en fous
J'ai rendez-vous avec vous.
La lumière que je préfère
C'est celle de vos yeux jaloux,
Tout le restant m'indiffère,
J'ai rendez-vous avec vous.
Monsieur mon propriétaire
Comme je lui dévaste tout,
Me chasse de son toit, oui mais de son toit,
Moi je m'en fous
J'ai rendez-vous avec vous.
La demeure que je préfère
C'est votre robe à froufrous,
Tout le restant m'indiffère,
J'ai rendez-vous avec vous.
Madame ma gargotière
Comme je lui dois trop de sous
Me chasse de sa table, oui mais de sa table,
Moi je m'en fous
J'ai rendez-vous avec vous.
Le menu que je préfère
C'est la chair de votre cou
Tout le restant m'indiffère,
J'ai rendez-vous avec vous.
Sa majesté financière
Comme je ne fais rien à son goût,
Garde son or, or de son or, moi je m'en fous
J'ai rendez-vous avec vous.
La fortune que je préfère
C'est votre cœur d'amadou
Tout le restant m'indiffère,
J'ai rendez-vous avec vous.

I Have a Rendez-vous With You

My Lord, the solar star,
As I don't admire him enough,
Has taken his fire away from me,
Yes, but I don't care about his heat,
I have a rendez-vous with you.
The light that I love best
Comes from your jealous eyes,
All the rest leaves me cold,
I have a rendez-vous with you.
My landlord,
As I ransacked everything,
Drove me from under his roof,
Yes, but I don't care about his dwelling,
I have a rendez-vous with you.
The home that I love best
Is your swishing dress,
I'm unmoved by all the rest,
I have a rendez-vous with you.
Madame, who sells her seedy snacks,
As I owe her too much money,
Has driven me away from her table,
Yes, but I don't care about her table,
I have a rendez-vous with you.
The dish that I love best
Is your neck's tender flesh,
The rest doesn't whet my appetite,
I have a rendez-vous with you.
The high and mighty financier,
As I do nothing to please him,
Keeps his gold to himself,
Yes, but I don't care about his gold,
I have a rendez-vous with you.
The fortune that I want to keep
Is the coals of your heart that can light like a flame
All the rest leaves me cold,
I have a rendez-vous with you.

Put the number of the flag in the appropriate box.

2 *Japon* 5 *Canada* 6 *Union soviétique* 3 *États-Unis*

1 *Grande-Bretagne* 4 *Suissc*

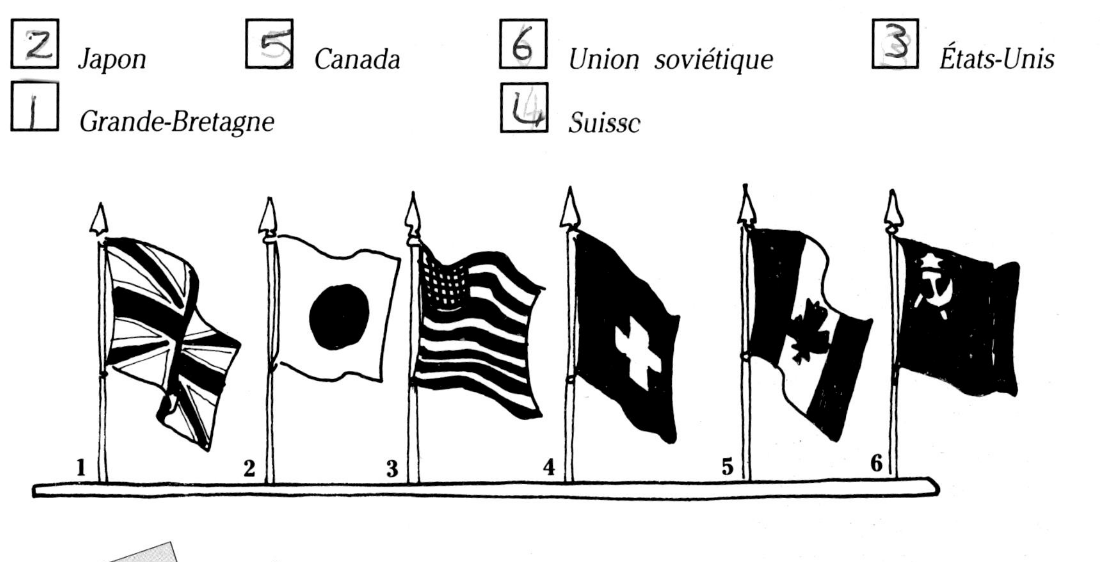

N° 2

Where would you see the objects in the illustration ? Put the numbers in the appropriate box beside each city.

6 *Venise* 1 *Londres* 4 *Rome* 5 *Bruxelles* 3 *Le Caire*

2 *Paris*

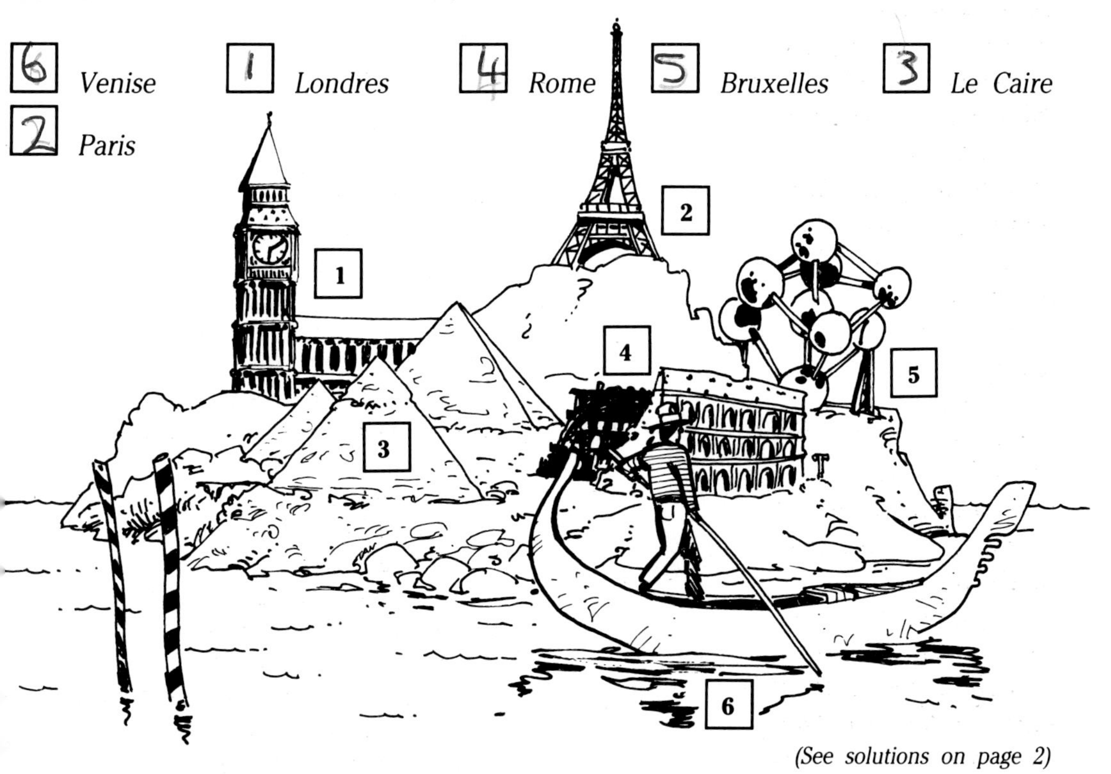

(See solutions on page 2)

1.2 CONTACTS

 *Listen*

A L'HÔTEL

A Paris, à la réception de l'hôtel Méridien, dans le 17e arrondissement, près de la place de l'Étoile

Le réceptionniste : *Bonsoir, Madame.*

La cliente : *Bonsoir, Monsieur. J'ai réservé une chambre pour deux nuits. Je suis de la société Sony.*

Le réceptionniste : *Très bien, Madame. Votre nom, s'il vous plaît ?*

La cliente : *Otsuka.*

Le réceptionniste : *Un instant, s'il vous plaît. Otsuka... Otsuka ?... Je suis désolé, Madame. Je n'ai pas ce nom.*

La cliente : *Comment ? Mais c'est impossible ! Ma secrétaire a réservé.*

Le réceptionniste : *Otsuka ?... Vous pouvez épeler, s'il vous plaît ?*

La cliente : *O-T-S-U-K-A. Akiko Otsuka !*

Le réceptionniste : *Non, je n'ai pas de chambre au nom de Otsuka. Mais... excusez-moi, quel est votre prénom ?*

La cliente : *Akiko.*

Le réceptionniste : *Ah, je comprends ! Otsuka est votre nom de famille et Akiko votre prénom !*

La cliente : *Exactement.*

Le réceptionniste : *Sur le registre vous êtes inscrite à Akiko. Vous avez bien une réservation pour deux nuits.*

La cliente : *Ah, bon !*

Le réceptionniste : *Excusez-moi, Madame. Veuillez remplir cette fiche, s'il vous plaît... Merci, Madame !...*
Voilà votre clé. C'est la chambre 430, au quatrième étage.

La cliente : *C'est bien la chambre 430 ?*

Le réceptionniste : *Oui, oui. C'est au quatrième étage et l'ascenseur est au fond du hall, à droite.*

La cliente : *Merci.*

Le réceptionniste : *Bonne soirée, Madame !*

[• •] Listen and repeat
(You may look at the translation on page 3 in the booklet.)

c de Triomphe et la Place de l'Etoile

2. Réception dans un hôtel ancien

3. Réception dans un hôtel moderne

1.2 WORDS

hôtel (M) — hotel
réception (F) — reception desk
arrondissement (M) — arrondissement (an administrative division of a French city)
place (F) — square
réceptionniste (M ou F) — receptionist
client(e) — client, customer, (hotel) guest
chambre (F) — bedroom
nuit (F) — night
prénom (M) — first name, Christian name
nom de famille (M) — surname
nationalité (F) — nationality
registre (M) — register
réservation (F) — reservation, booking
fiche (F) — in a hotel, I.D. form
clé (F) — key
étage (M) — floor, storey
ascenseur (M) — lift, elevator
hall (M) — foyer, hall, lobby

---

chambre individuelle (F) — single room
chambre double (F) — double room
lit (M) — bed
rez-de-chaussée -R.C.- (M) — ground floor

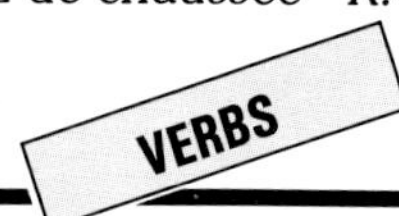

réserver — to reserve, to book

avoir — to have
pouvoir — to be able, can
épeler — to spell
comprendre — to understand
remplir — to fill, to fill in
compter — to count ***(1)***

impossible — impossible
sûr(e) — sure, certain

---

complet(ète) — full
cher(ère) — dear, expensive

---

premier(ère) — first
deuxième — second
troisième — third
quatrième — fourth
cinquième — fifth
sixième — sixth
septième — seventh
huitième — eighth
neuvième — ninth
dixième — tenth
vingtième — twentieth

REMEMBER... REMEMBER... REMEMBER... REMEMBER... REMEMBER

(1) *For reference all numbers are written in French at the bottom of each page. —* ***(2)*** *A statement can be transformed into a question simply by giving it a rising intonation (see grammar page 46). —* ***(3)*** *« Bonjour » : when you go into shops, it is customary to say « bonjour » before addressing people. « Monsieur » and « Madame » are much more frequently used in French than « Sir » and « Madam » in English. They can be dropped in very informal situations, but when in doubt it is best to use them. « Mademoiselle » is used for teenage girls and youg unmarried women.*

HOW TO SAY IT

1. ASKING SOMEONE'S SURNAME

Quel est votre nom ? — What's your surname ?
Comment vous appelez-vous ? — What's your name ?
Votre nom, s'il vous plaît ? — Your name, please ? ***(2)***

2. ASKING SOMEONE'S FIRST NAME

Quel est votre prénom ? — What's your first name ?
Votre prénom, s'il vous plaît ? — Your first name, please ?

3. ASKING ABOUT SPELLING

Vous pouvez épeler, s'il vous plaît ? — Could you spell that, please ?
Comment ça (cela) s'écrit ? — How is that spelt ?

4. GREETING SOMEONE

a) formally

Bonjour Madame/Monsieur — Good morning/good afternoon ***(3)***
Bonsoir Madame/Monsieur — Good evening

b) informally

Bonjour — Hello (morning, afternoon)
Bonsoir — Hello (evening)

5. SAYING GOODBYE

Au revoir (Madame, Monsieur) — Goodbye
Bonsoir — Good night (early in the evening)
Bonne nuit — Good night (late in the evening)
A tout à l'heure — See you later (the same day)
A bientôt — See you soon
A ce soir/à demain — See you tonight/tomorrow
A jeudi — See you on Thursday

6. GIVING SOMEONE YOUR GENERAL GOOD WISHES

Bonne journée ! — Have a nice day !
Bon après-midi ! — Have a nice afternoon !
Bonne soirée ! — Have a nice evening !

7. APOLOGISING

Pardon / *Excusez-moi* — I'm sorry
Je suis (vraiment) désolé(e) — I'm (terribly) sorry

8. EXPRESSING SURPRISE

Comment ? — Pardon ? (What ?)
C'est impossible ! — That's impossible !
C'est incroyable ! — That's incredible !
Ce n'est pas vrai ! — That's can't be true !

1.2 ORAL PRACTICE

1. SEE PAGE 16

SPELLING IN FRENCH

Listen

(CHURCHILL)

C-H-U-R-C-H-I-LL

NOW, SPELL THE FOLLOWING SURNAMES:

(CHURCHILL) — (JAEGER) — (KENNEDY) — (ROBERTSON) — (O'REILLY) — (PHILLIPS) — (WILLIAMSON)

2. SEE PAGE 18

NUMBERS

Listen :

(chambre 15/1er étage)

— Je suis à la chambre 15 au premier étage.

NOW, SAY WHERE YOUR HOTEL ROOM IS:

(chambre 15/1er étage) — (chambre 22/2e étage) — (chambre 36/3e étage) — (chambre 48/4e étage) — (chambre 51/5e étage) — (chambre 69/6e étage) — (chambre 75/7e étage) — (chambre 80/8e étage).

3. GRAMMAR : SEE PAGE 46

ASKING PEOPLE TO REPEAT

Listen :

(Je suis Mme Dubois)

— Pardon, quel est votre nom ?

(Je suis française)

— Pardon, quelle est votre nationalité ?

NOW, ASK PEOPLE TO REPEAT THEIR NAMES OR NATIONALITIES:

(Je suis Mme Dubois), (Je suis française) — (Je suis M. Verret), (Je suis belge) — (Je suis M. Santos), (Je suis espagnol) — (Je suis Mme Barre), (Je suis canadienne) — (Je suis Mademoiselle Brown), (Je suis américaine)

4. GRAMMAR : SEE PAGE 46

VERB PRACTICE : THE VERB « AVOIR »

Listen :

(Je)

— J'ai la chambre 102.

(Elle)

— Elle a la chambre 102.

NOW, GIVE THE CORRECT FORM OF THE VERB « AVOIR », ACCORDING TO THE SUBJECT:

(je) — (elle) — (vous) — (il) — (nous) — (M. et Mme Dévé) — (tu) — (je) — (M. et Mme Laubeuf)

5. GRAMMAR : SEE PAGE 46

INTONATION QUESTIONS

Listen :

(Elle a une chambre)

— Elle a une chambre ?

(Il est au 4e étage)

— Il est au 4e étage ?

NOW, TURN THE FOLLOWING STATEMENTS INTO QUESTIONS BY CHANGING THE INTONATION:

(Elle a une chambre) — (Il est au 4e étage) — (Elle a une réservation) — (Elle est de la société Sony) — (C'est au fond du hall) — (Elle est réceptionniste) — (Il travaille à l'hôtel) — (Elle est japonaise).

6. GRAMMAR : SEE PAGE 46

NEGATIVE SENTENCES WITH THE VERB « ÊTRE »

Listen :

(Vous êtes japonais ?)

— Non, je ne suis pas japonais.

(Il est ingénieur ?)

— Non, il n'est pas ingénieur.

NOW, ANSWER THE FOLLOWING SENTENCES WITH THE VERB « ÊTRE » IN THE NEGATIVE FORM:

(Vous êtes japonais ?) — (Il est ingénieur ?) — (Nous sommes au 8e étage ?) — (Vous êtes américain ?) — (Il est à la B.N.P. ?) — (Il est directeur ?) — (Vous êtes à Paris ?) — (Elle est chez Renault ?) — (Je suis à la chambre 15 ?)

HOTELS

For the business traveller in a hurry, France offers the usual comfortable, convenient and reliable hotel chains : the Sofitel, Novotel, Frantel and many others. For the traveller with more time on his hands and an appetite to taste the country, France, true to her individualistic self, offers a varied range of reasonably priced hotels, each with its own distinct personality.

AFTER DARK *The atmosphere of one of the many small reasonably priced family hotels can be a delight. But there are some words of warning. First, do ask to have a look at your room (this is quite acceptable in France). Rooms can vary enormously within the same hotel, and late arrivals can find themselves bundled into a rickety bed in an attic the size of a closet. While checking the room, look in the cupboards for the pillows* (oreillers). *The French can be careless about them, and it's no good looking for them after midnight. A word also about the hours after dark. France's wonderful lighting system must be responsible for many a broken foreign limb. The* minuterie, *as its name suggests, gives you light for just 30 seconds ! So do press it on every floor, or you may find yourself crawling to your room on all fours in the dark.*

A ROOM FOR TWO *Another word of advice : when travelling around France, definitely take along a* Michelin *guide and, if possible, an affable travelling companion, not only for the obvious reasons, not even because France can be so blatantly romantic : it's simply a question of money. In France you pay by the room, not the person, so your partner can cut your costs by half. Incidentally, the price of a room does not always include breakfast, so if you want your croissant and* grand crème *(white coffee), you'll have to pay extra. But hotel prices in France are still way below those of Britain and the United States.*

STREET SYMPHONIES *If you haven't chosen your room carefully, you may find you need that early morning coffee more than you had anticipated. French traffic is not the quietest in the world, especially in Paris, where from midnight onwards on a Saturday night the streets echo to a symphony of shouts and a selection of French vocabulary that you won't find in the grammar books. Either bring your earplugs* (boules Quiès) *or ask for a room that doesn't look on to the street (* sur cour *instead of* sur rue*).*

Having said all this, French hotels still remain among my favourites in the world : the good old-fashioned high beds, the freshness of well-laundered clean cotton sheets, the smell of strong coffee and bread from the local boulangerie — the old world still lives on, even in the middle of modern industrial cities, to say nothing of the small village hotels and the grands châteaux, *that boast, not only delightful accommodation, but often some of the best, and most reasonably priced, French cuisine.*

The range and number of hotels per town mean that booking is not normally a problem, but do beware of the south coast in summer and Paris in September (when many of the trade fairs are held). The bridges on the Seine can be beautiful to look at after midnight, but they're not much fun to sleep under. □

N° 1 ⊡ Listen

Listen to the people on the cassette introducing themselves and then circle the place where they're from on the map.

Listen

Listen to the room numbers and find the right key.

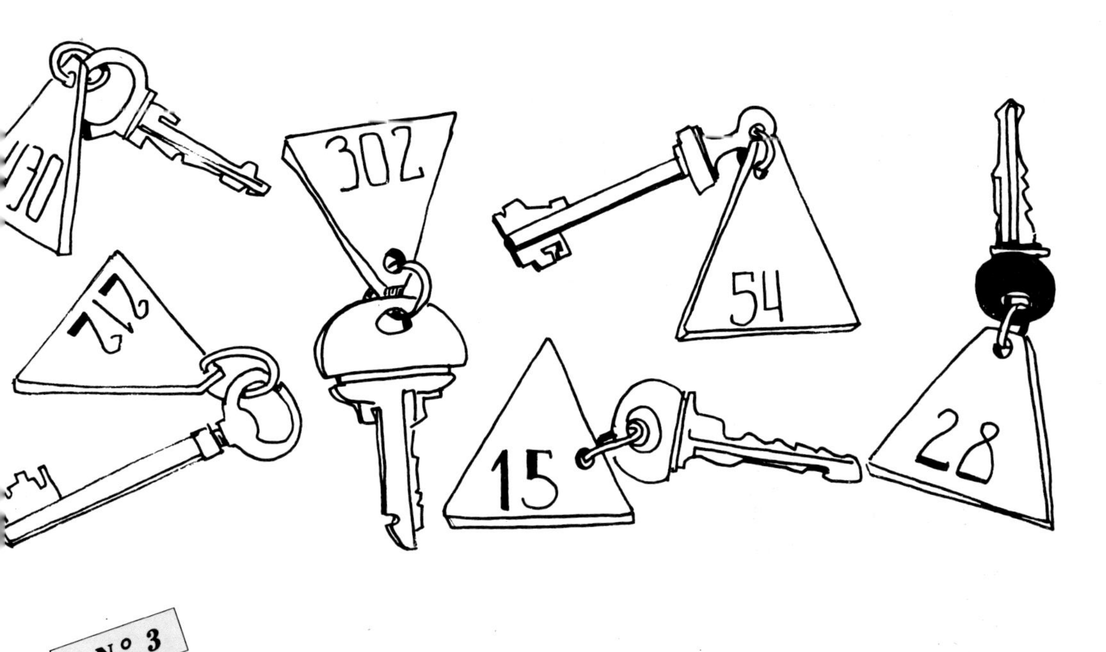

N° 3

Fill in the blanks with the correct nationalities, and another word will appear in the grey column.

1. *American*
2. *Japanese (feminine)*
3. *Italian*
4. *German (feminine)*
5. *French*
6. *English (feminine)*
7. *Mexican (feminine)*
8. *Australian*
9. *Canadian (feminine)*
10. *Spanish (feminine)*
11. *Senegalese*
12. *British*
13. *Belgian*

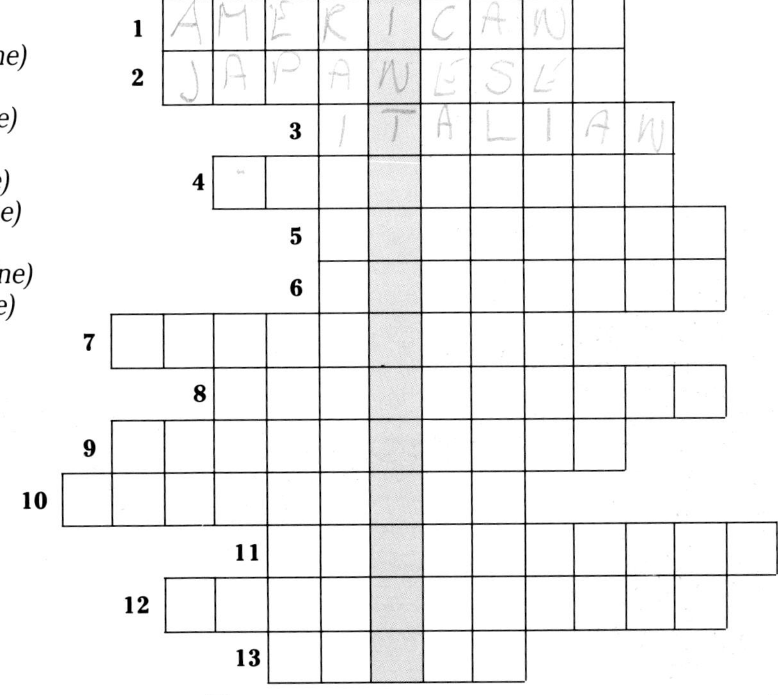

(See solutions on page 4)

1.3 CONTACTS

[• •] *Listen*

DANS UN CAFÉ AUX HALLES

Un homme et une femme assis au bar font connaissance

Le garçon : *Madame ?*

Elle : *Je voudrais un jus d'orange, s'il vous plaît.*

Le garçon : *Bien Madame... Et pour vous, Monsieur ?*

Lui : *Un demi et un paquet de Gitanes filtre.*

Lui : *Pardon Madame, est-ce que vous avez du feu ?*

Elle : *Non, je suis désolée, je ne fume pas.*

Lui : *Ah, je n'ai pas de chance !*

Le garçon : *Tenez, Monsieur ! Voilà une boîte d'allumettes.*

Lui : *Merci beaucoup.*

Elle : *Excusez-moi, vous habitez à Paris ?*

Lui : *Non, mais je connais bien Paris. Pourquoi ?*

Elle : *Je vais au Salon du prêt-à-porter et je ne sais pas exactement où c'est.*

Lui : *Tiens, vous travaillez dans la mode !*

Elle : *Oui, je suis journaliste pour un magazine suisse. Et vous, qu'est-ce que vous faites ?*

Lui : *Je suis responsable des achats pour des magasins de prêt-à-porter au Canada.*

Elle : *Ah, vous travaillez aussi dans la mode ! Vous êtes canadien ?*

Lui : *Non, pas du tout. Je travaille au Canada mais je suis français. Et vous, vous êtes suisse ?*

Elle : *Oui, oui.*

Lui : *Et vous habitez où ?*

Elle : *Devinez !*

Lui : *A Genève ?*

Elle : *Non. A Lausanne. Et vous ?*

Lui : *J'habite Ottawa. Mais je voyage beaucoup.*

Elle : *Evidemment !*

Lui : *Vous savez, je vais aussi au Salon. Je peux vous emmener si vous voulez.*

Elle : *Volontiers.*

Lui : *Je connais de très bons restaurants à côté du Salon. On pourrait déjeuner ensemble.*

Elle : *Pourquoi pas ?*

Lui : *Je m'appelle Frédéric Millau. Tenez, voilà ma carte !*

Elle : *Moi, je m'appelle Françoise Mungler. Mais je n'ai pas de carte de visite sur moi, je suis désolée.*

Lui : *Ce n'est pas grave !...*

[• •] Listen and repeat
(You may look at the translation on page 4 in the booklet.)

1. Centre Beaubourg (Pompidou)
2. Intérieur d'un café parisien traditionnel
3. Forum des Halles
4. Grand couturier parisien
5. Place dans le quartier des Halles
6. Terrasse de café en face du Forum

1.3 WORDS

homme (M) — man
femme (F) — woman
jus d'orange (M) — orange juice ***(1)***
demi (M) — beer (about half a pint)
paquet (M) — pack, packet
Gitanes filtre (F) — Gitane filter cigarettes
boîte (F) — box
allumette (F) — match
salon (M) — trade fair
prêt-à-porter (M) — off the peg
mode (F) — fashion
journaliste (M ou F) — journalist
magazine (M) — magazine
magasin (M) — shop
restaurant (M) — restaurant
carte de visite (F) — business card ***(1)***

---

café (M) — cup of (black) coffee
express (M) — small cup of strong black coffee
thé (M) — cup of tea
crème (M) — cup of white coffee
bière (F) — beer
verre de vin (M) — glass of wine
jus de fruit (M) — fruit juice
cigarette (F) — cigarette
briquet (M) — lighter

suisse — Swiss
canadien(ne) — Canadian
bon(ne) — good

VERBS

vouloir — to want, to wish
fumer — to smoke
habiter — to live ***(2)***
aller — to go
connaître — to know ***(3)***
savoir — to know ***(3)***
faire — to do, to make
deviner — to guess
voyager — to travel
emmener — to take (someone) somewhere
déjeuner — to have lunch

---

boire — to drink
manger — to eat
dîner — to have dinner
prendre son petit déjeuner — to have breakfast
dire — to say, to tell
donner — to give

faire connaissance — to meet (someone)
avoir du feu — to have a light
avoir de la chance — to be lucky
tiens ! — really ***(4)***
tenez — here you are ***(4)***
voilà — there it is, there you are
pas du tout — not at all
évidemment — obviously
ce n'est pas grave — it doesn't matter

REMEMBER... REMEMBER... REMEMBER... REMEMBER... REMEMBER

(1) *Notice the different word order in English and French in the following examples: un jus d'orange (orange juice); un jus de fruit (fruit juice); une carte de visite (a business card).* — ***(2)*** *« Habiter »: you can say « habiter à Paris » or « habiter Paris ».* — ***(3)*** *These two French verbs correspond to the English verb « to know ». « Savoir » means to know facts. « Connaître » means to be acquainted with people and things, or with places you have visited.* — ***(4)*** *« Tiens » and « tenez » are both derived from the verb « tenir »,*

HOW TO SAY IT

1. ASKING WHERE SOMEONE LIVES

Où est-ce que vous habitez ? / *Vous habitez où ?* — Where do you live ?
Vous habitez en Angleterre ? — Do you live in England ?
Vous venez d'où ? — Where do you come from ?
D'où êtes-vous ? — Where are you from ?

2. SAYING WHERE YOU LIVE OR WHERE YOU COME FROM

J'habite en Suisse — I live in Switzerland
Je suis d'Ottawa — I come from Ottawa

3. ASKING ABOUT SOMEONE'S OCCUPATION

Quelle est votre profession ? — What's your job ? ***(5)***
Qu'est-ce que vous faites ? — What do you do ?
Vous travaillez dans la mode ? — Do you work in fashion ?

4. ORDERING FOOD AND DRINK

Je voudrais un café — I would like a coffee
Un jus de fruit, s'il vous plaît — A fruit juice, please
Un demi (s'il vous plaît) — A beer (please)

5. OFFERING HELP

Vous voulez que je vous emmène ? — Would you like me to give you a lift ?
Je peux vous emmener, si vous voulez — I can give you a lift, if you like

6. ACCEPTING OFFERS

Oui, merci — Yes, please
Volontiers / *Avec plaisir* / *Je veux bien* / *D'accord* — I would be glad to ***(6)***

REMEMBER... REMEMBER... REMEMBER... REMEMBER... REMEMBER

*meaning « to hold ». — **(5)** « Quelle est votre profession ? » is only used in very formal situations. — **(6)** These expressions can be used interchangeably.*

1.3 ORAL PRACTICE

1. GRAMMAR : SEE PAGE 46

SAYING WHAT PEOPLE DO FOR A LIVING. VERB PRACTICE : VERBS ENDING IN -ER

Listen :

(Vous travaillez dans la mode) (— je)
— Je travaille dans la mode.
(Madame Leblanc)
— Madame Leblanc travaille dans la mode.

NOW, COMPLETE THE SENTENCES, CHANGING THE VERBS AS NECESSARY :

(Vous)
(je) — (Madame Leblanc) — (nous) — (vous) — (je) — (Chantal et Sophie) — (tu) — (nous) — (vous)

2. GRAMMAR : SEE PAGE 43

ASKING PEOPLE WHERE THEY ARE GOING

Listen :

(le Salon)
— Vous allez au Salon ?
(la réception)
— Vous allez à la réception ?

NOW, ASK QUESTIONS LIKE THESE USING AU/À LA/ À L' :

(le Salon) — (la réception) — (le restaurant) — (l'hôtel) — (la banque) — (l'usine) — (le bureau) — (la chambre 10) — (le café)

3. SEE PAGE 27

ORDERING FOOD AND DRINK

Listen :

(un jus d'orange)
— Je voudrais un jus d'orange, s'il vous plaît.
(un demi)
— Je voudrais un demi, s'il vous plaît.

NOW, USE « JE VOUDRAIS » TO ORDER THE FOLLOWING

(un jus d'orange) — (un demi) — (un café) — (un paquet de Gitanes) — (un thé) — (un sandwich) — (un crème) — (un verre de vin) — (un jus de fruit)

4. GRAMMAR : SEE PAGE 43

COUNTRIES : MASCULINE, FEMININE AND PLURAL

Listen :

(le Canada)
— Il habite au Canada.
(la France)
— Il habite en France.

NOW, USE « AU », « EN » OR « AUX », ACCORDING TO EACH COUNTRY :

(le Canada) — (la France) — (le Japon) — (l'Angleterre) — (les États-Unis) — (l'Allemagne) — (la Suisse) — (le Sénégal)

5. GRAMMAR : SEE PAGE 46

QUESTIONS

Listen :

(Vous avez du feu ?)
— Est-ce que vous avez du feu ?
(Il est journaliste ?)
— Est-ce qu'il est journaliste ?

NOW, TRANSFORM THE QUESTIONS :

(Vous avez du feu ?) — (Il est journaliste ?) — (Elle habite aux États-Unis ?) — (Ils viennent d'Allemagne ?) — (Vous connaissez Jacques ?) — (Elles vont à l'hôtel ?) — (Vous pouvez épeler ?) — (Il dirige la société ?) — (Vous avez une chambre ?)

6. GRAMMAR : SEE PAGE 45

ANSWERING IN THE NEGATIVE FORM

Listen :

(Vous fumez ?)
— Non, je ne fume pas.
(Vous êtes français ?)
— Non, je ne suis pas français.

NOW, ANSWER THE FOLLOWING QUESTIONS USING THE NEGATIVE FORM :

(Vous fumez ?) — (Vous êtes français ?) — (Vous travaillez à Bordeaux ?) — (Vous allez au Salon ?) — (Vous habitez à Bruxelles ?) — (Vous savez où c'est ?) — (Vous connaissez Londres ?) — (Vous déjeunez au restaurant ?) — (Vous êtes ingénieur ?)

A FRENCH INSTITUTION

CAFÉS : LOVE THEM OR HATE THEM *French cafés are like yoghurt or snails : you either love them or you hate them. The café lover will tell you that the café is the most versatile place in the world, and he's probably right. You can go simply for rest and refreshment. You can put on a fancy hat and go "to see and be seen" (boring if repeated but fun once in a while). You can go to discuss business, meet friends, chat, write your novel (where would Sartre, Hemingway and Joyce have been without their local café ?). Or you can go just to be alone. For me, one of the delights of the French café is to sit for hours with a coffee (nobody hassles you to consume more than one drink) and simply watch the world go by on the boulevards.*

HELL ON EARTH *But for the Californian health-and-meditation freak, the café must be hell on earth. The anti-smoking brigade that has taken over the rest of the world seems to have passed through France largely unnoticed. Not only do a great proportion of French people smoke, they also generally choose their cigarette brands with great care. None of this ultra-mild stuff. Here it's the good old Gauloise, dark tobacco, full of nicotine and tar, without filters. There are no non-smoking areas in cafés or restaurants, but the confirmed non-smoker can always find a pavement table in the open air. Too bad if it's November. For peace of mind, too, the café might not be the ideal place to hang around. Most of them have tiled floors, plastic tables spaced about two centimetres apart, and an awful lot of steel and enamel. Waiters are invariably over-worked and rush around clattering glasses and trays at high speed. Maybe it's all that strong coffee that sets the café pulse so high.*

WHAT TO ORDER ? *The choice is yours. If you're hungry, you can have a snack :* croque-monsieur *(a toasted ham sandwich with melted cheese on top), a long sandwich made with crispy French bread, a salad or a full meal. If you're thirsty, you can order anything from fruit juices and hot drinks to the real hard stuff. Licensing laws in France are idyllic for the would-be alcoholic : wine and spirits are served at any time of the day or night, and many cafés stay open until two or three in the morning, so you don't have to hurry. If you want a French aperitif, try a "kir" — a delicious mixture of dry white wine and* cassis *(blackcurrant liqueur). For those with stronger heads there's always* pastis, *the aniseed drink that they say kills any kind of germ (and practically everything else in your body).*
Then there are all the usual spirits that come in generous measures, nice and high in the glass, at, alas, equally high prices. If you're still sober after your couple of café hours (actually, people consume much less in a French café than in an English pub or American bar) and you want to pay, don't worry about tipping : 15 % service is automatically added to the bill, but you can leave a little extra if you're feeling generous. If the waiter is busy, and you have the right change, it's quite acceptable simply to leave the money on the table, and wander out into the streets — or on to the next café. □

1.3 TAKE A BREAK

N° 1

Listen

Where are the people on the cassette ? Put the number of each sentence next to the appropriate place.

N° 2

Find the names of the professions that are hidden in the grid below. Words may be written horizontally, vertically, diagonally, forwards or backwards.

médecin/publiciste/architecte/agent de voyage/dentiste/éditeur.

W	E	Z	X	G	L	A	D	N	T	I	L	Z	O
U	R	G	P	M	H	K	R	W	L	M	P	U	B
Z	V	I	A	R	C	H	I	T	E	C	T	E	N
R	X	O	L	Y	D	B	U	A	M	X	L	W	Y
U	I	A	B	D	O	C	Q	L	D	E	A	T	O
E	N	K	N	O	L	V	I	B	Z	R	O	R	D
T	D	I	P	M	E	D	E	C	I/	N	I	C	K
I	O	V	X	A	O	Z	U	D	G	T	N	V	X
D	M	N	O	P	W	R	P	O	I	R	S	I	E
E	L	Q	I	R	N	V	K	L	Z	N	U	P	B
S	I	E	S	D	E	N	T	I	S	T	E	R	S
N	P	L	N	A	V	Q	L	M	T	K	I	G	Y
M	E	T	S	I	C	I	L	B	U	P	W	Z	A

N° 3

In each of the following lists, there is one item that belongs to a different category. Circle the "odd man out" in each list.

1. *Japonais, Français, Anglaise, Chinois, Algérien.*

2. *Une eau minérale, une orange pressée, un citron pressé, une eau minérale, un ballon de rouge.*

3. *Un café, un thé au lait, un thé citron, un petit crème, un jus de fruit.*

4. *Un comédien, une journaliste, une touriste, un photographe, une styliste de mode, un plombier.*

5. *Bonjour, s'il vous plaît, salut, bonsoir, bonne nuit.* *(See solutions on page 5-6)*

1.4 CONTACTS

⊡ *Listen*

LA SEINE

Deux amies se rencontrent à un « cocktail » sur un bateau-mouche

Anne : *Tiens, Caroline, tu es là ! Quelle bonne surprise ! Comment vas-tu ?*

Caroline : *Très bien. Et toi ?*

Anne : *Ça va, merci.*

Caroline : *Qu'est-ce que tu fais maintenant ? Tu es toujours dans l'informatique ?*

Anne : *Oui, toujours.*

Caroline : *Dis-moi, tu connais le jeune homme près du bar ?*

Anne : *Bien sûr ! C'est Jean-Pierre.*

Caroline : *Jean-Pierre ? Qui est-ce ?*

Anne : *C'est mon adjoint. Il travaille avec moi depuis six mois.*

Caroline : *Tu choisis bien tes collaborateurs ! Il a l'air charmant.*

Caroline : *Qu'est-ce qu'il fait exactement ?*

Anne : *Il est responsable du service des achats.*

Caroline : *Dis donc ! Mais il est jeune ! Il a quel âge ?*

Anne : *Il a trente-sept ans.*

Caroline : *Trente-sept... Il fait plus jeune... Il est marié ?*

Anne : *Non, il est célibataire.*

Caroline : *Mais c'est très intéressant !*

Anne : *On peut prendre un verre avec lui, si tu veux.*

Caroline : *Volontiers... Attends une minute ! Tu as un miroir ?*

. . . .

Anne : *Jean-Pierre, je vous présente une de mes amies, Caroline Davout.*

Jean-Pierre : *Enchanté !*

Anne : *Jean-Pierre Legrand, mon adjoint.*

Caroline : *Ravie de faire votre connaissance.*

Jean-Pierre : *Vous prenez quelque chose ?*

Anne : *Je veux bien une coupe de champagne.*

Jean-Pierre : *Et vous, Mademoiselle ?*

Caroline : *Je vais prendre un jus de fruit.*

Jean-Pierre : *Tenez !*

Anne : *Merci.*

Caroline : *Merci beaucoup.*

Jean-Pierre : *Il fait chaud, ici !*

Caroline : *Il y a trop de monde. On peut monter sur le pont !*

Jean-Pierre : *Bonne idée !*

Anne : *Moi, je vous laisse. Je vais dire bonjour aux Mercier. A tout à l'heure !*

⊡ Listen and repeat
(You may look at the translation on page 6 in the booklet.)

1. Bateau-mouche sur la Seine

2. Vue aérienne de la Seine, au centre de Paris

1.4 WORDS

ami(e) — friend
jeune homme (M) — young man
adjoint(e) — assistant
collaborateur(trice) — colleague
coupe de champagne (F) — glass of champagne
pont (M) — bridge

---

collègue (M ou F) — colleague
supérieur(e) — superior
service financier — finicial departement
service des achats — sales departement

---

monsieur (M) — gentleman
dame (F) — lady
jeune fille (F) — young lady
jeune femme (F) — young woman
des jeunes gens (M) — young people, youth

charmant(e) — charming
jeune — young
marié(e) — married
célibataire — single
intéressant(e) — interesting
amusant(e) — funny

---

veuf(ve) — widower, widow
divorcé(e) — divorcee

---

vieux (vieille) — old ***(1)***
âgé(e) — elderly ***(1)***

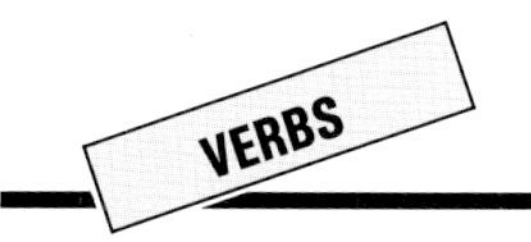

se rencontrer — to meet
choisir — to choose
attendre (quelqu'un) — to wait (for someone
monter — to go up
laisser — to let, to leave

---

descendre — to go down

avoir l'air — to seem, to appear
quelle bonne surprise ! — what a nic surprise !
bien sûr — of course
prendre un verre — to have a drink ***(2)***
faire la connaissance (de quelqu'un) — to make the acquaintance of, to get to know (someone
il fait chaud — it is hot
dire bonjour — to say hello

---

dire au revoir — to say goodbye

REMEMBER... REMEMBER... REMEMBER... REMEMBER... REMEMBER

(1) *« vieux » and « vieille » are less tactful than « âgé ». —* ***(2)*** *« prendre » means "to have" when referrin to food and drink. —* ***(3)*** *French introductions are usually much more formal than English ones.*

HOW TO SAY IT

1. ASKING PEOPLE HOW THEY ARE

Bonjour, comment allez-vous ?
Bonjour, comment vas-tu ? — Hello. How are you ?
Très bien, merci, et vous ?
Très bien, merci, et toi ? — Very well/fine thank you, and you ?

2. ASKING ABOUT SOMEONE

Qui est-ce ? — Who is that ?
Il a quel âge ? — How old is he ?
Il est marié ? — Is he married ?

3. TALKING ABOUT SOMEONE

C'est Jean-Pierre — This/that is Jean-Pierre
Il a 37 ans — He is 37 (years old)
Il est célibataire — He is single

4. TALKING ABOUT SOMEONE'S APPEARANCE

Il fait jeune — He looks young
Il a l'air charmant — He seems nice

5. INTRODUCING SOMEONE *(3)*

Je vous présente Caroline Davout — Let me introduce Caroline Davout
Permettez-moi de vous présenter Caroline Davout — May I introduce you to Caroline Davout ?
Vous connaissez Caroline ? — Do you know Caroline ?

6. BEING INTRODUCED *(3)*

Enchanté(e) — How do you do ?
(Je suis) très heureux(se) de faire votre connaissance
(Je suis) ravi(e) de faire votre connaissance — I am delighted to meet you

1.4 ORAL PRACTICE

1. GRAMMAR : SEE PAGE 41

POSSESSIVE ADJECTIVES : MON, TON, SON ETC.

Listen :

(J'ai un collaborateur)
— Voilà mon collaborateur.
(J'ai des collaborateurs)
— Voilà mes collaborateurs.

NOW, IDENTIFY PEOPLE IN THE SAME WAY, USING THE APPROPRIATE FORM OF THE POSSESSIVE ADJECTIVE :

(J'ai un collaborateur) — (J'ai des collaborateurs) — (Françoise a un collaborateur) — (Alain et Hervé ont un collaborateur) — (Vous avez un collaborateur) — (Nous avons des collaborateurs) — (André a des collaborateurs) — (J'ai une collaboratrice) — (Corinne et Martine ont des collaboratrices) — (Stéphane a une collaboratrice) — (Nous avons une collaboratrice)

2. GRAMMAR : SEE PAGE 46

TALKING ABOUT PEOPLE'S AGES

Listen :

(Elle a 40 ans)
— Mais non, elle n'a pas 40 ans !
(Il a 18 ans)
— Mais non, il n'a pas 18 ans !

NOW, QUESTION PEOPLE'S AGES IN THE SAME WAY. REMEMBER THE SENTENCE IS NOT COMPLETE WITHOUT THE WORD « ANS » :

(Elle a 40 ans) — (Il a 18 ans) — (Ils ont 17 ans) — (Elle a 60 ans) — (Il a 51 ans) — (Ils ont 35 ans) — (Elle a 6 ans) — (Il a 92 ans)

3. GRAMMAR : SEE PAGE 35

GIVING INFORMATION ABOUT OTHER PEOPLE

Listen :

(Patrick)
— C'est Patrick.
(informaticien)
— Il est informaticien.
(35 ans)
— Il a 35 ans.

NOW, TALK ABOUT THE FOLLOWING PEOPLE SAYING WHAT THEIR JOBS AND AGES ARE :

(Patrick), (informaticien), (35 ans) — (Jeanne), (secrétaire), (42 ans) — (M. et Mme Delage), (50 ans), (comptables) — (Christian), (45 ans), (directeur)

4. GRAMMAR : SEE PAGE 46

ASKING PEOPLE TO REPEAT INFORMATION

Listen :

(C'est Mme Lefort)
— Qui est-ce ?
(Elle est journaliste)
— Qu'est-ce qu'elle fait ?
(Elle a 46 ans)
— Elle a quel âge ?

NOW, ASK FOR THE FOLLOWING INFORMATION TO BE REPEATED : NAMES, JOBS AND AGES

(C'est Mme Lefort) — (Elle est journaliste) — (Elle a 46 ans) — (Il est ingénieur) — (Il a 37 ans) — (C'est M. Youcef) — (C'est Mlle Li-Wang) — (Elle est secrétaire) — (Elle a 22 ans) — (Il est réceptionniste) — (Il a 58 ans)

5. GRAMMAR : SEE PAGE 47

VERB PRACTICE : THE VERBS « VOULOIR » AND « PRENDRE »

Listen :

(vous), (prendre)
— Vous prenez une coupe de champagne.
(Jérôme), (vouloir)
— Jérôme veut une coupe de champagne.

NOW, COMPLETE THE SENTENCES, PUTTING THE VERBS IN THE CORRECT FORM :

(vous), (prendre) — (Jérôme), (vouloir) — (Caroline et Anne), (prendre) — (nous), (vouloir) — (vous), (vouloir) — (je), (prendre) — (tu), (vouloir) — (Agnès), (prendre) — (Aude et Jean), (vouloir)

6. GRAMMAR : SEE PAGE 46

GIVING INFORMATION ABOUT YOURSELF

Listen :

(Jean-Pierre, français, 38 ans, Belgique)
— Je m'appelle Jean-Pierre, je suis français, j'ai 38 ans et je travaille en Belgique.

NOW, IMAGINE YOU ARE EACH OF THE FOLLOWING PEOPLE. GIVE INFORMATION ABOUT YOURSELF IN THE SAME WAY :

(Jean-Pierre, français, 38 ans, Belgique) — (Marcel suisse, 25 ans, Luxembourg) — (Bernadette, française 48 ans, Sénégal) — (Annick, belge, 19 ans, France) — (Omar Diop, sénégalais, 32 ans, Allemagne) — (Patricia, canadienne, 41 ans, Italie)

LE COCKTAIL

FOOD AND DRINK Le cocktail *is an Anglo-Saxon import to which the French have added a gastronomically Gallic touch. In short this means that most French cocktail parties could easily pass themselves off as buffet dinners. Instead of nibbling on peanuts and potato chips you will find yourself feasting on salmon sandwiches,* pâté en croûte, *and dainty* petits fours. *But don't overdo it : after a cocktail party guests invariably drift off in small groups and head for the nearest restaurant. In France, if you haven't sat down at a table to eat, you haven't really eaten.*

For an American, the drinks offered at a French cocktail party — or bar for that matter — may prove disappointing. Apart from such staples as screwdrivers (known simply as vodka-orange *in French) and gin and tonics, French people don't drink* "cocktails". *They drink champagne, wine, Scotch, or a mild bittersweet drink called* "Martini" *(no relation to the dry martini !). My suggestion is to forget the traditional cocktail and drink the champagne. When in France . . .*

THE ART OF THE GAB AND THE GARB *Food and drink are all very well, but what do you say and do at a French cocktail party ?*

Since French people are generally more formal than English people and much more formal than Americans, you many find yourself hard pressed for conversational partners unless you already know a few people at the party. French people don't usually strike up conversations with perfect strangers — even at social gatherings. They never walk up to each other with American directness and say, "Hi, I'm Joe. I'm in insurance. What's your line ?" They wait to be introduced — a custom which has the disadvantage of keeping up social barriers and the advantage of preserving privacy.

And, oh yes, one more thing. Don't overdress. French women rarely wear evening gowns. They seem to strive (as do the men) for the "négligé chic" *look — layer upon layer of elegant clothes draped with casual art over the body Or else a simple, elegant décollete with one striking accessory.*

Don't be alarmed by all the dos and don'ts of French cocktail party behaviour. In France, as everywhere else in the world, most rules and barriers start to break down after the third drink. □

1.4 TAKE A BREAK

N° 1

Listen

Listen to the people talking about themselves and their work, and then put the number of the person beside the corresponding photo.

N° 2

Read the interviews. Then put the corresponding number next to the appropriate illustration and headline.

1. *Je m'appelle Marcel Marcellin. Normalement, je travaille dans un café près de l'Étoile. J'espère bien être le premier à l'arrivée.*

2. *Mon nom est Ling Huang. Je suis d'origine chinoise. Je travaille chez Lagerfeld. Cette année, le style est international : des jupes sud-américaines avec des chemisiers à l'orientale... C'est très joli !*

3. *C'est un grand jour pour moi et pour toute l'équipe. Nous travaillons depuis six mois. Il y a des Allemands, des Anglais, des Français... Moi, je m'appelle Patrick Ducos. Je suis informaticien et je m'occupe des ordinateurs de contrôle en vol.*

4. *Je me présente : Rafaëla Anconina. Je suis d'origine italienne. Je suis comédienne. C'est la première fois que je viens ici. C'est très bien mais il y a trop de monde !*

40e FESTIVAL DE CANNES
clic
clic
NOUVELLE COLLECTION D'ÉTÉ : SUPER !

GRANDE COURSE DES GARÇONS DE CAFÉ
qui va gagner ?*
(* Every year in Paris, about 200 waiters compete in a race in which they carry trays full of wine-glasses)

(See solutions on page 7)

1.5 CONTACTS

Listen

RECHERCHE D'EMPLOI

Réponse à une offre d'emploi

Paris, le 1er juin 1987.

Monsieur le Directeur,

Suite à l'annonce parue dans l'Expres du mercredi 28 mai, je vous soumets ma candidature au poste de responsable commercial.

Vous trouverez ci-joint mon curriculum vitae. Je pense qu'il retiendra votre attention.

Je me tiens, bien sûr, à votre entière disposition pour un entretien.

Dans l'attente d'un prochain con

Je vous prie de croire, Monsieur le Directeu à l'expression de mes sentiments disting

P. Pinaud

CURRICULUM VITAE

Nom : PINAUD
Prénom : Patrick
Date de naissance : 14 avril 1955 à Clermont-Ferrand (63)
Situation de famille : marié, 2 enfants
Nationalité : française
Adresse : 79, rue de Sèvres, 75007 PARIS
Téléphone : 42.61.75.70

FORMATION

1973 : Baccalauréat, série C, lycée Charlemagne, Paris.
1973-1975 : Classe préparatoire des écoles de commerce
1975-1978 : Ecole supérieure de Commerce de Reims.
Juin 1978 : Diplôme de l'Ecole supérieure de Reims.

EXPERIENCE PROFESSIONNELLE

1977 : Stage à l'usine PUK de St Jean de l'Isère (service des achats)
1978 : Stagiaire au service Prêts internationaux de la BNP à Paris.
1978/1879 : Coopérant au service économique de l'Ambassade de France à Séoul (Corée du Sud) dans le cadre du service national
Octobre 1979/Juillet 1981 : Chargé de Mission au service financier de l'Oréal.
Depuis août 1981 : Attaché à la direction générale de l'Oréal, Responsable des filiales étrangères

LANGUES ETRANGERES
Anglais courant (lu, parlé et écrit)
Allemand parlé.

1. *Préparation d'un C.V.*
2. *Kiosque à journaux*
3. *Boîte aux lettres*
4. *Lecture du courrier*

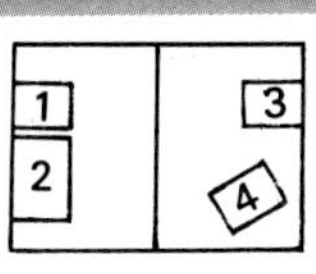

1.5 WORDS

emploi (M) — job
offre d'emploi (F) — job advertisement
(petite) annonce (F) — classified advertisement
candidature (F) — application
poste (M) — job, position
entretien (M) — interview
enfant (M ou F) — child
adresse (F) — address
rue (F) — street
formation (F) — training, studies
diplôme (M) — degree, diploma
expérience (F) — experience
stage (M) — course, training programme
stagiaire (M ou F) — someone doing a course or on a training programme
coopérant (M) — someone doing non-military national service
ambassade (F) — embassy
chargé(e) de mission — project manager
attaché(e) — attaché (diplomatic services)
direction générale (F) — senior management
filiale (F) — branch, subsidiary
langue (étrangère) (F) — (foreign) language

---

jour (M) — day ***(1)***
lundi — Monday
mardi — Tuesday
mercredi — Wednesday
jeudi — Thursday
vendredi — Friday
samedi — Saturday
dimanche — Sunday
mois (M) — month
janvier — January
février — February
mars — March
avril — April
mai — May
juin — June
juillet — July
août — August
septembre — September
octobre — October
novembre — November
décembre — December

---

chômage (M) — unemployment
lettre (F) — letter
courrier (M) — mail

VERBS

soumettre (une candidature) — to apply for (a job)
trouver — to find
penser — to think
parler — to speak

---

comprendre — to understand
écrire — to write
signer — to sign

REMEMBER... REMEMBER... REMEMBER... REMEMBER... REMEMBER

(1) *Months and days are not capitalized —* ***(2)*** *You can use this form if you've met the person at least once. —* ***(3)*** *When writing to the head of an organization, the French will often address the person by his title. —* ***(4)*** *These expressions which roughly mean « please accept this sincere expression of my esteem » must be used in business letters, however formal they may seem. — You must repeat the opening form of address at the end of your letter : Monsieur — Veuillez croire, Monsieur ; Chère Madame — Veuillez croire,*

HOW TO SAY IT

1. GIVING A DATE OF BIRTH

Je suis né(e) le 14 avril 1955 — I was born on April 14th, 1955
Je suis né(e) en mars — I was born in March

2. GIVING AN ADDRESS

J'habite 79, rue de Sèvres — I live at 79 rue de Sèvres
J'habite dans le 7ᵉ arrondissement — I live in the 7th district

3. STARTING A LETTER

a) formally

Monsieur/Madame,... — Dear Sir/Madam,
Messieurs,... — Dear Sirs,
Cher Monsieur,... — Dear Sir, ***(2)***
Chère Madame,... — Dear Madam,
Monsieur le Président,... — Dear Mr..., ***(3)***
Madame la Directrice,... — Dear Mrs...,

b) informally

Cher Paul/Chère Catherine,... — Dear Paul/Catherine,
Chers amis,... — Dear Friends,

4. ENDING A LETTER

a) formally *(4)*

Veuillez croire, Monsieur, / *Je vous prie de croire, Monsieur,* / *Croyez, Monsieur,* — *à l'expression de mes sentiments* — *distingués* / *respectueux* / *les meilleurs*

— Yours faithfully, Yours sincerely,

b) informally *(5)*

Amitiés, amicalement — Best wishes, Warm wishes,

Je t'embrasse / *Baisers* — Love

REMEMBER... REMEMBER... REMEMBER... REMEMBER... REMEMBER

*chère Madame, etc. — If you are writing to someone in an important position or much older than yourself, the appropriate adjective is « respectueux ». For someone you like it is « les meilleurs » ; otherwise use « distingués ». — **(5)** « Baisers » is a noun meaning « kisses ». The verb « baiser », used in 17th and 18th century literature, no longer means to kiss, but something much more vulgar !*

1.5 ORAL PRACTICE

1. GRAMMAR : SEE PAGE 43

SAYING WHERE YOU LIVE

Listen :

(79, rue de Sèvres)
— J'habite 79, rue de Sèvres.
(Paris)
— J'habite à Paris.
(7e)
— J'habite dans le 7e.

NOW, PRACTICE SAYING WHERE YOU LIVE.

(79, rue de Sèvres) — (Paris) — (7e) — (Marseille) — (30, bd St-Germain) — (6e) — (Bordeaux) — (12, avenue Leclerc) — (Lyon) — (3e)

2. GRAMMAR : SEE PAGE 44

DATES OF BIRTH

Listen :

(Elle - 17 décembre)
— Elle est née le 17 décembre.
(Elle - 1962)
— Elle est née en 1962.

NOW, MAKE SENTENCES GIVING THE FOLLOWING DATES OF BIRTH :

(elle - 17 décembre) — (elle - 1962) — (Vincent - janvier) — (vous - 29 février) — (Pierre et Étienne - 1946) — (tu - 15 octobre) — (nous - août) — (je - 1971)

3. GRAMMAR : SEE PAGE 45

ANSWERING IN THE NEGATIVE FORM

Listen :

(Vous êtes marié ?)
— Non, je ne suis pas marié.
(Elle va à l'hôtel ?)
— Non, elle ne va pas à l'hôtel.

NOW, ANSWER THE FOLLOWING QUESTIONS IN THE NEGATIVE FORM :

(vous êtes marié ?) — (elle va à l'hôtel ?) — (vous habitez à Lyon ?) — (il travaille chez Michelin ?) — (vous parlez espagnol ?) — (elle choisit ses collaborateurs ?) — (il comprend l'allemand ?) — (vous connaissez mon adjoint ?)

4. GRAMMAR : SEE PAGE 46

GIVING INFORMATION ABOUT PEOPLE

Listen :

(Pinaud Patrick)
— Il s'appelle Patrick Pinaud.
(nationalité française)
— Il est français.
(adresse : 79, rue de Sèvres)
— Il habite 79, rue de Sèvres.
(langues parlées : anglais, allemand)
— Il parle anglais et allemand.

NOW, GIVE THE FOLLOWING PEOPLE'S NAMES, NATIONALITIES AND ADDRESSES AND SAY WHICH FOREIGN LANGUAGES THEY SPEAK :

(Pinaud Patrick), (nationalité française), (adresse : 79, rue de Sèvres), (langues parlées : anglais, allemand) — (Santos Maria), (nationalité espagnole), (adresse : 5, rue de la Banque), (langues parlées : anglais, français) — (Müller Hans), (nationalité allemande), (adresse : 3, Berliner strasse), (langues parlées : anglais, russe)

5. GRAMMAR : SEE PAGE 46

TALKING ABOUT AGE, MARITAL STATUS AND FAMILY

Listen :

(Jean, 25 ans) (marié) (2 enfants)
— Jean a 25 ans.
— Il est marié et il a deux enfants.

NOW, TALK ABOUT THE FOLLOWING PEOPLE :

(Jean, 25 ans), (marié), (2 enfants) — (Chantal, 38 ans), (divorcée), (1 enfant) — (Didier, 40 ans), (marié), (4 enfants)

6. GRAMMAR : SEE PAGE 47

VERB PRACTICE : VERBS ENDING IN -IR

Listen :

(je) - (remplir)
— Je remplis une carte.
(vous) - (choisir)
— Vous choisissez une carte.

NOW, COMPLETE THE SENTENCES CHANGING THE VERB AS NECESSARY :

(je) (remplir) — (vous) (choisir) — (François) (choisir) — (nous) (remplir) — (Charles et Sylvie) (choisir) — (tu) (remplir) — (vous) (remplir) — (je) (choisir)

EDUCATION

The French educational system seems to have been designed for the student who "always-knew-that-he-or-she-wanted-to-be-an-engineer-and-build-bridges-when-he-or-she-grew-up". Aspiring bridge builders even have their own school, one of the famous grandes écoles, Les Ponts et Chaussées. *After completing his secondary studies and passing the* baccalauréat *examination, a student who wants to go on to higher education has one of two choices: university or the* grandes écoles.

THE UNIVERSITY *Since French universities practise open admissions and are open to all holders of the* baccalauréat *diploma, they are normally regarded as less prestigious than the* grandes écoles, *which have a limited number of highly coveted places. All the universities are state run and practically free. It is unusual for students to go away to a university in a distant part of the country; instead, many students live at home and attend their local university. University degrees are roughly equivalent to British and American degrees, but the system keeps changing — each Minister of Education tries to go down in history for his own particular Reform. In any case, here's a rough guide:*

licence *(three years) = B.A. or B.Sc.*
maîtrise *(one year after the* licence*) = M.A. or M.Sc.*
doctorat de 3e cycle *(three years after the* maîtrise*)*
doctorat d'état *(six or seven years after the* maîtrise*)*

THE "INSTITUT UNIVERSITAIRE TECHNOLOGIQUE" *Similar to Britain's "sandwich courses", which combine academic studies with practical industrial or commercial experience,* I.U.T.*s are becoming increasingly popular, since many employers prefer graduates who have already acquired work experience. Usually, a course at an* I.U.T. *consists of two years of academic study in a university and six to twelve months working in a company (this part is called a* "stage"*). The two- to three-year course leads to a* Diplôme Universitaire Technologique, *now frequently preferred by employers to the traditional* licence.

THE "GRANDE ÉCOLE" *The* grandes écoles *are comparable in status to Oxbridge in Britain and the Ivy League colleges in the United States. Admissions are by highly competitive examinations (students who wish to apply must spend an additional year or two after the* bac *preparing for the entrance exams in a special* cours préparatoire*) and fees are often high. Most students at the* grandes écoles *are from upper middle class backgrounds. Another characteristic of the* grandes écoles *is that they are all highly specialized: the* École Nationale d'Administration (E.N.A.) *trains the nation's civil servants (a large number of French politicians on the left and on the right are* E.N.A. *graduates); the* École des Hautes Études Commerciales (H.E.C.) *trains future business managers; the* École Polytechnique *produces engineers, and so on. Besides the handful of well-known* grandes écoles, *there are many new, less prestigious private* "écoles" *which aspire to being* "grandes".
The advantages of going to the grandest of the grandes écoles *are obvious. Graduates are sure to find well-paid jobs and to benefit from the old-boy network of their* école. *Though male-dominated for decades, the* grandes écoles *have recently been admitting more women, so we may soon be able to speak of an old-girl network as well.*

THE "LYCÉE" *Specialization is not the exclusive prerogative of* the grandes écoles. *At the age of 15, secondary school students in the* lycées *must choose one of several programmes, strongly emphasizing one of the following: philosophy, languages, economics, maths or science.*
So our aspiring bridge builder would have had to choose mathematics at the age of 15, go on to a cours préparatoire *at 18, and be admitted at 19 or 20 to the three-year course at* Les Ponts et Chaussées. *A feat which requires more foresight than many 15- or even 18-year-olds are capable of mustering.* □

* *A Ph.D is higher than a* doctorat de 3e cycle *and lower than a* doctorat d'état, *for which there is no equivalent.*

Listen **_Non, je ne regrette rien_**

Édith Piaf (paroles de Michel Vaucaire et musique de Charles Dumont)
Publié avec l'autorisation de la Société SEMI

Non, rien de rien
Non, je ne regrette rien
Ni le bien qu'on m'a fait
Ni le mal, tout ça m'est bien égal
Non, rien de rien
Non, je ne regrette rien
C'est payé, balayé, oublié
Je me fous du passé
Avec mes souvenirs, j'ai allumé le feu
Mes chagrins, mes plaisirs
Je n'ai plus besoin d'eux
Balayés les amours avec leur trémolo
Balayé pour toujours
Je repars à zéro
Non, rien de rien, non, je ne regrette rien
Ni le bien qu'on m'a fait, ni le mal
Tout ça m'est bien égal
Non, rien de rien, non, je ne regrette rien
Car ma vie, car mes joies
Aujourd'hui
Ça commence avec toi

No Regrets

No, nothing, nothing at all
I regret nothing
Not the good that people have done me
Nor the bad, it all means nothing to me
Nothing
I regret nothing
It's all paid up, swept up, forgotten
The past means nothing to me
I've lit a bonfire of my memories
All my sorrows, all my joys
I have no more need of them
All my loves, all their madness
They're all swept up
I'm back to square one
No, nothing, nothing at all
I regret nothing
Not the good that people have done me
Nor the bad, it all means nothing to me
Because my life, my joy
Begins here, today
With you

STREET TALK · STRAIGHT TALK
SALUT FRÉDO. A VA? T'AS PAS A PÊCHE!
BOF! J'SUIS CREVÉ. JE BOSSE COMME UN DINGUE.
DIS-MOI, C'EST QUI LE MEC DE LAURA? TU CONNAIS?
OUI. C'EST FRANÇOIS, UN POTE À MOI.
AIT UOI?
RIEN, IL GLANDE. IL CHERCHE DU BOULOT.
FAUT QUE JE TE LAISSE. J'AI UN RANCART, JE SUIS À LA BOURRE.
SALUT!
BONJOUR FRÉDÉRIC, OMMENT- LLEZ-VOUS? OUS N'AVEZ S L'AIR U FORME.
EN EFFET, JE SUIS TRÈS FATIGUÉ. JE TRAVAILLE ÉNORMEMENT.
VOUS CONNAISSEZ L'AMI DE MADEMOISELLE LAURA?
OUI. C'EST FRANCOIS. UN DE MES AMIS
QU'EST-CE QU'IL FAIT?
PAS GRAND CHOSE. IL CHERCHE DU TRAVAIL.
JE DOIS VOUS QUITTER. J'AI UN RENDEZ-VOUS ET JE SUIS TRÈS PRESSÉ.
AU REVOIR.

1 WRITTEN PRACTICE

1.1

COMPLETE: *Je .... anglaise — Mon nom .... Rose Thomson — Je .... chez Danone — Je m' .... Francis Duval — Vous .... agronome ? — Il .... ingénieur.*

TRANSLATE: *Elle est française — Elle s'appelle Catherine — Elle travaille chez Chanel — Il s'occupe des études techniques — Il vient de Tokyo — Michel est ingénieur à Marseille.*
My name is Corinne Bellefeuille — I am Canadian and I am director of technical studies — Jane is English — She is a computer scientist — I am in charge of the commercial department.

1.2

COMPLETE: *J' .... la chambre 430 — Elle n' .... pas votre nom — Je .... suis .... japonaise, je .... chinoise — 4 581 F : quatre ....*

TRANSLATE: *Bonsoir Monsieur — Excusez-moi Madame, c'est bien l'Hôtel Méridien ? — Pardon, vous pouvez épeler, s'il vous plaît ? — Je suis désolé, je n'ai pas votre nom — Bonne soirée, Madame.*
Good morning, Madam — Here is your key — My first name is Philippe, my surname is Dominique — Could you spell your first name, please ? — Goodbye, have a good day — Thank you, Madam.

1.3

COMPLETE: *Je vais .... musée du Louvre — Tu n'habites pas .... France — Ils vont .... réception — Vous travaillez .... Chili — Nous allons .... États-Unis — Nos bureaux sont ....Amsterdam — J'ai une chambre .... Hôtel Bristol.*

TRANSLATE: *Où est-ce que vous habitez ? — Il vient de Zurich — Qu'est-ce que vous faites dans la vie ? — Je peux vous emmener au Salon — Je veux bien, merci — Je voudrais un café et un jus d'orange.*
He works in Geneva, but he doesn't live in Switzerland — They're not Canadian, they're French — They aren't going to the hotel, they're going to the restaurant — I'd like a cup of tea, please.

1.4

COMPLETE by writing the verbs in brackets in the appropriate form: *Je (aller) .... à Nice ce soir — Ils (prendre) .... un verre — Vous (ne pas connaître) .... le Moulin Rouge ? — Qu'est-ce qu'elle (faire) .... ? — Elle (ne pas savoir) .... où c'est.*

TRANSLATE: *J'ai trente-deux ans et je suis marié — Quel âge avez-vous ? — Il a l'air jeune — Je ne suis pas dans l'informatique — Je suis ravie de faire votre connaissance — C'est Bernard, mon collaborateur.*
Hello, Yves. How are you ? Fine, thank you — Let me introduce you to my assistant, François Brasseur — What will you have ? I'll have a glass of champagne, please.

1.5

COMPLETE: *Il .... marié et il .... deux enfants — Elle est née .... 1986, ... novembre — J'ai un congrès .... Chicago .... 18 septembre — Nous travaillons .... le 8e arrondissement — Elle .... 41 ans — Il fait un stage .... Danemark.*

TRANSLATE: *Je suis né à Bruxelles, le 10 novembre 1948 — Je parle trois langues et j'ai un diplôme de commerce — J'habite 17, rue du Bac dans le 7e — Nous faisons un stage à l'usine Péchiney.*
You were born on September 1st, 1954, in London — He is married and he has one child — She is thirty-five years old — I speak two foreign languages — We live in Paris, at 71, rue Lafayette.

(Check your answers on page 38 of your booklet)

IMPROVE

PROFESSIONS

adjoint (M) — assistant
analyste financier (M) — a financial analyst
analyste programmeur (M) — a program analyst
architecte (M) — architect
assistant (M) — assistant
attaché commercial (M) — commercial representative
attaché de direction (M) — managerial assistant
auditeur (M) — auditor
avocat (M) — barrister
cadre (M) — executive
chef d'entreprise (M) — company director
chef de produit (M) — product manager
chef de projet (M) — project manager
chef des ventes (M) — sales manager
chef du personnel (M) — personnel manager
chirurgien (M) — surgeon
chômeur (M) — an unemployed person
comptable (M) — accountant
contremaître (M) — foreman
contrôleur (M) — controller
contrôleur de gestion (M) — financial controller
consultant (M) — consultant
coordinateur (M) — coordinator
délégué (M) — delegate
dentiste (M) — dentist
économiste (M) — economist
écrivain (M) — writer
employé (M) — employee, clerk
expert-comptable (M) — chartered accountant
juge (M) — judge
juriste (M) — jurist
ingénieur commercial (M) — engineer in charge of sales
ingénieur électronicien (M) — electronics engineer
ingénieur informaticien (M) — computer engineer
ingénieur logiciel (M) — software engineer
ingénieur système (M) — systems engineer
inspecteur (M) — inspector
instituteur (M) — school teacher
magistrat (M) — magistrate
médccin (M) — doctor
notaire (M) — notary
ouvrier (M) — a worker, labourer
président (M) — president
professeur (M) — teacher
pupitreur (M) — computer operator
responsable (M) — person in charge
secrétaire général (M) — deputy director
sous-directeur (M) — deputy director
sténodactylo (M) — shorthand typist
technicien (M) — technician

COUNTRIES AND NATIONALITIES

La France — France
français (e) — French
L'Angleterre — England
anglais (e) — English
L'Ecosse — Scotland
écossais (e) — Scottish
L'Irlande — Ireland
irlandais (e) — Irish
L'Islande — Iceland
islandais (e) — Icelandic
La Hollande — Holland
hollandais (e) — Dutch
La Finlande — Finland
finlandais (e) — Finnish
La Pologne — Poland
polonais (e) — Polish
Le Japon — Japan
japonais (e) — Japanese
Le Liban — Lebanon
libanais (e) — Lebanese
Le Pakistan — Pakistan
pakistanais (e) — Pakistani
Le Portugal — Portugal
portugais (e) — Portuguese
La Suède — Sweden
suédois (e) — Swedish
La Chine — China
chinois (e) — Chinese
Le Pays de Galles — Wales
gallois (e) — Welsh
Le Danemark — Denmark
danois (e) — Danish
L'Italie — Italy
italien (ne) — Italian
L'Algérie — Algeria
algérien (ne) — Algerian
L'Egypte — Egypt
égyptien (ne) — Egyptian
L'Autriche — Austria
autrichien (ne) — Austrian
L'Inde — India
indien (ne) — Indian
La Tunisie — Tunisia
tunisien (ne) — Tunisian
La Libye — Lybia
libyen (ne) — Lybian
La Palestine — Palestine
palestinien (ne) — Palestinian
La Syrie — Syria
syrien (ne) — Syrian
La Norvège — Norway
norvégien (ne) — Norwegian
L'Arabie Saoudite — Saudi Arabia
saoudien (ne) — Saudi Arabian
Le Canada — Canada
canadien (ne) — Canadian
Le Vénézuéla — Venezuela
vénézuélien (ne) — Venezuelan
Le Brésil — Brazil
brésilien (ne) — Brazilian
Le Chili — Chile
chilien (ne) — Chilean
Le Viêt-nam — Vietnam
Vietnamien (ne) — Vietnamese
Israël — Israel
israélien (ne) — Israeli
La Belgique — Belgium
belge — Belgian
La Yougoslavie — Yugoslavia
yougoslave — Yugoslav
La Suisse — Switzerland
suisse — Swiss
La Russie — Russia
russe — Russian
L'URSS — USSR
soviétique — Soviet
La Grèce — Greece
grec (que) — Greek
La Turquie — Turkey
turc (turque) — Turkish
Les États-Unis — The United States
américain (e) — American
Le Maroc — Morocco
marocain (e) — Moroccan
Le Mexique — Mexico
mexicain (e) — Mexican
L'Allemagne — Germany
allemand (e) — German
L'Espagne — Spain
espagnol (e) — Spanish
La Grande-Bretagne — Great Britain
britannique — British

I. TEST YOURSELF

1. WRITE THE CORRECT FORM : CORRECT FORM

Les intervenants épèlent leur/ses *nom* ....
Il travaille en/au *Canada* ....
Vous être/êtes *agronome* ....
Il est/es *américain* ....
Françoise présente son/sa *adjoint* ....
Alain donne son/sa *carte de visite* ....
Il est japonais/japonaise ....
Je suis comptable/un comptable ....

2. WRITE THE CORRECT FORM : CORRECT FORM

J'habite en/aux *États-Unis* ....
Il travaille en/dans *l'aéronautique* ....
Je viens le 2/2e *septembre* ....
Il est/a *vingt-cinq ans* ....
Vous êtes ingénieur pour/chez *Renault* ....
Elle est directeur/directrice ....
J'ai un congrès le/en *10 juillet* ....
Je suis né dans/en *1922* ....
Ça va bien/bon ....

3. WRITE OUT THE FOLLOWING NUMBERS IN FULL :

14 ....
9 ....
100 ....
21 ....
19 ....
98 ....
75 ....
42 ....

4. FILL IN THE BLANKS :

Comment allez- .... *?*
Elle .... *française*
Je vais .... *États-Unis*
Il est né .... *4 octobre 1950*
Gertrud habite .... *Allemagne, elle est* ....
Vous .... *comptable* .... *Yves Saint-Laurent*
Il .... *18* ...., *il* .... *jeune*
Elle .... *peut* .... *venir*

5. ADJECTIVES OF NATIONALITY

ex : Made in France – c'est français
Now continue giving the adjective of nationality :

Made in France ....
Made in USA ....
Made in Senegal ....
Made in England ....
Made in Spain ....
Made in Japan ....
Made in Germany ....
Made in Canada ....
Made in Switzerland ....
Made in Mexico ....
Made in Italy ....

6. MATCH THE FOLLOWING ANSWERS TO THE APPROPRIATE QUESTIONS :

1. *18 ans*
2. *C'est la directrice du service commercial*
3. *Elle travaille dans la mode*
4. *Je m'appelle Alain Garand*
5. *Jean-Claude Thomas*
6. *Avec 2 "p" et 2 "l"*
7. *Je suis sénégalais*
8. *A Marseille*
9. *Marc*
10. *Bien, merci, et vous-même ?*

A. *Il habite où ?*
B. *Quel est votre nom ?*
C. *Vous venez d'où ?*
D. *Il a quel âge ?*
E. *Comment allez-vous ?*
F. *Qu'est-ce qu'elle fait ?*
G. *Qui est-ce ?*
H. *Comment vous appelez-vous ?*
I. *Ça s'écrit comment ?*
J. *Votre prénom, s'il vous plaît ?*

7. COMPLETE THE SENTENCES USING ONE OF THE VERBS FROM THE LIST IN ITS APPROPRIATE FORM :

connaître – déjeuner – remplir – avoir – réserver – s'appeler – être – aller – habiter – comprendre – travailler

Vous arrivez à l'hôtel et vous .... une fiche.
Je voudrais .... une chambre pour deux nuits.
Dimanche nous .... à Paris.
Vous pouvez épeler ? Je ne .... pas.
Qui est ce jeune homme ? Je ne le .... pas.
Il est directeur, il .... chez Peugeot.
Je .... mariée et j .... 3 enfants.
Quel est votre nom ? Je .... Dumoulin.
Nous .... rue de Grenelle.
Il est midi, je vais ....

(Check your answers on page 39 of your booklet)

Mr. MARTIN AND MONSIEUR DANIEL

These days I'm afraid to fall asleep. I do everything I can to put off the dreaded moment : I read, I do the Times crossword puzzle, I make myself sandwiches out of all the leftovers in the fridge. But it's no use. Every night at about 3.00 or 3.30 a.m. I'm overcome by drowsiness and I doze off. And then the nightmare begins. And it's always the same. Night after night.

In my dream, I'm in the bathroom, shaving. I peer into the mirror and examine the face that stares back at me. I see a grey-faced man, no longer young but not yet old, with thinning hair. He has an honest, friendly-looking face and worry lines around his mouth.

Then, suddenly, as I stand there in my bathrobe complacently appraising myself, the nightmare begins. The face in the mirror becomes animated and breaks into a wide grin. The honest though rather blank expression becomes mischievous, almost sinister. I can feel my heart beating faster and my eyes opening in terror. He seems amused at my horrified expression and winks at me, slowly and deliberately. That wink seems to suggest depths, unknown to me, of . . . is it evil or simply vulgarity ? As I continue to stare, paralyzed by fear, the face in the mirror opens its mouth (revealing two gold canines) and says in a deep voice :

« Bonjour, je suis Martin Daniel. J'ai 34 ans... » My schoolboy French is rusty ; his sounds practically flawless, at least to my untrained ears. "Hold it !" I shout. "You've got it all wrong . . . and backwards. *My* name is Daniel Martin. That's pronounced Mar*tin* not Martain. And I'm 43 years old. And will you please stop winking at me !"

« Aha ! Monsieur Martin n'aime pas les clins d'œil ! Monsieur Martin est trop sérieux. Beaucoup trop sérieux. Vous devriez apprendre à rire. Dans la vie il faut rigoler, comme on dit en français ! »

And then, every night, the same thing happens. The face in the mirror — my reflection, if I can still call it that — starts to laugh, loudly and deeply. And, as he says, *« Venez avec moi. On va rigoler »*, his arm reaches out of the frame of the mirror . . .

The arm belongs to me, but it's wearing a cheap-looking bracelet with the name Martin Daniel engraved on it in Gothic lettering. A strangled scream forms itself in my throat, and I run out of the bathroom. At that moment, of course, the image disappears from the mirror, and no evidence of my horrible nightmare remains — except for yesterday, when the cheap-looking bracelet with Martin Daniel engraved on it, fell neglected on the washbasin.

Quickly throwing a towel over the mirror, I stuffed the bracelet into my bathrobe pocket, and said "I'm stronger than you, Martin Daniel. I can make you disappear."

* * *

The next day, I received a strange letter. It was addressed to Daniel Martin, Esq., in a fine spidery hand. The envelope had a French stamp on it depicting a painting by one of the impressionists. It hadn't been postmarked, so there was no way of telling when or where it had been posted. I tore open the envelope, and read in the same spidery hand that had addressed the envelope:

Cher Monsieur,

Je suis de passage dans votre ville, et j'aimerais beaucoup faire votre connaissance. J'espère qu'il vous sera possible de venir au rendez-vous que je vous propose le 14 janvier à 21 heures. Je serai à une table au fond de la salle. Je porte toujours un imperméable noir avec un chapeau de feutre noir — mais ce n'est vraiment pas la peine de vous donner toutes ces précisions. Vous allez me reconnaître tout de suite ! A bientôt ! Amicalement,

Martin Daniel

Needless to say, I was disturbed and upset by this letter. Then I decided it was all some sort of huge practical joke and the only sensible thing to do was to go to the Café Français on the appointed day. At least, I thought, I would clear up the mystery of Martin Daniel and return his ID bracelet, which was still in my bathrobe pocket where I had left it.

I reread the letter stopping at the phrase, *« le 14 janvier à 21 heures »*. "That's tonight !" I exclaimed. "Mr. Daniel doesn't believe in giving one much warning." But I was curious, and a bit frightened.

At half past eight, or *vingt heures trente* as Martin Daniel would say, I got on the tube, and rode out to Soho. At nine o'clock sharp I had found the *Café Français* and was pushing open the door. It was done up to look like a Belle Epoque French cafe, with a big zinc counter and Toulouse Lautrec posters on the walls. I walked to the back of the cafe, looked around for the man in the black hat and raincoat, and, when I didn't see him, took a seat facing a Belle Epoque mirror with an ornate frame. The French, I had noticed during trips to the continent, put mirrors up everywhere — in lobbies, waiting rooms, cafes and restaurants. Why anyone would constantly want to be checking up on his appearance I really don't know.

Instead of studying myself in the mirror, I studied the menu. As was to be expected in a place calling itself *« Le Café Français »*, this was in French. My eye ran down the usual list of *« boissons alcoolisées — bière, vin rouge, vin blanc, calvados... — et non alcoolisées — eaux minérales, jus de fruits, citron ou orange pressés, café, café crème, thé, chocolat... »*

Given my present nervous state, I concentrated on the *« boissons alcoolisées »*. By the time the waiter walked over to me and asked, *« Vous voulez commander, Monsieur ? »* I was ready with my order : *« Un ballon de Bordeaux, s'il vous plaît. »* I answered in French. "After all," I thought to myself, "if he's going to inflict his Cockney-accented French on me, I may as well give him a dose of my rusted schoolboy . . ." There my thoughts froze. While I had been thinking to myself I had glanced up into the ornate Belle Epoque mirror. And there was my reflection, suddenly elegant . . . in a black raincoat and a black hat. I looked down at myself. I was still wearing my dirty tan raincoat.

TO BE CONTINUED...

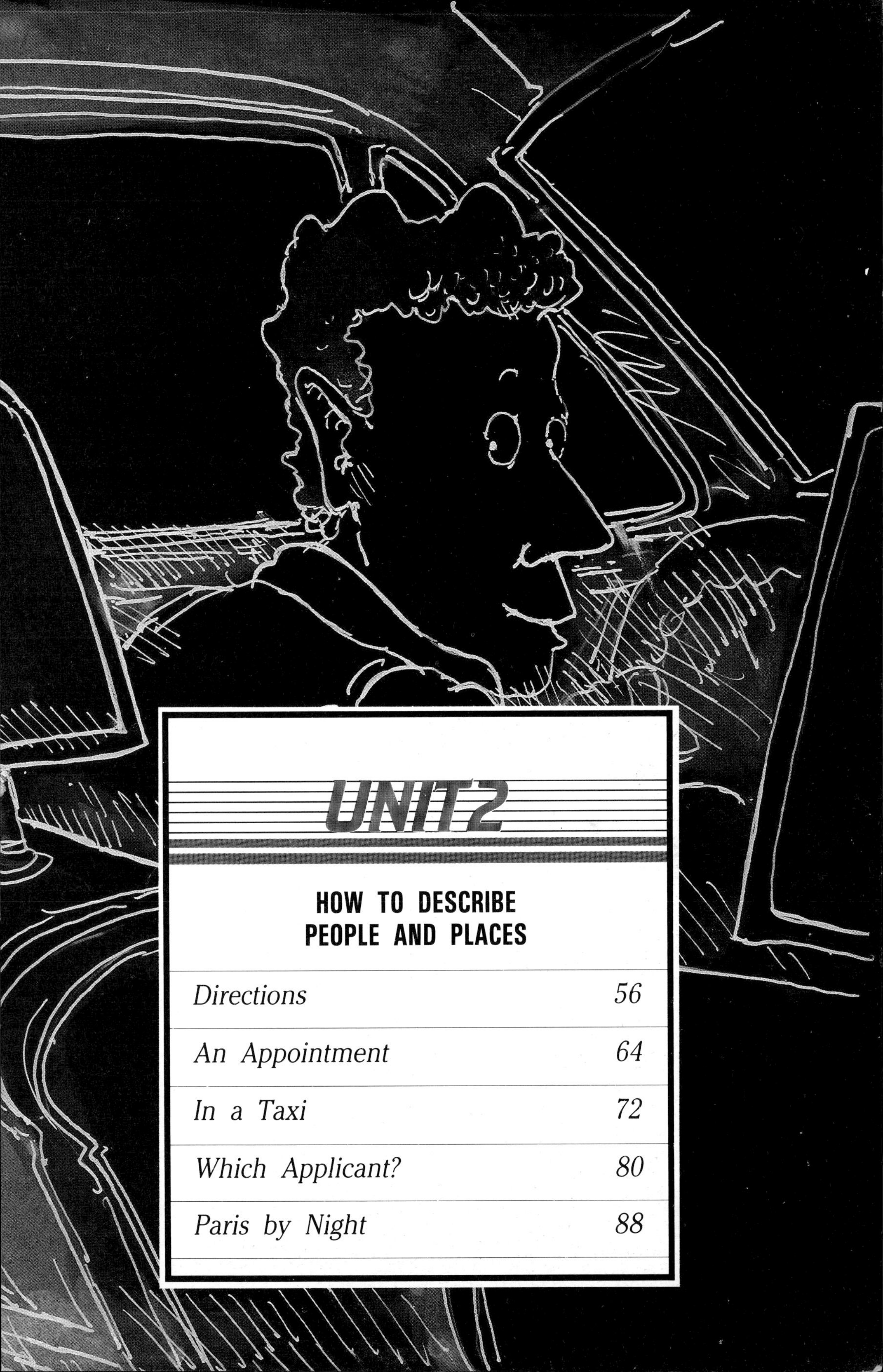

UNIT 2

HOW TO DESCRIBE PEOPLE AND PLACES

2.1 CONTACTS

Listen

ITINÉRAIRES

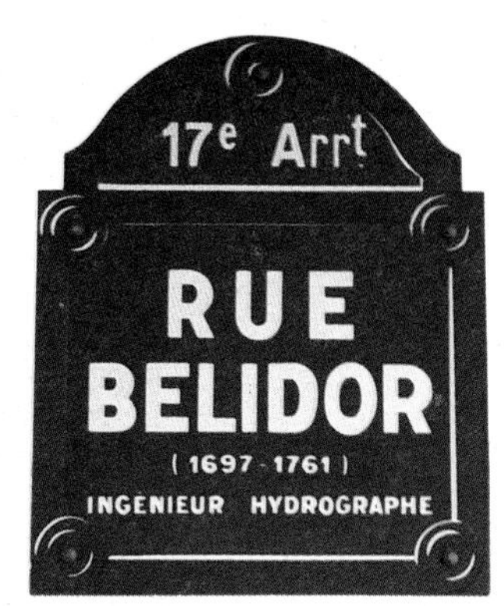

Monsieur Fortin doit se rendre au service export d'une entreprise

A la station Pasteur

M. Fortin : *Je voudrais un ticket, s'il vous plaît.*

Employé de la RATP : *1re ou 2e classe ?*

M. Fortin : *1re classe. S'il vous plaît, pour la Porte Maillot, je prends quelle ligne ?*

Employé : *Vous prenez d'abord la ligne 12, direction Porte de la Chapelle.*

M. Fortin : *Pardon, quelle direction ?*

Employé : *Direction Porte de la Chapelle. Vous changez à Concorde et ensuite vous prenez la ligne 1, direction Pont de Neuilly.*

M. Fortin : *Merci.*

A la sortie du métro Porte Maillot

M. Fortin : *Pardon Madame, la rue Bellidor s'il vous plaît ?*

Une passante : *Je ne sais pas, je ne suis pas du quartier.*

M. Fortin : *Excusez-moi.*

...

M. Fortin : *Madame, s'il vous plaît, est-ce que vous savez où se trouve la rue Belidor ?*

Une autre passante : *La rue Belidor ? Oui. Vous remontez l'avenue ; au premier feu rouge, tournez à gauche et prenez le boulevard Gouvion Saint-Cyr.*

M. Fortin : *Excusez-moi, je n'ai pas compris le nom.*

La passante : *Gouvion Saint-Cyr. Continuez tout droit et vous trouverez la rue Belidor sur votre droite ; c'est la première ou la deuxième.*

M. Fortin : *Est-ce que c'est loin ?*

La passante : *Non, c'est à cinq minutes à pied.*

M. Fortin : *Je vous remercie.*

La passante : *Je vous en prie.*

Dans un immeuble

M. Fortin : *Le service étranger, c'est bien ici ?*

La gardienne : *Ah non, Monsieur, vous vous trompez d'étage ! C'est au deuxième. Qui cherchez-vous ?*

M. Fortin : *Mme Letellier, du service export.*

La gardienne : *Mme Letellier ? Elle est au bureau 205 ; c'est à gauche en sortant de l'ascenseur, tout au bout du couloir.*

M. Fortin : *Merci, Madame.*

La gardienne : *A votre service.*

Listen and repeat
(You may look at the translation on page 10 in the booklet.)

1. Plaque de rue, à Paris
2. Bouche de métro en face du Palais des Congrès
3. Bouche de métro Art Nouveau, à Montmartre
4. Couloir de métro avec panneaux de stations et correspondances
5. Quai de la station Sèvres-Babylone, 6e arrondissement

2.1 WORDS

itinéraire (M) — itinerary
entreprise (F) — company, business
station de métro (F) — underground station
ticket (M) — ticket ***(1)***
direction (F) — direction
sortie (F) — exit
avenue (F) — avenue
boulevard (M) — boulevard
feu (rouge) (M) — traffic light
immeuble (M) — building
couloir (M) — corridor

route (F) — road
carrefour (M) — intersection, crossroads
entrée (F) — way in, entrance
changement (M) — change
quai (M) — platform (station)
départ (M) — departure
arrivée (F) — arrival
billet (M) — ticket
bicyclette (F) (vélo [M]) — bicycle ***(2)***
cheval (M) — horse ***(2)***
voiture (F) — car ***(2)***
bus (M) — bus ***(2)***
train (M) — train ***(2)***
avion (M) — plane ***(2)***
bateau (M) — ship ***(2)***

devoir — must, to have to
se rendre — to go (formal), to visit (places)
changer — to change
remonter — to go back up
tourner — to turn
continuer — to continue, to keep on
(se) trouver — to be situated, to find oneself
remercier — to thank
se tromper (de) — to make a mistake
chercher — to look for
sortir — to go out

suivre — to follow
traverser — to cross
passer — to pass, to walk past
descendre — to go down (a street), to get off (a train, bus...)
entrer (dans) — to go in, enter
s'en aller — to go away
perdre — to lose
trouver — to find
retourner — to return, to go back

d'abord — first
ensuite — then
être du quartier — to live in the district
à pied — on foot
faire demi-tour — to go back the way one came
être perdu — to be lost

REMEMBER... REMEMBER... REMEMBER... REMEMBER... REMEMBER

(1) *When you want to take the metro or the bus you have to buy a « ticket ». For all other kinds of transport (trains, planes, ships, etc.) you need a « billet ».* — ***(2)*** *See grammar page 44.* — ***(3)*** *« je suis désolé(e) » is a commonly used expression meaning « I'm sorry » — It is stronger than « je regrette », but not as strong as a literal translation might suggest.*

HOW TO SAY IT

1. GIVING DIRECTIONS

Continuez tout droit — Keep going straight on
Vous remontez l'avenue — Go back up the avenue
Il faut prendre le boulevard — You have to go along the boulevard
C'est à gauche/à droite — It's on the left/on the right
C'est à 100 m à droite — It's a 100 m farther on, on the right
C'est au bout de la rue — It's at the end of the street
C'est assez loin — It's quite a long way
C'est tout près — It's very near here
C'est à cinq minutes à pied — It's 5 minutes on foot
C'est ici ! — It's right here

2. SAYING YOU DON'T KNOW SOMETHING

Je ne sais pas — I don't know
Excusez-moi, je ne suis pas d'ici — I'm sorry, but I'm a stranger here
Je suis désolé(e), je ne suis pas du quartier — I'm sorry, but I don't live in the district ***(3)***
Je ne connais pas le quartier — I don't know this area
Je ne comprends pas — I don't understand

3. ASKING SOMEONE TO REPEAT SOMETHING

Pardon (quelle direction) ? — Pardon (which way ?)
Excusez-moi, je n'ai pas compris (le nom) — Excuse me, I didn't understand (the name)
Comment ? — Pardon ?
Qu'est-ce que vous dites ? — What did you say ?
Vous pouvez répéter, s'il vous plaît ? — Could you repeat that, please ?

4. THANKING PEOPLE

Merci — Thanks/thank you
Je vous remercie — Thank you very much
C'est très gentil — That's very kind of you

5. RESPONDING TO THANKS

Je vous en prie — Not at all
Ce n'est rien / *De rien* / *Il n'y a pas de quoi* — You're welcome / Don't mention it
A votre service — Glad to be of service

2.1 ORAL PRACTICE

1. GRAMMAR : SEE PAGE 45

ANSWERING IN THE NEGATIVE FORM

Listen :

(Vous êtes du quartier ?)
— Non, je ne suis pas du quartier.
(Vous changez à Concorde ?)
— Non, je ne change pas à Concorde.

NOW, ANSWER THE FOLLOWING QUESTIONS IN THE NEGATIVE FORM

(Vous êtes du quartier ?) — (Vous changez à Concorde ?) — (Il prend le métro ?) — (Je continue tout droit ?) — (Vous comprenez ?) — (Elle remonte l'avenue ?) — (Ils savent où c'est ?) — (Est-ce que c'est loin ?).

2. GRAMMAR : SEE PAGE 47

GIVING DIRECTIONS AND INSTRUCTIONS : THE IMPERATIVE

Listen :

(Nous tournons à droite ?)
— Oui, tournez à droite.

NOW, CONFIRM WHAT THESE PEOPLE SAY, USING THE IMPERATIVE FORM

(Nous tournons à droite ?) — (Nous traversons le pont ?) — (Nous changeons à l'Opéra ?) — (Nous descendons à Montparnasse ?) — (Nous allons par là ?) — (Nous prenons la rue du Bac ?) — (Nous remontons l'avenue ?)

3. GRAMMAR : SEE PAGE 47

VERB PRACTICE : REFLEXIVE VERBS

Listen :

(Je)
— Je me trompe d'étage.
(Nous)
— Nous nous trompons d'étage.

NOW, TRANSFORM THE SENTENCES USING THE PROMPT WORDS

(Je) — (Nous) — (Tu) — (Sophie) — (Yves) — (les Mercier)

4. GRAMMAR : SEE PAGE 44

SAYING HOW LONG IT TAKES TO REACH A PARTICULAR DESTINATION

Listen :

(5 mn, pied)
— C'est à 5 mn à pied.
(10 mn, métro)
— C'est à 10 mn en métro.

NOW, TELL PEOPLE HOW LONG IT WILL TAKE TO REACH THEIR DESTINATION

(5 mn, pied) — (10 mn, métro) — (20 mn, voiture) — (2 mn, bus) — (25 mn, taxi) — (10 mn, vélo) — (5 mn, pied) — (35 mn, train)

5. GRAMMAR : SEE PAGE 46

FORMING QUESTIONS : ASKING PEOPLE TO REPEAT THINGS

Listen :

(Je cherche Mme Letellier)
— Pardon, qui cherchez-vous ?
(Je m'appelle Girouy)
— Pardon, comment vous appelez-vous ?

NOW, ASK PEOPLE TO REPEAT THE FOLLOWING INFORMATION

(Je cherche Mme Letellier) — (Je m'appelle Girouy) — (J'habite à Mulhouse) — (Je viens du Canada) — (Je connais Jean-François) — (J'ai seize ans) — (Je suis né au Havre)

6. SEE PAGE 59

ASKING FOR DIRECTIONS

Listen :

(Excusez-moi Madame, je cherche la rue Bellidor)
— Pardon Madame, la rue Bellidor s'il vous plaît ?

NOW, ASK FOR DIRECTIONS IN THE SAME WAY

(Excusez-moi Madame, je cherche la rue Bellidor) — (Excusez-moi Monsieur, je cherche la gare de Lyon) — (Excusez-moi Madame, je cherche l'Opéra) — (Excusez-moi Monsieur, je cherche les Champs-Elysées) — (Excusez-moi Madame, je cherche le Faubourg St-Honoré) — (Excusez-moi Monsieur, je cherche la Villette)

GETTING AROUND

The answer is simple: quickly, cheaply, comfortably. Whatever you love or hate about the country, you have to admit that when it comes to eating, drinking, and getting from A to B, it can't be rivalled.

Take Parisian transport (yes, do take it — it's infinitely simpler, and often quicker, than driving): Paris must have one of the best and cheapest underground systems in the world, with the possible exception of Moscow.

Just look for the signs saying "Métro" (these are often the original beautiful wrought-iron ones from the turn of the century), go down innumerable steps (yes, the Paris métro is not built for those with weak leg muscles) and get your ticket. If you're staying for longer than ten days, and are going to do a lot of exploring, it's worth investing in a Carte Orange, which gives you unlimited travel on buses and métro for a month (it's on sale at the beginning of the month, so don't buy one on the 31st). If you're staying for a shorter period, buy a carnet (ten tickets at a reduced rate) which can be used on both buses and métro.

"MÉTRO" There is the Formule 1, which offers a day's unlimited travel on second-class bus, métro, and RER in central Paris, and the suburbs. Also, the Paris-Sésame ticket, which covers unlimited travel (first class) in Paris and its surroundings for two-, four- and seven-day periods. Now you've got your tickets, all you have to do is get on the train — preferably one going in the right direction.

THE MÉTRO MAP It looks like a multi-coloured spider, but in fact it's all fairly simple. You just look for the terminus of the route your station is on, and follow the signs. Métro trains are fast and regular, stations are close together, trains run until 12.45 at night, and, unless you're in some unsalubrious part of town, there are usually enough people around to make it safer than the London underground, to say nothing of the New York subway. Do hold on to your handbag or wallet, though, especially in the crowded rush-hour compartments.

If you hate the idea of missing the sights and sounds of the boulevards by going underground, Paris has an equally excellent bus service. Indeed, one of the great delights is that practically everywhere is within half an hour's reach, and practically everything en route is a feast for foreign eyes. Even if you have to face a journey out to the not-so-exciting suburbs, it is nothing like the ordeal it can become in other capital cities. A fast, modern train network, the RER, offers a quick, comfortable service to the outskirts of Paris. And, to the amazement of those used to travelling on British Rail, the trains run about every ten minutes and — miracle of miracles — they are nearly always on time.

If you're feeling rushed or rich, there are always taxis. They're fast (too fast, some would say) and not too expensive. But they're not always easy to find, especially when you really need them, and most Parisian taxi drivers seem to be afflicted by a permanent bad temper, usually manifested to their customers by a series of grudging growls. And don't be misled by the taxi drivers' dogs, those sweet little bundles of fur that sit next to their masters and mistresses in the front seats. They're probably trained to bite, or at least to snarl, especially at foreigners. Like owner, like dog.

ON FOOT Finally, if you've got the time and the energy, by far the best way to travel is on foot. Get a good map, and wander. Allow double the time you normally take to cover distances — there are so many tiny boutiques, cake shops, clothes shops and characters en route that a stop every few yards is almost obligatory.

Do be careful when crossing the roads. At best, Parisian drivers are fast. At worst, they can be maniacal. Even they seem to realise their tendencies, but it doesn't stop them making life hell for the foreign pedestrian. As the old saying of Parisian drivers goes: "To aim at a pedestrian on a street is sport, but to aim at him on a zebra crossing is sadism." Having said all that, you can still measure the pleasure of your stay by the shoe leather you have used up. With all its modern technological transport, Paris remains the domain of the idle wanderer (the French have a lovely word for it — le flâneur). Fare forward, flâneur ! □

2.1 TAKE A BREAK

Listen ***Les feuilles mortes***

Juliette Gréco

Oh je voudrais tant que tu te souviennes
Des jours heureux où nous étions amis
En ce temps-là la vie était plus belle
Et le soleil plus brûlant qu'aujourd'hui
Les feuilles mortes se ramassent à la pelle
Tu vois, je n'ai pas oublié
Les feuilles mortes se ramassent à la pelle
Les souvenirs et les regrets aussi
Et le vent du nord les emporte
Dans la nuit froide de l'oubli
Tu vois, je n'ai pas oublié
La chanson que tu me chantais
C'est une chanson qui nous ressemble
Toi qui m'aimais, moi qui t'aimais
Nous vivions tous les deux ensemble
Toi qui m'aimais, moi qui t'aimais
Mais la vie sépare ceux qui s'aiment
Tout doucement sans faire de bruit
Et la mer efface sur le sable
Les pas des amants désunis

The Dead Leaves

Oh, I so want you to remember
Those happy days when we were friends
Life was sweeter then
And the sun stronger than now
They're gathering up the dead leaves in shovels
You see, I haven't forgotten
They're gathering up the dead leaves in shovels
Along with the memories, the regrets
And the north wind is carrying them
Into the cold night of forgetfulness
You see, I haven't forgotten
The song you would sing for me
It's a song that's just like us
You loved me, and I loved you
We lived, the two of us together
You who loved me, I who loved you
But life comes between those who love
Very gently, noiselessly
And the sea washes away
The footprints of the separated lovers
From the sand

How well can you find your way around on the Paris underground? Look at the metro map (page 00), and follow the instructions below. You will find yourself in front of some of the monuments marked on the map on the facing page. Write the name of the monument in the blank beside the corresponding directions.

1. Vous êtes à la station Chaussée d'Antin. Vous prenez la direction Mairie d'Ivry et vous descendez à Châtelet. Ensuite vous prenez la correspondance Porte d'Orléans; c'est à 7 stations.

2. Vous prenez la direction Charles de Gaulle. C'est à 11 stations.

3. Vous prenez la direction Nation jusqu'à Trocadéro. Ensuite vous marchez un peu.

4. Vous prenez la direction Mairie de Montreuil jusqu'à Franklin D. Roosvelt. Ensuite vous prenez la correspondance Château de Vincennes. Vous descendez à Châtelet et vous marchez un peu.

5. Vous prenez la direction Pont de Neuilly et vous descendez.

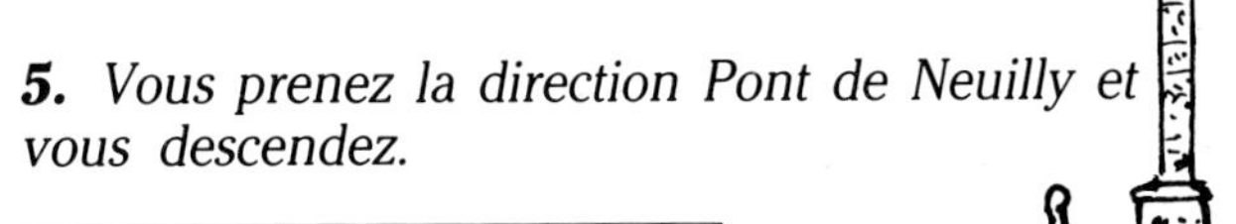

(See solutions on page 11)

2.2 CONTACTS

[• •] *Listen*

UN RENDEZ-VOUS

Monsieur Philippon, qui travaille dans une agence de presse, téléphone à Madame Lefèvre, attachée de presse de la société Durabel

M. Philippon : *Allô, la société Durabel ?*
Une dame : *Ah non, Monsieur, vous faites erreur ; quel numéro demandez-vous ?*
M. Philippon : *Le 48.06.66.90.*
La dame : *Ici c'est le 48.06.70.90.*
M. Philippon : *Oh, excusez-moi.*
La dame : *Je vous en prie.*

La standardiste : *Durabel, j'écoute.*
M. Philippon : *Bonjour Madame, je voudrais parler à Mme Lefèvre, s'il vous plaît.*
La standardiste : *Vous avez son numéro de poste ?*
M. Philippon : *Oui, c'est le 320.*
La standardiste :*Ne quittez pas, je vous la passe.*

M. Philippon : *Allô ? Allô, Mme Lefèvre ?*
La secrétaire : *Mme Lefèvre est en réunion. C'est de la part de qui, s'il vous plaît ?*
M. Philippon : *De la part de M. Philippon. Je voudrais prendre rendez-vous avec elle.*

La secrétaire : *Je suis sa secrétaire ; j'ai son agenda. Je vais noter le rendez-vous si vous voulez. Voyons... la semaine prochaine ?*
M. Philippon : *Non, je préfère cette semaine.*
La secrétaire : *Mercredi à 9 h 00, ça va ?*
M. Philippon : *Ah, ce n'est pas possible, le mercredi matin je suis toujours pris.*
La secrétaire : *Et cet après-midi à 17 h 00 ?*
M. Philippon : *Attendez, j'ai un rendez-vous à 15 h 00 et un autre à 18 h 00...*
Non, je n'ai pas le temps ! Mais je suis libre jeudi, en fin de journée.
La secrétaire : *Jeudi à 17 h 30 ?*
M. Philippon : *C'est parfait.*
La secrétaire : *Bon, je note. Rappelez-moi votre nom, s'il vous plaît.*
M. Philippon : *Philippon.*
La secrétaire : *Vous pouvez épeler, s'il vous plaît ?*
M. Philippon : *P.H.I.L.I.P.P.O.N.*
La secrétaire : *Merci Monsieur, je transmettrai à Mme Lefèvre.*
M. Philippon : *Merci beaucoup, Madame.*
La secrétaire : *Au revoir, Monsieur.*

[• •] Listen and repeat
(You may look at the translation on page 12 in the booklet.)

1. *Cabine téléphonique*
2. *Demande de rendez-vous*
3. *Rendez-vous impossible !*
4. *Réunion dans une entreprise*

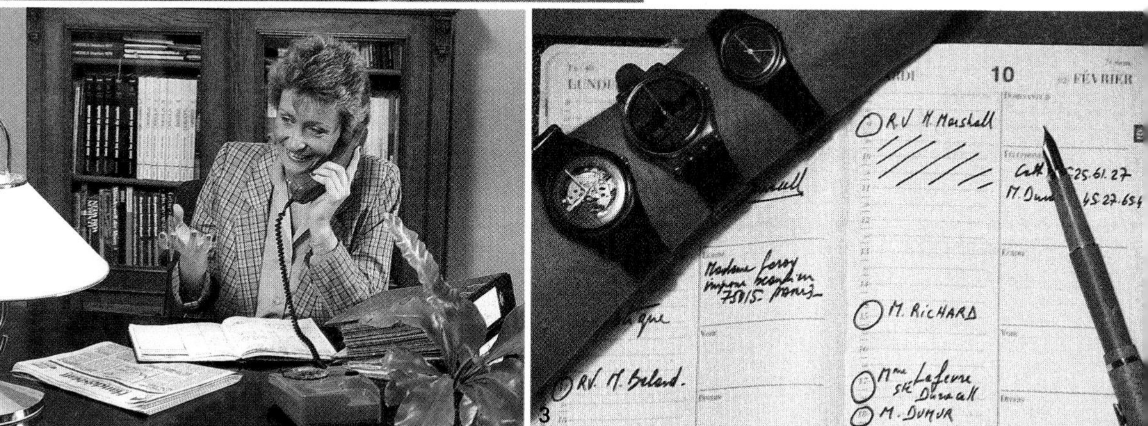

2.2 WORDS

rendez-vous (M) — appointment
agence (F) — agency
agence de presse (F) — press agency
attaché(e) de presse — a public relations officer
numéro (M) — number
standardiste (M ou F) — switchboard operator
numéro de poste (M) — extension
poste (M) — extension
réunion (F) — meeting
agenda (M) — diary
semaine (F) — week
heure (F) — hour
matin (M) — morning
journée (F) — day **(1)**
jour (M) — day
après-midi (M ou F) — afternoon
an (M) — year
année (F) — year
téléphone (M) — telephone
annuaire (M) — telephone directory
appel (M) — (phone) call
communication (F) — (phone) call
standard (M) — switchboard

téléphoner (à quelqu'un) — to telephone someone
demander (quelque chose à quelqu'un) — to ask (someone for something)
écouter — to listen to
noter — to make a note of something
préférer — to prefer
rappeler — to remind someone (of something)
transmettre — to pass on a message
appeler (quelqu'un) — to call (someone)
rappeler (quelqu'un) — to call (someone) back
décrocher — to pick up the receiver
raccrocher — to hang up
entendre — to hear

au revoir — goodbye
allô — hello
être en réunion — to be in a meeting
prendre rendez-vous — to make an appointment
être pris — to be busy
être libre — to be free
avoir le temps — to have time
en fin (de) — at the end of
faire erreur — to make a mistake
passer (quelqu'un à quelqu'un) — to put someone through
être en communication — to be on the phone
être en ligne — to be on the line
aujourd'hui — today
demain — tomorrow
hier — yesterday
après-demain — the day after tomorrow
avant-hier — the day before yesterday

REMEMBER... REMEMBER... REMEMBER... REMEMBER... REMEMBER

(1) *When you wish to talk about a specific number of days, you must use the word « jour » (il travaille depuis dix jours). If, on the other hand, you are referring to something that happened within a particular day you use « journée » (il a fait beau toute la journée). The same rule applies for* matin/matinée, an/année soir/soirée.

HOW TO SAY IT

1. MAKING A PHONE CALL

Allô, Madame Lefèvre ? — Hello, is that Mrs. Lefèvre ?
Allô, la société Duracel ? — Hello, is that Duracel ?
Allô, le 48.06.66.90 ? — Hello, is that 48.06.66.90 ?
Allô, je suis bien chez Madame Lefèvre ? — Hello, is that Mrs. Lefèvre's residence ?

2. ANSWERING A CALL

Oui, c'est moi / *Oui, j'écoute* — Yes, speaking
Monsieur Dévé à l'appareil — Mr. Dévé speaking
Oui, c'est bien ici — Yes, that's right
Non, vous faites erreur / *Non, c'est une erreur* / *Non, vous vous trompez (de numéro)* — No, you've got the wrong number
Non, il n'y a pas de Monsieur/Madame X ici ! — No, there's no one here by that name

3. ASKING FOR A SPECIFIC PERSON

Mme Lefèvre, s'il vous plaît ? — Mrs. Lefèvre, please ?
Je voudrais parler au directeur — I'd like to speak to the director
Est-ce que je pourrais parler à Jacqueline ? — Could I speak to Jacqueline ?
Vous pouvez me passer M. Philippon ? — Could you put me through to Mr. Philippon ?

4. ASKING WHO IS CALLING

C'est Monsieur/Madame... ? / *Vous êtes Monsieur/Madame.. ?* — Is that Mr./Mrs... ?
Qui est à l'appareil ? / *C'est de la part de qui ?* — Who's calling ?

5. ANSWERING A REQUEST

Oui, je vous le/la passe — Yes, I'll put you through
Oui, ne quittez pas — Yes, hold on, please
Oui, un instant je vous prie — Yes, one moment, please

Non, il/elle n'est pas là — No he/she isn't in
C'est occupé... — It's engaged
Il est en ligne... / *Il est en communication...* — He is on another line
Vous patientez s'il vous plaît — Could you hold on, please ?
Non il/elle est absente — No, he/she is away
Non il/elle est en réunion — No, he/she is in a meeting
Il n'y a plus personne — Everyone's gone

2.2 ORAL PRACTICE

1. GRAMMAR : SEE PAGE 46

VERB PRACTICE : THE VERB « ALLER »

Listen :

(Je)

— Je vais à l'agence.

(Nous)

— Nous allons à l'agence.

(M. Philippon)

— M. Philippon va à l'agence.

NOW, CHANGE THE FORM OF THE VERB « ALLER », USING THE PROMPTS

(Je) — (Nous) — (M. Philippon) — (Tu) — (Vous) — (Mme Lefèvre) — (Les clients) — (Je) — (Véronique et Michel)

2. GRAMMAR : SEE PAGE 40

ASKING FOR SOMEONE ON THE TELEPHONE

Listen :

(Henri Dubois)

— Je voudrais parler à Henri Dubois, s'il vous plaît.

(Responsable)

— Je voudrais parler au responsable...

NOW, ASK TO SPEAK TO THE FOLLOWING PEOPLE. REMEMBER TO USE THE DEFINITE ARTICLE WHEN NECESSARY

(Henri Dubois) — (Responsable) — (Ingénieur) — (Directrice) — (Attaché de presse) — (Anne Perrot) — (Directeur des achats) — (Cliente) — (Monsieur Serval)

3. GRAMMAR : SEE PAGE 47

POLITE REQUESTS :

Listen :

(Épelez !)

— Vous pouvez épeler, s'il vous plaît ?

(Répétez !)

— Vous pouvez répéter, s'il vous plaît ?

NOW, ASK PEOPLE TO DO THE FOLLOWING, USING THE POLITE FORM

(Épelez !) — (Répétez !) — (Venez !) — (Sortez !) — (Descendez !) — (Transmettez !) — (Écrivez !) — (Choisissez !)

4. GRAMMAR : SEE PAGE 44

TELLING THE TIME :

Listen :

(Il est exactement 18 h 15 mn)

— Il est déjà 6 heures et quart !

(Il est exactement 15 h 30 mn)

— Il est déjà 3 heures et demie !

NOW, EXPRESS THE FOLLOWING TIMES IN THE ALTERNATIVE WAY, USING THE 12-HOUR CLOCK

(Il est exactement 18 h 15 mn) — (Il est exactement 15 h 30 mn) — (Il est exactement 20 h 45 mn) — (Il est exactement 12 h) — (Il est exactement 9 h 15mn) — (Il est exactement 23 h) — (Il est exactement 11 h 55 mn) — (Il est exactement 00 h) — (Il est exactement 5 h 40 mn)

5. SEE PAGE 67

CONFIRMING TELEPHONE NUMBERS AND ASKING FOR SOMEONE

Listen and look at the phone number :

(Roger Lafosse — 42.72.23.86)

— Allô le 42.72.23.86 ? M. Lafosse, s'il vous plaît.

NOW, YOU CHECK THE TELEPHONE NUMBERS AND ASK FOR THE FOLLOWING PEOPLE

(Roger Lafosse 42.72.23.86) — (Alain Butaro 78.37.84.50) — (Sophie Dumoyer 44.00.33.54) — (Françoise Martin 83.21.81.14) — (Christian Ferr 73.90.11.87) — (Jean Bertrand 31.97.33.27) — (Yves Jonon 39.46.55.35)

6. GRAMMAR : SEE PAGE 44

TIMETABLES :

Listen :

(Casablanca 08 h 15/mardi)

— L'avion pour Casablanca part mard. matin.

(Caracas 23 h 59/jeudi)

— L'avion pour Caracas part jeudi soir.

NOW, YOU GIVE THE DESTINATIONS AND DAYS OF THE FOLLOWING FLIGHT

(Casablanca 08 h 15/mardi) — (Caracas 23 h 59/jeudi — (Johannesburg 22 h 40/dimanche) — (Annecy 19 h 30/mercredi) — (Tokyo 6 h 55/lundi) — (Cayenne 10 h 20/vendredi)

MÉTRO-BOULOT-DODO

There is a phrase in French slang that says it's all : "Métro, boulot, dodo" — commute, work, sleep. Contrary to the myth of the light-hearted, pleasure-loving Latins, the French work schedule can be gruelling for those accustomed to an eight-hour day with tea breaks.

In France, the day begins early, with most offices waking up at around 8.00 or 8.30 and finishing nine hours later, with a 45-minute break for lunch, often in the company canteen. But the higher you go in the hierarchy, the later the day begins. Some Parisian "cadres" (executives) have earned the evil reputation of rolling into the office at around 10.00, taking a leisurely three-hour lunch break, and clocking off well-fed and sleepy from the afternoon's excesses, well before six. This is not strictly true, either. Many French marriages must have been sorely tested by an overtime routine that keeps busy executives in their offices until 7.00 or 8.00 in the evening.

BUSINESS IS BUSINESS But it's not all grind. Two great pleasures alleviate the lot of the French employee. The first is the Business Lunch — rarely a snack, never a sandwich. It is a ritual of fine surroundings and good taste — literally. Whether in a local café, bistro or luxury restaurant, you can expect your French host to tuck happily into an entrée and main course, washed down by a bottle of something delicious, followed by dessert and the essential strong black coffee that hopefully undoes some of the damage caused by that extra glass of Beaujolais. To an Anglo-Saxon palate, it is sometimes a mystery how any work gets done at all : the mornings are spent starving after a practically non-existent breakfast at the crack of dawn (they say that, statistically, more road accidents occur at 11.30 a.m. than at any other time — when French stomachs are empty and tempers flare) and the afternoons are spent in a bloated state of euphoria.

BRIDGES AND LONG WEEK-ENDS The other great alleviator is the holiday. On average, the French worker officially gets five weeks holiday a year, divided into a winter and summer break. Officially, in fact, the French work force, regardless of individual religious convictions, benefits from a whole panoply of national holidays. In May and November, when the deities are particularly active, the norm is a four-day week. Then there is that other wonderful invention : "Le Pont" (the bridge). "On fait le pont" means that, if the holiday falls on a Tuesday or Thursday, the preceding Monday or follow ing Friday get thrown in into the bargain, and the week gets whittled down to three days. Then, of course, there's August, when total paralysis hits the country as everyone takes off on their annual month's vacation. So — if your main goal is really to go to France to get some serious work done (but whoever goes to France only for work ?) the best months are January, March and possibly a bit of September. Work hard (when you're there, that is), eat well, play a lot. The recipe's not so bad, n'est-ce pas ? □

N° 1 [• •] Listen

Listen to the radio advertisements, then fill in the right numbers after each one.

- *Les numéros gagnants du loto* ....

- *« La Belle Époque », la plus belle brasserie de Paris. Ouvert après minuit : crustacés coquillages. Réservations au* ....

- *Salle 1 « Tombe les filles et tais-toi » de Woody Allen. Séances à* .... *le film* ....*minutes après*

- *Vous perdez vos cheveux ? Appelez-nous au* ....

N° 2

Put the missing words in the blanks on the grid ; another word will appear in the grey column.

1. *Hold the line, please.*
Ne .... pas, s'il vous plaît.
2. *I'm sorry, her line's engaged.*
Elle est .... (two words)
3. *Who's calling, please ?*
C'est .... de qui ? (three words)
4. *Hold on, I'll put you through.*
Ne quittez pas, je vous la ....
5. *What's her extension ?*
Quel est son .... ?
6. *It's 810.*
C'est le .... (write out in full).
7. *I'm sorry, there's no answer.*
Ça ne .... pas.
8. *Would you like to hold the line ?*
Voulez-vous ....?
9. *No thank you. I'll call back later.*
Non, merci. Je ....

N° 3

Mme Dutheil's secretary has mixed up her appointments. Can you rewrite the items on the left in the blank diary on the right ?

9.00 Déjeuner avec M. Bartolli.
10.00 Cocktail-Présentation des nouveaux produits.
12.30 Réunion avec la direction commerciale.
14.30 Courrier.
18.30 Préparation des documents pour la réunion avec la direction commerciale.
20.30 Dîner chez les Bonnard.

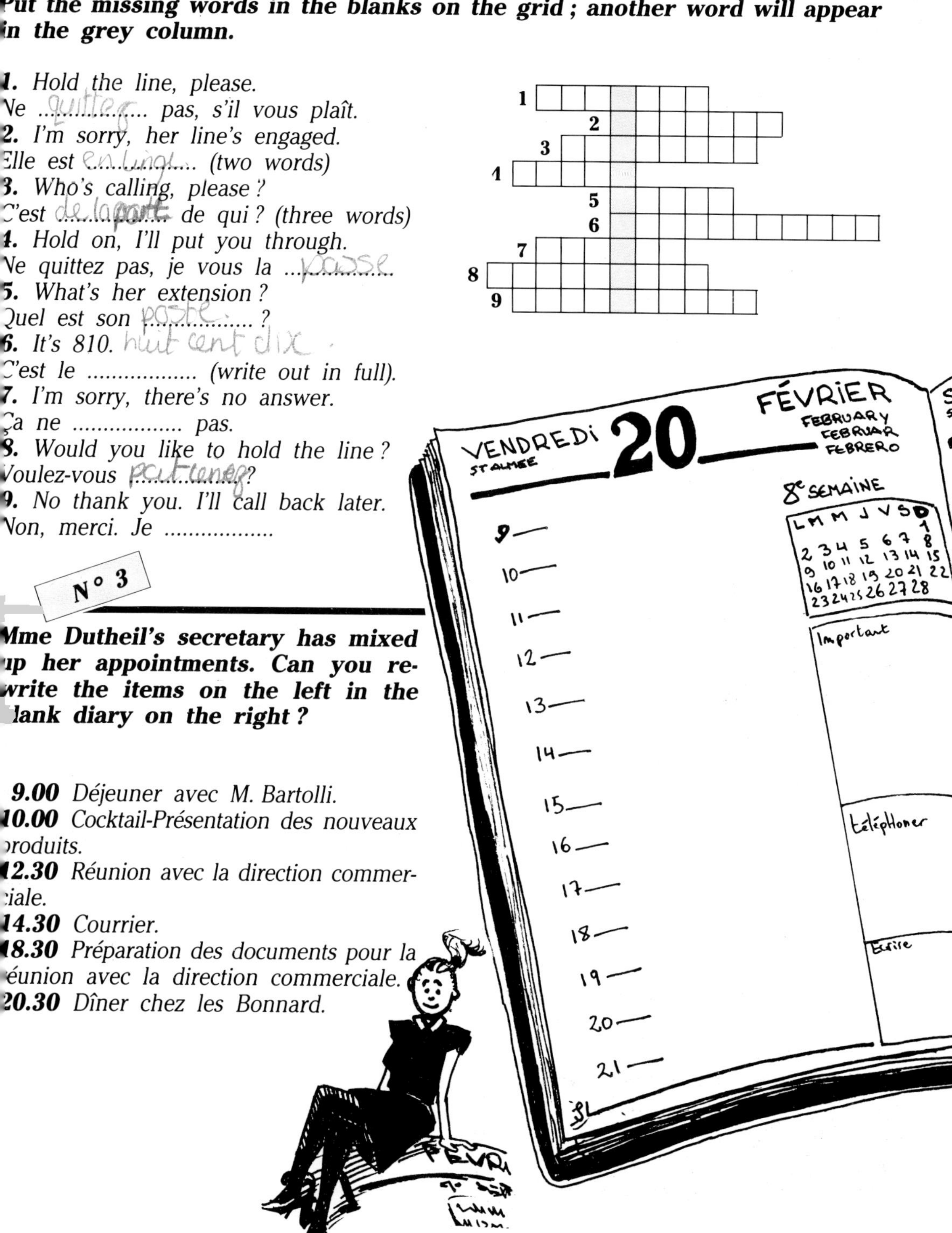

(See solutions on page 13)

2.3 CONTACTS

[• •] *Listen*

EN TAXI

Monsieur Philippon est en retard à son rendez-vous Il prend un taxi

M. Philippon : *Bonjour Monsieur, 17 rue La Rochelle, s'il vous plaît.*
Le chauffeur de taxi : *C'est près de la tour Montparnasse ?*
M. Philippon : *Oui, c'est juste derrière.*

Le chauffeur : *Quel sale temps ! Depuis deux jours il y a du vent et en plus aujourd'hui il fait froid.*
M. Philippon : *Vous savez, vous avez de la chance, ici. J'arrive de Suède : là-bas il fait – 10° en ce moment et il neige depuis deux mois.*
Le chauffeur : *Vous êtes suédois ? Vous parlez bien français pour un Suédois.*
M. Philippon : *Je ne suis pas suédois ; je suis français, mais je vis en Suède depuis quinze ans.*

Le chauffeur : *Et ça vous plaît, la Suède ?*
M. Philippon : *Oui, beaucoup ; j'ai un travail qui m'intéresse... et puis ma femme est suédoise !*
Le chauffeur : *Ah, je comprends ! Et l'hiver, vous aimez ? Il fait nuit très tôt, là-bas ?*
M. Philippon : *Oui, vers trois heures et demie, mais on est habitué. En Suède les maisons sont très agréables, on aime bien rester chez soi ; on lit beaucoup, on écoute de la musique et on ne se couche pas tard, vous savez.*
Le chauffeur : *Vous habitez à Stockholm*
M. Philippon : *Non, j'habite dans la ban lieue au bord d'un lac, en pleine forêt on peut faire du ski derrière la maiso et l'été, avec les enfants, on se baign dans le lac.*
Le chauffeur : *Alors vous n'aimez pa Paris ?*
M. Philippon : *Si, j'aime bien, c'est un très belle ville, mais je préfère la cam pagne ; j'ai horreur du bruit et de l foule.*

Le chauffeur : *Ça y est ! Un embouteillage Ah, je vous jure !*
M. Philippon : *Vous avez l'heure, s'il vou plaît ?*
Le chauffeur : *Oui, il est quatre heures Vous êtes pressé ?*
M. Philippon : *Assez, oui.*
Le chauffeur : *Bon. Alors, il vaut mieu prendre le métro. C'est direct et vou serez à Montparnasse dans dix minutes*
M. Philippon : *Vous avez raison. Je vou dois combien ?*
Le chauffeur : *Ça fait 50 F.*
M. Philippon : *Vous me faites une fiche s'il vous plaît.*
Le chauffeur : *Voilà Monsieur, et bonn journée.*
M. Philippon : *Merci, au revoir.*

[• •] Listen and repeat
(You may look at the translation on page 13 in th booklet.)

1. *Embouteillage Place de la Concorde, à Paris*
2. *Station de taxis*
3. *Taxi parisien « pas libre »*
4. *Compteur de taxi*
5. *Tour Montparnasse*

2.3 WORDS

NOUNS

chauffeur de taxi (M) — taxi driver
temps (M) — weather or time ***(1)***
vent (M) — wind
travail (M) — work
femme (F) — woman, wife
hiver (M) — winter
maison (F) — house
banlieue (F) — suburb
lac (M) — lake
forêt (F) — forest
été (M) — summer
ville (F) — town
campagne (F) — country(side)
bruit (M) — noise
foule (F) — crowd
embouteillage (M) — traffic jam
fiche (F) (de taxi) — receipt (for taxi ride)
automne (M) — autumn
printemps (M) — spring
saison (F) — season
parent (M) — parent

ADJECTIVES

agréable — pleasant
beau (belle) — handsome, beautiful
direct(e) — direct
froid(e) — cold
chaud(e) — hot

VERBS

prendre (un taxi, un bus) — to take (a taxi, bus)
arriver — to arrive, to happen
neiger — to snow
vivre — to live
intéresser — to interest
aimer — to like, to love
rester — to stay
lire — to read
se coucher — to go to bed
se baigner — to go swimming
partir — to leave, to depart
adorer — to love, to adore
détester — to hate, to detest
pleuvoir — to rain

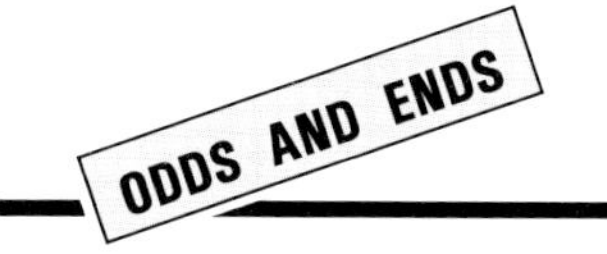

ODDS AND ENDS

être en retard — to be late
devoir de l'argent (à quelqu'un) — to owe money
il y a du vent — it's windy
il fait froid — it's cold ***(2)***
il fait nuit — it's dark, it gets dark
tôt — early
tard — late
faire du ski — to ski
avoir horreur (de) — to hate, to loathe
avoir l'heure — to have the time (refers to watch, clock)
être pressé(e) — to be in a hurry
avoir raison — to be right
être à l'heure — to be on time
être en avance — to be early
il fait jour — it's light, it gets light
avoir tort — to be wrong
faire du sport — to play sports
jouer au tennis — to play tennis
jouer d'un instrument — to play an instrument
faire de la voile — to sail
faire du bateau — to sail
faire du cheval — to ride
faire de la natation — to swim

HOW TO SAY IT

1. ASKING AND SAYING WHAT SOMEONE LIKES

Vous aimez Paris ? — Do you like Paris ?
Vous aimez le ski ? — Do you like skiing ?
Ça vous plaît, la Suède ? — Do you like Sweden ?
J'aime rester chez moi — I like staying at home
J'aime bien la musique — I like music a lot ***(3)***
J'aime beaucoup Stockholm — I like Stockholm very much
J'adore le cinéma — I love the cinema
Ce film me plaît beaucoup — I like this film very much

2. SAYING WHAT YOU DON'T LIKE

Je n'aime pas les grandes villes — I don't like big cities
Je déteste les embouteillages — I hate traffic jams
J'ai horreur du bruit — I can't stand noise
Cette ville ne me plaît pas du tout — I don't like this city at all
Je n'aime pas beaucoup le ski — I don't like skiing very much

3. SAYING WHAT YOU PREFER

Je préfère la campagne — I prefer the country
J'aime mieux les petites villes — I prefer small towns

4. GIVING ADVICE

Il vaut mieux prendre le métro — It would be better to take the metro
Je vous (je te) conseille de prendre un taxi — I'd advise you to take a taxi
Vous devriez (tu devrais) prendre le bus — You should take the bus
Vous feriez (tu ferais) mieux de prendre l'avion — You would be better off taking the plane
A votre (à ta) place, je prendrais le train — If I were you, I would take the train

REMEMBER... REMEMBER... REMEMBER... REMEMBER... REMEMBER

(1) *The word « temps » can be translated as either « weather » or « time ». However, to ask the time in French you say « Quelle heure est-il ? ». The question « Quel temps fait-il ? » means « What is the weather like ? » —* ***(2)*** *When talking about the weather, the expression « il fait » is used to say : it is hot, cold, mild, etc. (see improve 2 page 97). If you want to say that a person is hot or cold, the verb « avoir » is used : il a chaud, j'ai froid, etc. In all other cases, the verb « être » is used : mon café est froid, cette omelette est chaude. —* ***(3)*** *After verbs such as « aimer », « adorer » you must use the definite article when referring to things in general : « j'aime* la *musique ».*

2.3 ORAL PRACTICE

1. GRAMMAR : SEE PAGE 44

DURATION : SAYING HOW LONG YOU HAVE BEEN DOING SOMETHING

Listen :

(Vous vivez en Suède ? — 15 ans)
— Oui, je vis en Suède depuis 15 ans.
(Vous connaissez Marie ? — 1980)
— Oui, je connais Marie depuis 1980.

NOW, YOU SAY HOW LONG YOU HAVE BEEN DOING THE FOLLOWING

(Vous vivez en Suède ?) (15 ans) — (Vous connaissez Marie ?) (1980) — (Vous faites du ski ?) (10 ans) — (Vous attendez Michel ?) (2 heures) — (Vous êtes marié ?) (26 ans) — (Vous allez sur la Côte d'Azur ?) (1981)

2. GRAMMAR : SEE PAGE 46

VERB PRACTICE : THE VERB « FAIRE »

Listen :

(Je) — (ski)
— Je fais du ski.
(Vous) — (voile)
— Vous faites de la voile.

NOW, COMPLETE THE FOLLOWING SENTENCES PUTTING THE VERB « FAIRE » IN THE CORRECT FORM

(Je) (ski) — (Vous) (voile) — (Marcel) (bateau) — (Tu) (gymnastique) — (Les enfants) (cheval) — (Je) (natation) — (Nous) (vélo) — (Vous) (danse)

3. SEE PAGE 75

DISCUSSING LEISURE ACTIVITIES :

Listen :

(Je fais du ski)
— Ah bon, vous aimez le ski ?
(Je joue au tennis)
— Ah bon, vous aimez le tennis ?

NOW, COMMENT ON WHAT PEOPLE DO IN THEIR FREE TIME

(Je fais du ski) — (Je joue au tennis) — (Je fais du cheval) — (Je joue au golf) — (Je joue du piano) — (Je fais de la danse) — (Je joue de la guitare) — (Je fais de la natation) — (Je joue au football)

4. GRAMMAR : SEE PAGE 47

SAYING WHAT YOU LIKE DOING :

Listen :

(On reste à la maison)
— On aime rester à la maison.
(On écoute de la musique)
— On aime écouter de la musique.

NOW, SAY WHAT YOU (AND YOUR FAMILY) LIKE DOING

(On reste à la maison) — (On écoute de la musique) — (On lit) — (On fait du ski) — (On se baigne dans le lac) — (On se couche tôt) — (On prend l'avion) — (On va au restaurant)

5. SEE PAGE 75

SAYING WHAT YOU LIKE AND DISLIKE :

Listen :

(Les grandes villes, vous n'aimez pas ?)
— Ah non, je déteste les grandes villes !
(La campagne, vous aimez ?)
— Ah oui, j'adore la campagne !

NOW, CONFIRM WHAT YOU LIKE AND DISLIKE

(Les grandes villes, vous n'aimez pas ?) — (La campagne, vous aimez ?) — (La forêt, vous aimez ?) — (La banlieue, vous n'aimez pas ?) — (Le vent, vous n'aimez pas ?) — (Le soleil, vous aimez ?) — (Le métro, vous n'aimez pas ?) — (Le ski, vous aimez ?)

6. GRAMMAR : SEE PAGE 47

VERB PRACTICE : REFLEXIVE VERBS IN THE NEGATIVE FORM

Listen :

(Vous vous couchez tard ?)
— Non, je ne me couche pas tard.
(Il se trompe d'étage ?)
— Non, il ne se trompe pas d'étage.

NOW, ANSWER THE FOLLOWING QUESTIONS IN THE NEGATIVE FORM

(Vous vous couchez tard ?) — (Il se trompe d'étage ?) — (Vous vous baignez dans le lac ?) — (Elle s'appelle Anne-Marie ?) — (Je me trompe de bureau ?) — (Nous nous occupons des achats ?) — (Les enfants se lèvent tard ?)

THE WEATHER

A SAFE TOPIC OF CONVERSATION *"When two Englishmen meet their first talk is of the weather," observed Samuel Johnson. In France, the first talk is often of food and wine, but the weather comes a close second. It is always a safe topic of conversation, especially before* le week-end *when the middle classes are contemplating their weekly escapades to their country homes* (la maison de campagne).

France is blessed with a great variety of climates, so depending where you go you can encounter any sort of weather from grey skies and nordic temperatures in the north to Mediterranean sunshine and warmth in the south. But wherever you go, you will find the pleasant outdoor habits of the Mediterranean, for the sunny south has somehow spread its habits to the rest of the country : Paris, for example, is not really any warmer or dryer than London, yet the sidewalk café is as much a part of life in Paris as it is on the Côte-d'Azur. Although you will hear people grumbling about the weather, as they do elsewhere in the world, the French — or at least French café owners — are endowed with unflagging optimism. At the first timid appearance of a pale springtime ray of sunshine, café tables and chairs are carried outside. If surprised by a downpour, everyone rushes indoors and, when the rain stops, the garçon de café *simply sponges some of the water off the chairs and greets a new batch of customers intent on getting a headstart on their summer tans* (le bronzage).

"BRONZER" *Thanks to France's varied climatic zones, it is possible to* bronzer *in continental France for most of thc year. In the winter, thousands of ski buffs head for the slopes in the Alps and the Pyrenees. It has become very popular, and very chic, to take a week's holiday in the winter to go skiing. In February (the most popular season for skiing) city streets suddenly become dotted with brown faces, owl-like from skiing with goggles.*

Sun-worshippers who aren't satisfied with the limited tan afforded by the slopes and want the total tan that will make neighbours and co-workers pale with envy can always try one of France's distant départements *in the Caribbean or the Indian Ocean. There they will find sun during Europe's dreariest months.*

PARIS IN THE SPRING *Paris and the rest of the country are often very beautiful in the spring, yet anyone planning a springtime holiday should remember that March and April are the rainiest months on the Mediterranean. Late summer and early autumn are often the best seasons in the south. Known as the* arrière-saison, *late summer is the time of the year to relax in the golden afternoon sunshine, tour the winegrowing country, and meet and talk to the local people, who are much friendlier and less harried than in the peak tourist months of July and August.*

Southern France is the only part of the country that has fairly stable, predictable weather — that is, it's nearly always pleasant and sunny. Elsewhere the weather is changeable and unpredictable (making the weatherman's job an unenviable one). Perhaps that's why it's such a constant topic of conversation : the sun, and the clouds and the wind are always doing something to remind you of their existence. □

N° 1

Listen

Listen to our reporters and guess where they're speaking from. To help you, a few key words in each report have been translated. Then, put the right numbers in the boxes next to the places listed below.

un lac — a lake
une forêt — a forest
la neige — snow
le froid — cold
un loup — a wolf
un défilé de mode — a fashion show
un grand couturier — a famous fashion designer
une pierre — a stone
l'art — art
l'histoire — history
une église — a church
une planche à voile — a windsurf board
la mer — the sea
une vague — a wave
une vedette — a star
une fête — a party

☐ *Hawaii*
☐ *Tokyo*
☐ *Rome*
☐ *Cannes*
☐ *Canada*

N° 2

Describe today's weather in France, using the meteorological map and the key below. Write sentences using the model:

A Marseille, il fait un temps ensoleillé avec beaucoup de vent du sud-ouest ; la température est de 23° C.

TEMPS ENSOLEILLÉ

TEMPS NUAGEUX AVEC DES ÉCLAIRCIES

PLUIE

ORAGES

TEMPS BRUMEUX

VENT

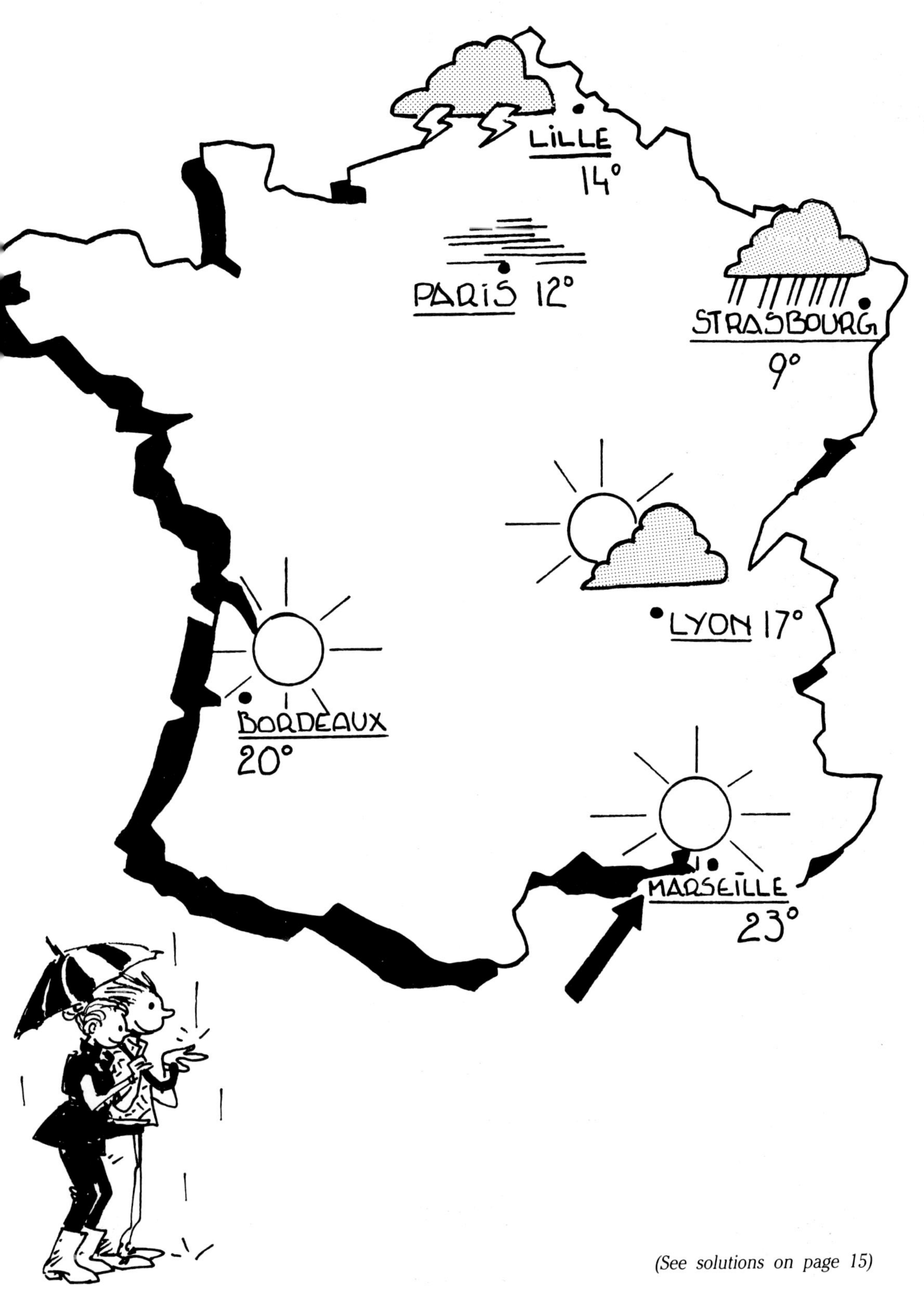

(See solutions on page 15)

2.4 CONTACTS

[• •] *Listen*

QUEL CANDIDAT CHOISIR ?

Monsieur Vabret, directeur du personnel, va voir Monsieur Launay, le président-directeur général

M. Launay, P.-D.G. : *Oui, entrez.*
M. Vabret, D. : *Bonjour Monsieur Launay.*
P.-D.G. : *Bonjour Monsieur Vabret, asseyez-vous, je vous en prie.*
D. : *Merci.*

P.-D.G. : *Alors, vous l'avez trouvé, notre futur directeur export ?*
D. : *Je crois que oui. J'ai deux candidats qui me semblent très intéressants. Tenez, si vous voulez regarder leurs curriculum vitae.*

P.-D.G. : *Il a l'air bien, ce Jacques Leclerc. Je vois qu'il a beaucoup d'expérience.*
D. : *Oui, j'ai discuté avec lui ; visiblement il connaît bien les problèmes de la vente ; il saura animer une équipe de vendeurs et il s'intéresse aux nouvelles technologies.*
P.-D.G. : *En plus, il est célibataire : il pourra voyager facilement. Il parle bien anglais ?*
D. : *Il n'est pas vraiment bilingue mais il parle correctement. Il parle aussi espagnol.*
P.-D.G. : *Vous voyez autre chose ?*
D. : *A mon avis, c'est un jeune homme un peu trop réservé...*

P.-D.G. : *Et Mademoiselle Lefranc, elle n'est pas trop jeune pour le poste ? Elle n'a que 32 ans ! Qu'est-ce que vous en pensez ?*
D. : *Moi, elle m'a impressionné ; elle est diplômée de l'ESSEC, elle a de l'allure, elle est souriante et elle a beaucoup de charme.*
P.-D.G. : *Et vous pensez qu'elle est capable de s'imposer ?*
D. : *Oui, tout à fait, elle a une forte personnalité.*
P.-D.G. : *Elle parle vraiment trois langues ?*
D. : *Oui, couramment.*
P.-D.G. : *Et pour les déplacements ?*
D. : *Elle est très disponible et elle adore voyager.*

P.-D.G. : *Si je comprends bien, vous préférez Mlle Lefranc ? Bon, convoquez-les tous les deux pour mardi après-midi.*
D. : *Bien, Monsieur.*
P.-D.G. : *A propos, vous sortez avec nos clients brésiliens ce soir ?*
D. : *Oui, je dois les emmener dîner à « La Closerie des Lilas » et ensuite nous allons au Crazy Horse.*
P.-D.G. : *Au Crazy Horse!! Alors, bonne soirée !... et à demain.*

[• •] Listen and repeat
(You may look at the translation on page 15 in the booklet.)

1. Quel est le candidat idéal ? 2. Réunion de travail
3. La Closerie des Lilas : restaurant parisien dans le 14ᵉ arrondissement

2.4 WORDS

candidat(e) — applicant, candidate
président-directeur général (PDG) (M) — company president
directeur du personnel (M) — personnel manager
personnel (M) — staff
expérience (F) — experience
problème (M) — problem
vente (F) — sales, selling
équipe (F) — team
vendeur(euse) — salesperson
technologie (F) — technology
ambition (F) — ambition
poste (M) — position
acheteur(euse) — buyer
représentant(e) — representative

nouveau (nouvelle) — new
réservé(e) — reserved
diplômé(e) — a graduate of
souriant(e) — cheerful
fort(e) — strong
disponible — available
intelligent(e) — intelligent
timide — shy
sympathique — likeable
antipathique — unpleasant, disagreeable
ouvert(e) — open
gentil(le) — nice
ambitieux(se) — ambitious
sérieux(se) — serious
désagréable — unpleasant
grand(e) — tall
petit(e) — short
gros(se) — fat
maigre — thin
joli(e) — pretty
mince — slim

s'asseoir — to sit down
sembler — to seem, to appear
voir — to see
discuter — to talk, to discuss
animer — to lead, to organize (a group)
s'intéresser — to be interested in
manquer (de) — to lack
impressionner — to make a good impressio
s'imposer — to assert oneself
convoquer — to summon, to ask to a meetin
sortir (avec) — to go out (with)
se lever — to get up
croire — to think, to believe ***(1)***
regarder — to look at
acheter — to buy
vendre — to sell

aller voir quelqu'un — to visit someone ***(2***
à mon avis — in my opinion
avoir de l'allure — to be striking
avoir du charme — to be charming
à demain — see you tomorrow
avoir l'air — to look
taper à la machine — to type

HOW TO SAY IT

1. ASKING SOMEONE FOR AN OPINION

u'est-ce que vous pensez de Jacques ? — What do you think of Jacques ?
ous pensez qu'il est intelligent ? / *ous croyez qu'il est intelligent ?* — Do you think he's intelligent ? ***(1)***
votre avis, c'est bien ? — Is it good, in your opinion ?
uel est votre avis ? — What's your opinion ?

2. GIVING AN OPINION

e pense que c'est un bon vendeur / *e crois que c'est un bon vendeur* / *e trouve que c'est un bon vendeur* — I think he's a good salesman
mon avis, c'est un bon vendeur — In my opinion he's a good salesman
est anglais, je pense/je crois — He's English, I think
e pense que oui/non — I think so/I don't think so

3. TALKING ABOUT WHAT YOU CAN DO

parle espagnol — He speaks Spanish
connaît les problèmes de la vente — He knows all about sales
est bilingue — He's bilingual
sait animer une équipe — He knows how to manage a team
est capable d'animer une équipe — He is able to manage a team
e suis bon en anglais — I'm very good at English
ous êtes doué(e) pour le commerce — You are very good at selling

4. TALKING ABOUT YOUR INTERESTS

s'intéresse aux nouvelles technologies / *es nouvelles technologies l'intéressent* — He's interested in modern technology
e suis passionné par l'informatique / *'informatique me passionne* — I'm very interested in computer science

REMEMBER... REMEMBER... REMEMBER... REMEMBER... REMEMBER

1) *« Penser », « croire » and « trouver », are always followed by « que » when they are used to express pinions. —* ***(2)*** *In French « visiter » is used exclusively for places and monuments, never for people : « on end visite à quelqu'un » or « on va voir quelqu'un »*

2.4 ORAL PRACTICE

1. GRAMMAR : SEE PAGE 41

ADJECTIVES : MASCULINE AND FEMININE FORMS

Listen :

(Il est grand)

— Oui, mais elle aussi, elle est grande.

NOW, TRANSFORM THE ADJECTIVES FROM THE MASCULINE TO THE FEMININE FORM

(Il est grand) — (Il est sérieux) — (Il est charmant) — (Il est disponible) — (Il est intéressant) — (Il est intelligent) — (Il est travailleur) — (Il est bilingue) — (Il est ambitieux)

2. SEE PAGE 83

VERB PRACTICE : EXPRESSING OPINIONS

Listen :

(Je) — (penser)

— Je pense qu'il est bilingue.

(Vous) — (croire)

— Vous croyez qu'il est bilingue.

NOW, MAKE SIMILAR SENTENCES USING THE FOLLOWING PROMPT WORDS

(Je) (penser) — (Vous) (croire) — (Gisèle) (être sûr) — (Je) (croire) — (Tu) (savoir) — (Nous) (penser) — (Vous) (voir) — (Frédéric) (croire)

3. GRAMMAR : SEE PAGE 41

DESCRIBING PEOPLE : MASCULINE AND FEMININE FORMS OF ADJECTIVES

Listen :

(Il) (sérieux)

— Il est sérieux.

(jeune femme) (sérieuse)

— C'est une jeune femme sérieuse.

NOW, DESCRIBE THE FOLLOWING PEOPLE

(il) (sérieux) — (jeune femme) (sérieuse) — (elle) (charmante) — (candidat) (intéressant) — (il) (intelligent) — (directeur) (travailleur) — (elle) (informaticienne)

4. SEE PAGE 83

VERB PRACTICE : THE VERBS « DEVOIR » « POUVOIR », « VOULOIR » AND « SAVOIR »

Listen :

(Florence) — (savoir)

— Florence sait animer une équipe.

(Je) (devoir)

— Je dois animer une équipe.

NOW, CHANGE THE FOLLOWING USING THE PROMPT WORDS AND PUTTING THE VERBS INTO THEIR CORRECT FORMS

(Florence) (savoir) — (Je) (devoir) — (Vous) (pouvoir) — (Vous) (devoir) — (Anne) (vouloir) — (Nous) (pouvoir) — (Les ingénieurs) (devoir) — (Nous) (savoir) — (Je) (pouvoir) — (Les candidats) (vouloir)

5. GRAMMAR : SEE PAGE 43

RELATIVE PRONOUNS : « QUI »

Listen :

(J'ai une candidate — Elle semble intéressante)

— J'ai une candidate qui semble intéressante.

NOW, LINK THE FOLLOWING SENTENCES WITH THE RELATIVE PRONOUN « QUI »

(J'ai une candidate. Elle semble intéressante) — (J'ai un ami. Il est bilingue) — (Vous avez une amie. Elle adore voyager) — (J'ai 2 collaborateurs. Ils sont célibataires) — (J'ai une vendeuse. Elle a une forte personnalité) — (Ce sont des techniciens. Ils s'intéressent à l'informatique)

6. GRAMMAR : SEE PAGE 45

POSITION OF ADVERBS

Listen :

(Elle parle anglais ? — bien)

— Oui, elle parle bien anglais.

(Elle travaille ? — beaucoup)

— Oui, elle travaille beaucoup.

NOW, ANSWER THE FOLLOWING QUESTIONS PLACING THE ADVERB IN THE CORRECT POSITION

(Elle parle anglais ?) (bien) — (Elle travaille ?) (beaucoup) — (Il sort ?) (souvent) — (Vous fumez ?) (toujours) — (Vous voyagez ?) (quelquefois) — (Elle joue du piano ?) (bien)

TRAVEL AND LANGUAGES

Everyone in France, except for the self-employed, has a minimum annual holiday of five weeks. Although many stay in France and devote their holiday to lolling on a beach or fixing up an old house they may have purchased in the countryside, about 12 percent hop on a plane (often a charter) and fly off to distant lands. Group travel is less popular in France than it is in Britain or the United States. The individualistic French traveller generally prefers to strike out in twos or threes.

Abroad, you will find French travellers in the remotest of places. Although many middle class, middle-aged French travellers may choose the traditional tour bus circuit, there is a hardier breed of French traveller, often of the "baba cool" (the French expression for "aging hippy") variety, who will be found on local buses on dusty Indian roads — and he or she will often be the only tourist for miles around. The French, though they have a reputation for complaining about foreign food and arguing about prices, are generally well regarded abroad. Often, because I was carrying the French edition of the Blue Guide, I have been taken for a French tourist in various countries, from Brazil to India, and I must say that people were generally much friendlier than when they took me for an English or American tourist. The French abroad retain their reputation of being a cultured people intent on discovering the country they are visiting and learning about its people.

Although every year campaigns are launched to encourage the French to travel outside of the busy summer months of July and August, they have so far been largely unsuccessful — though some travellers now set off in mid-June or September. The result is not only that Paris and other major cities are deserted in July and especially August, but that all flights are booked up months in advance. Paris's airports are to be avoided, especially on the 1st, 15th and 31st July and August (as many people take their holidays from the 1st to the 31st or from the 15th to the 15th). Since many French factories and some businesses (including restaurants) shut down completely during some or all of August, many employees cannot really choose when to take their holidays.

"PARLEZ-VOUS FRANÇAIS ?"

The French may not be the world's best linguists (they are certainly not multilingual as are the citizens of smaller countries such as Holland or Denmark), but that doesn't stop them from visiting far-flung places. The younger generation can usually get by with English, the lingua franca of today's traveller, since the study of English is now obligatory in French schools. Older people, many of whom speak only French, can always rely on sign-language, in which they are perfectly fluent, thanks to the expressiveness of Gallic gestures. Although efforts are periodically made to encourage the study of other languages besides English, German and Spanish, few schools are equipped to teach Russian, Chinese, Arabic or even Italian. The result is that as an English-speaker you will often be able to communicate in your own language. But that doesn't mean that you shouldn't learn French ! The man in the street and the typical garçon de café *do not often speak English, and even in business circles you will find that people are pleased to discover that you have made the effort to learn their language, and will, consequently, be warmer and friendlier — and more likely to make a deal with you.* □

2.4 TAKE A BREAK

Nº 1 Listen

Listen to the film previews on your cassette, and then write down the numbers of the previews that correspond to the film posters below.

Read the following classified ads, then look at the pictures and ID cards below. Match the advertiser with the appropriate person who might answer the ad.

1. *Urgent. Ingénieur allemand cherche appartement trois pièces. Paris ou région parisienne.*
Tél. : 42.78.34.67 après 19 h.

FICHE D'IDENTITÉ

Nom : Yoshio Mitzumaki
Age : 22 ans
Nationalité : japonaise
Profession : étudiant en architecture

2. *Directrice service export souhaite apprendre le japonais. Cherche professeur langue maternelle japonaise.*
Tél. : 46.48.89.04

FICHE D'IDENTITÉ

Nom : Geneviève de Beaumont
Age : 54 ans
Nationalité : française
Profession : agent immobilier

3. *Jeune homme, 23 ans, sportif. Cherche personnes (hommes ou femmes) aimant la nature pour randonnées pédestres les week-ends aux alentours de Paris.*
Tél. : 45.34.67.26

FICHE D'IDENTITÉ

Nom : Marc Saint-Clair
Age : 27 ans
Nationalité : belge
Profession : musicien

4. *Jeune femme, 21 ans, blonde, yeux verts, 1 m 70. Cherche âme sœur 25/30 ans. J'aime la nuit, la ville, le cinéma, la musique, les discos.*
Tél. : 43.20.51.45

FICHE D'IDENTITÉ

Nom : Catherine Duvail
Age : 25 ans
Nationalité : française
Profession : professeur de gymmastique

(See solutions on page 16-17)

2.5 CONTACTS

 *Listen*

PARIS LA NUIT

Dépliant publicitaire

crazy horse de paris

12, av. george V
75008 paris - france

tel : 47.23.32.32 telex : 640 160

LE LIEU

Le Crazy Horse est situé au cœur de Paris, 12 avenue George V, dans le 8ᵉ arrondissement.

L'HEURE

Le Crazy Horse est ouvert tous les soirs, toute l'année.
Il offre deux représentations par soir : à 21 h 25 et 23 h 45, et trois représentations les vendredi et samedi à 20 h 30, 22 h 35 et 0 h 50.
Le spectacle dure 1 h 45 mn.

LES CONSOMMATIONS

Le prix comprend une demi-bouteille de champagne de grande marque par personne ou deux boissons. Le Crazy Horse ne sert pas de dîner mais seulement des boissons : champagne, vin, whisky, bière, jus de fruit et même Coca-Cola. Vous pouvez dîner près du Crazy Horse avant ou après le spectacle. Il y a de nombreux restaurants sur l'avenue George V ou sur la place de l'Alma, qui sont toujours ouverts à 7 heures du soir et souvent jusqu'à 2 heures du matin.

LE SPECTACLE

Le Crazy Horse propose le meilleur spectacle de nu du monde. La troupe comprend 24 danseuses, 3 ou 4 attractions de variétés et un orchestre de 4 musiciens.
Les artistes, qui sont des danseuses professionnelles de music-hall, sont aussi d'excellentes actrices. Elles sont très belles, mesurent 1,70 m, ne pèsent pas plus de 55 kg, ont de beaux yeux, une belle poitrine et une personnalité très marquée !

RÉSERVATION

Vous pouvez réserver dans toutes les agences ou au Crazy Horse en téléphonant directement.

1.-2. Crazy Horse

Paradis Latin

4. Lido

2.5 WORDS

lieu (M) — place
dépliant (M) — flyer
représentation (F) — performance
spectacle (M) — show
consommation (F) — drink consumed in a café, bar or club
prix (M) — price
(demi) bouteille (F) — (half) bottle
personne (F) — person
boisson (F) — drink
monde (M) — world
troupe (F) — theatrical or dance company
danseur(se) — dancer
variétés (F) — variety acts
orchestre (M) — band, orchestra
musicien(ne) — musician
artiste (F ou M) — performer
acteur (actrice) — actor (actress)
mètre (M) — metre
kilo (M) — kilo
œil (des yeux) (M) — eye (eyes)
pièce de théâtre (F) — play
théâtre (M) — theatre
cinéma (M) — cinema
opéra (M) — opera
ballet (M) — ballet
concert (M) — concert
dîner-spectacle (M) — dinner with a floor show
programme (M) — (theatre) programme
boîte de nuit (F) — nightclub

publicitaire — person who works in advertising
meilleur(e) — better
excellent(e) — excellent
nombreux(se) — numerous

---

ravissant(e) — very attractive
superbe — superb
laid(e) — ugly
affreux(se) — awful
pire — worse
mauvais(e) — bad

offrir — to offer, to give
durer — to last
comprendre — to include, to understand
servir — to serve
proposer — to suggest, to offer
mesurer — to measure
peser — to weigh

---

danser — to dance
chanter — to sing
s'amuser — to enjoy oneself

REMEMBER... REMEMBER... REMEMBER... REMEMBER... REMEMBER

(1) *In French when describing parts of the body you normally use the definite article (elle a les yeux bleus). —* ***(2)*** *1,70 m = 5'7" —* ***(3)*** *55 kg = 121 lbs. or 8st. 9 lb. —* ***(4)*** *In France, one uses the 24-hour clock : 7 heures means 7 a.m. ; 7 p.m. is 19 heures.*

HOW TO SAY IT

1. SAYING WHERE PLACES ARE

Le Crazy Horse est situé au cœur de Paris — The Crazy Horse is located in the heart of Paris
Le Crazy Horse est dans le 8e arrondissement ⎤
Le Crazy Horse se trouve dans le 8e ⎦ — The Crazy Horse is in the 8th district

2. DESCRIBING A PERSON

Elle est très belle — She's very beautiful
Elle a les yeux bleus — She has blue eyes **(1)**
Elle mesure 1 mètre 70 (soixante-dix) — She's 1 m 70 cm **(2)**
Elle pèse 55 (cinquante-cinq) kilos — She's 55 kilos **(3)**
Elle fait 1 mètre 80 (quatre-vingt) environ — She's about 1 m 80 cm **(2)**

3. INDICATING FREQUENCY

Le Crazy Horse est ouvert tous les soirs — The Crazy Horse is open every night
Il offre deux représentations par soir — There are two performances every evening
Elle danse tous les jours — She dances every day
Elles dansent deux fois par jour — They dance twice a day
Je dîne souvent avec lui — I often have dinner with him
Tu vas au cinéma de temps en temps ? — Do you go to the cinema from time to time ?

4. INDICATING DURATION

Le spectacle dure une heure quarante-cinq — The show lasts one hour and 45 minutes
Les restaurants sont ouverts de 7 h à 23 h — The restaurants are open from 7 p.m. to 11 p.m. **(4)**
Le spectacle commence à 22 h et finit à minuit — The show starts at 10 p.m. and finishes at midnight **(4)**

2.5 ORAL PRACTICE

1. GRAMMAR : SEE PAGE 41

ADJECTIVES IN THE PLURAL FORM :

Listen :

(Des restaurants) — (nombreux)
— Il y a de nombreux restaurants.

NOW, CHANGE THE FOLLOWING SENTENCES USING « IL Y A ». REMEMBER TO PLACE THE ADJECTIVE BEFORE THE NOUN

(Des restaurants) (nombreux) — (Des femmes) (belles) — (Des danseuses) (bonnes) — (Des artistes) (nouveaux) — (Des musiciens) (jeunes) — (Des quartiers) (beaux) — (Des théâtres) (vieux)

2. GRAMMAR : SEE PAGE 43

« TOUT », « TOUTE », « TOUS » AND « TOUTES »

Listen :

(La troupe est en voyage ?)
— Oui, toute la troupe est en voyage.

NOW, ANSWER IN THE AFFIRMATIVE, USING « TOUT », « TOUTE », « TOUS » OR « TOUTES » AS NECESSARY

(La troupe est en voyage ?) — (Les cafés sont ouverts le samedi ?) — (Les danseuses mesurent 1,70 m ?) — (Les places sont bien situées ?) — (Les musiciens sont français ?) — (Les boissons sont chères ?) — Le programme est en anglais ?)

3. GRAMMAR : SEE PAGE 43

RELATIVE PRONOUNS : « QUI »

Listen :

(Je connais un cabaret) (Il se trouve au centre de Paris)
— Je connais un cabaret qui se trouve au centre de Paris.

NOW, LINK THE FOLLOWING SENTENCES USING THE RELATIVE PRONOUN « QUI »

(Je connais un cabaret) (Il se trouve au centre de Paris) — (Je connais un cabaret) (Il est ouvert jusqu'à 3 h du matin) — (Je connais un cabaret) (Il est situé près des Champs-Elysées) — (Je connais un cabaret) (Il est fermé le lundi)

4. GRAMMAR : SEE PAGE 47

VERB PRACTICE : THE VERBS « DEVOIR » « POUVOIR » AND « SAVOIR » IN NEGATIVE SENTENCES :

Listen :

(Vous savez danser ?)
— Non, je ne sais pas danser.

NOW, ANSWER THE FOLLOWING SENTENCES IN THE NEGATIVE

(Vous savez danser ?) — (On peut dîner au Crazy Horse ?) — (Je dois réserver ?) — (Elle veut déjeuner ?) — (Je peux fumer ici ?) — (Vous savez aller au Crazy Horse ?) — (Il doit téléphoner ?) — (Vous voulez venir ?)

5. GRAMMAR : SEE PAGE 41

POSITION OF ADJECTIVES (BEAUTY, AGE, QUALITY AND SIZE)

Listen :

(Il cherche une danseuse) — (beau)
— Il cherche une belle danseuse.

NOW, REPEAT EACH SENTENCE ADDING THE ADJECTIVE AND CHANGING IT INTO THE FEMININE FORM AS NECESSARY

(Il cherche une danseuse) (beau) — (Il y a un orchestre) (nouveau) — (Donnez-moi une bouteille d'eau minérale) (petit) — (Qui est cette dame près du bar ?) (gros) — (Je ne connais pas ce musicien) (jeune) — (Je voudrais une chambre) (grand) — (C'est une marque de champagne) (vieux) — (J'ai réservé une table) (bon)

6. GRAMMAR : SEE PAGE 47

VERB PRACTICE : REFLEXIVE VERBS WITH « DEVOIR », « POUVOIR », « SAVOIR » AND « VOULOIR »

Listen :

(Vous vous trompez) (pouvoir)
— Vous pouvez vous tromper.
(Il se baigne) (vouloir)
— Il veut se baigner.

NOW, MAKE SENTENCES USING THE CORRECT FORM OF THE VERBS YOU HEAR. REMEMBER TO PUT THE REFLEXIVE VERB INTO ITS INFINITIVE FORM, BUT DO NOT CHANGE THE REFLEXIVE PRONOUN

(Vous vous trompez) (pouvoir) — (Il se baigne) (vouloir) — (Il s'occupe des clients) (savoir) — (Nous nous levons) (devoir) — (Hélène s'assied ici) (pouvoir) — (Tu te présentes) (savoir) — (Vous vous imposez) (vouloir)

PARIS BY NIGHT

They say that Paris never sleeps. This may be a slight exaggeration, but the traffic jams along the Boulevard Saint Michel at 3.00 a.m. on a Saturday and Sunday morning bear witness to a night life that can only be described as "animé".

WHAT TO DO IN PARIS AT NIGHT ? *The choice is yours — and your pocket's. There are, of course, the old favourites : the Moulin Rouge, the Lido, the Crazy Horse. Here, leggy, topless, perfectly-built young ladies glitter and glide against a background of moving scenery and flashing fountains. The problem with these monuments (the places, not the ladies) to French pleasure is that they are not French. The dancers probably come from Birmingham or The Hague, and the clientele from anywhere in the world except Paris. But do go there if you like the "grand spectacle" — if only to say you've been.*

HUNGRY ? *The choice is overwhelming. If you're down and out, try the Breton crêperies in Montparnasse. If you're richer, go to one of the good brasseries or La Coupole for traditional French cuisine. If you're loaded, head for the Tour d'Argent or Maxime's, and savour every mouthful of foie gras, lobster and Mouton Rothschild. These are, of course, extremes, but one thing is sure — whatever your budget, you won't go hungry.*

WANT SOME CULTURE ? *For real culture-vultures, there's the Comédie Française, where you can sit through a three-hour rendering of Racine on velvet seats and inspect the magnificent art work of the ceilings, even if you can't understand a word of what's going on on stage. If you are in a mood for something a little more lightweight, Paris is full of café-théâtres, where your food and drink are constantly being interrupted by a handful of actors and actresses doing sketches and skits, usually parodies of French politicians or celebrities, and totally incomprehensible to a non-native.*

If you'd rather stay away from the verbal side of things, there are innumerable jazz clubs and discos. Be prepared : while entrance fees are relatively low, drinks can cost a fortune, and one drink is obligatory, so, unless it's all on the expense account, go for the music or dancing, and not the alcohol. The only compensation is that the prices can spare you a horrible hangover.

For those who really can't do without that after-dinner coffee and cognac, the cafés along the Boulevard Saint Germain and Boulevard Montparnasse stay open until 2.00 or 3.00 a.m., so you can sip at your leisure (lovely on a balmy summer's night) and watch the night-owls saunter by in all their finery.

And for those really incurable romantics, the night must lead at some point to the Seine. You can have dinner by candlelight, as you float down the river on a glass-roofed boat (alas, with hundreds of other romantics) and watch the lights of the Bateaux Mouches cast shadows on the leaves of the trees on the Ile Saint-Louis. Afterwards walk through the Latin Quarter, and you're bound to come across street musicians, people selling paintings, jewellery and bric-à-brac. Or go to the Place Beaubourg and watch the fire-eaters and mime artists. Even the métro echoes with South American singers, violinists, and the odd folk enthusiast still hammering away at "Blowing in the Wind".

Above ground, on the main boulevards, the traffic is still getting in and out of jams, and the streets still resound with Gallic voices. So you see, you can do anything in Paris at night — except sleep, of course. □

Listen ***Il est cinq heures, Paris s'éveille***

Jacques Dutronc
(musique de Jacques Dutronc, paroles de Jacques Lanzmann et d'Anne Segalen)

Je suis le dauphin de la place Dauphine
Et la place Blanche a mauvaise mine
Les camions sont pleins de lait
Les balayeurs sont pleins de balais
Il est cinq heures
Paris s'éveille
Paris s'éveille
Les travestis vont se raser
Les strip-teaseuses sont rhabillées
Les traversins sont écrasés
Les amoureux sont fatigués
Il est cinq heures, Paris s'éveille (bis)
Le café est dans les tasses
Les cafés nettoient leurs glaces
Et sur le boulevard Montparnasse
La gare n'est plus qu'une carcasse
Il est cinq heures, Paris s'éveille (bis)
Les banlieusards sont dans les gares
A La Villette on tranche le lard
Paris by night regagne les cars
Les boulangers font des bâtards
Il est cinq heures, Paris s'éveille (bis)
La tour Eiffel a froid aux pieds
L'Arc de Triomphe est ranimé
Et l'Obélisque est bien dressé
Entre la nuit et la journée
Il est cinq heures, Paris s'éveille
Les journaux sont imprimés
Les ouvriers sont déprimés
Les gens se lèvent ils sont brimés
C'est l'heure où je vais me coucher
Il est cinq heures, Paris se lève
Il est cinq heures, je n'ai pas sommeil

Paris Wakens

I'm the prince of the Place Dauphine
And the square is pale and doesn't look well
The lorries are all loaded up with milk
The streetsweepers are all stacked up with broom
It's five in the morning
And Paris is waking up
Paris is waking up
The transvestites are going off to shave
The strippers have put all their clothes back on
The bolsters bear the imprints of the night
The lovers are running out of breath
It's five in the morning
And Paris is waking up
Paris is waking up
There's coffee in cups
And in the cafés, they're cleaning the mirrors
And on the boulevard Montparnasse
The old station is nothing more than a skeleton
It's five in the morning . . .
The commuters are in the stations
At La Villette, they're slicing the bacon
The "Paris-by-nighters" are getting back in thei
coaches
The bakers are baking their loaves
It's five in the morning . . .
The Eiffel Tower's got cold feet
The Arc de Triomphe's coming out of its sleep
And the Obelisk stands proudly
Between the night and the day
It's five in the morning . . .
The papers are printed
The workers feel jaded
The people are getting up, frustrated,
Now it's my bed time
It's five in the morning
Paris is getting up
And I'm not sleepy

STREET TALK · STRAIGHT TALK
BOUFFE ORS SOIR? SE FAIT OIS?
OH! LA BOUFFE, LES RESTOS. T'EN AS PAS MARRE TOI?
BON, ALORS UN CINOCHE?
NON. PAS LUNDI. C'EST BOURRÉ
JE PENSE À UN TRUC. SI ON ALLAIT PRENDRE UN POT CHEZ SYLVIE?
ET SI ON RESTAIT DANS NOTRE PIAULE, TOUS LES DEUX...
OUS DÎNONS N VILLE E SOIR? ANS UN HINOIS, AR XEMPLE.
LES REPAS, LES RESTAURANTS, TU N'ES PAS FATIGUÉE?
BON, ALORS ALLONS AU CINÉMA!
LUNDI IL Y A TROP DE MONDE.
J'AI UNE IDÉE. NOUS POURRIONS ALLER BOIRE QUELQUE CHOSE CHEZ SYLVIE.
POURQUOI NE RESTONS-NOUS PAS CHEZ NOUS, TOUS LES DEUX...

2 WRITTEN PRACTICE

2.1

COMPLETE. Choose the appropriate verb from the list: traverser, tourner, continuer, passer, prendre: *Je .... devant le Grand Palais — Je .... le Pont Alexandre-III — Je .... tout droit — Je .... à gauche devant les Invalides — Je .... la première à droite.*

TRANSLATE: *Pardon Monsieur, je voudrais aller au Louvre, quelle ligne est-ce que je prends ? Prenez direction Porte de Clignancourt, changez à Châtelet et prenez la ligne 1 — Merci — Je vous en prie The rue de Seine, please ? Excuse me, I don't understand, I'm a foreigner. To go to the Pompidou Centre you keep straight ahead and you turn right at the traffic lights.*

2.2

COMPLETE with cette, un, cet, à, au, la, en: *J'ai un rendez-vous .... huit heures — Je ne suis pas libre .... semaine prochaine mais je peux venir .... semaine — .... après-midi je vais .... cinéma — Je suis né .... mars 1963, ... lundi.*

TRANSLATE: *Allô Nicole ? — Oui, qui est à l'appareil ? — C'est Emmanuelle, je téléphone de Londres — Aujourd'hui, je n'ai pas le temps mais je suis libre le mercredi matin.*
I'd like to speak to Patrick — You've made a mistake, there's no one here by that name — Can you put me through to M. Guidimard ? — Who's calling ? — Stephane Pichon — M. Guidimard ? — Yes, speaking

2.3

COMPLETE with faire, être or avoir: *Je n'................. pas le temps, je .... pressé — Il .... 5 h 00, nous .... en retard — Ils .... horreur du ski, ils .... tort — Vous .... du ski, vous .... raison — Ça .... 50 F.*

TRANSLATE: *Nous n'habitons pas dans une grande ville — Depuis un an, nous vivons dans une petite maison, en pleine forêt, près d'un lac — Nous pouvons faire du sport — Il a horreur du bruit.*
Are you enjoying Lyons ? — I like music — You're late: it would be better to take a taxi — He likes the cinema very much — I prefer the theatre — You should take the tube.

2.4

COMPLETE. Put the word in brackets in the appropriate form: *Nous (devoir) .... être disponibles — Cette jeune femme est (ambitieux) .... — Elles (savoir) .... plusieurs langues — La (nouveau) .... comptable est charmante .... — Ils (pouvoir) .... voyager.*

TRANSLATE: *Ce soir, je sors avec la nouvelle secrétaire — Il sait animer une équipe de vendeurs — Je trouve que Françoise est très jolie — Je m'intéresse beaucoup à la technique.*
What do you think of the new director ? — She's very good — In my opinion, she knows her job well and she is capable of managing a team — What's more, she is very nice and charming.

2.5

COMPLETE with: les or par: *Je vais à New York une fois .... mois — Elle a .... yeux bleus et .... cheveux noirs — Je sors tous .... soirs — Il danse une fois .... jour.*

TRANSLATE: *Pour dîner, vous devez trouver un restaurant dans le quartier: le cabaret ne sert pas de repas — La danseuse qui est à gauche est très jolie — Les cafés qui sont sur cette avenue sont ouverts très tard. I don't go out every night, just from time to time — They start work at 9 a.m. and finish at 6 p.m. I'm 1 metre 80 and I weigh 90 kilos — The Opera is in the 9th district.*

(Check your answers on page 38 of your booklet)

IMPROVE

MEASURES

les mesures (F) — measures
gramme (M) — gramme
livre (F) — pound
demi-livre (F) — half pound
kilo (M) — kilo
litre (M) — litre
demi-litre (M) — half litre
millimètre (M) — millimetre
centimètre (M) — centimetre
décimètre (M) — decimetre
kilomètre (M) — kilometre
mètre (M) — metre
mètre carré (M) — square metre
mètre cube (M) — cubic metre

MONEY

argent (M) — money
billet (M) — bank note
monnaie (F) — change
pièce de monnaie (F) — coin
franc (M) — franc
demi-franc (M) — half franc
cinquante centimes — 50 Centimes
vingt centimes — 20 Centimes
dix centimes — 10 Centimes
cinq centimes — 5 Centimes
deux francs — 2 Francs
cinq francs — 5 Francs
dix francs — 10 Francs
vingt francs — 20 Francs
cinquante francs — 50 Francs
cent francs — 100 Francs
deux cents francs — 200 Francs
cinq cents francs — 500 Francs
chèque (M) — cheque
carnet de chèques (M) — cheque book
chéquier (M) — cheque book
carte de crédit (F) — credit card

BODY

corps (M) — body
tête (F) — head
cheveux (MPL) — hair
oreille (F) — ear
figure (F) / visage (M) — face
front (M) — forehead
œil (M) (PL : les yeux) — eye (eyes)
nez (M) — nose
bouche (F) — mouth
lèvre (F) — lip
langue (F) — tongue
dent (F) — tooth
joue (F) — cheek
menton (M) — chin
cou (M) — neck
nuque (F) — nape
épaule (F) — shoulder
bras (M) — arm
coude (M) — elbow
poignet (M) — wrist
main (F) — hand
doigt (M) — finger
ongle (M) — fingernail
dos (M) — back
poitrine (F) — chest
sein (M) — breast
ventre (M) — abdomen
sexe (M) — genitals
fesses (FPL) — buttocks
cuisse (F) — thigh
genou (M) — knee
jambe (F) — leg
cheville (F) — ankle
pied (M) — foot
orteil (M) — big toe
cœur (M) — heart
foie (M) — liver
estomac (M) — stomach
os (M) — bone
nerf (M) — nerve
muscle (M) — muscle
vertèbre (F) — vertebrae

WEATHER

temps (M) — weather
averse (F) — downpour
brouillard (M) — fog
brume (F) — mist
éclaircie (F) — break in the clouds
orage (M) — storm
nuage (M) — cloud
pluie (M) — rain
soleil (M) — sun
lune (F) — moon
température (F) — temperature
verglas (M) — frost
geler — to freeze
pleuvoir — to rain
beau — fine
bon — good
brumeux — misty
couvert — overcast
doux — mild
humide — damp, humid
mauvais — bad
nuageux — cloudy
orageux — stormy
pluvieux — rainy
sec — dry
frais — cool

2. TEST YOURSELF

1. WRITE THE CORRECT FORM: CORRECT FORM

Téléphonez la/à la *secrétaire* ....
Monsieur Fisher vit en/au *Texas* ....
Je voudrais parler aux/les *clients* ....
Il ne travaille pas chez/à *Peugeot* ....
Madame Dallas vient à/d' *Atlanta* ....
Vous aimez Grèce/la Grèce ....
Cet avion arrive du/de *Sénégal* ....
Vous devez dire bonjour à/au *directeur* ....
Elle adore États-Unis/les États-Unis ....
Vous habitez en/au *Allemagne* ....

2. WRITE OUT THE FOLLOWING TIMES:

12.00 ....
11.15 ....
4.45 ....
2.30 ....
5.20 ....
3.25 ....
10.35 ....
7.10 ....
8.40 ....
1.30 ....

3. FILL IN THE BLANKS WITH THE APPROPRIATE WORDS FROM THE LIST:

Qui demandez-vous — je vous en prie — allô — c'est de la part de qui — vous vous trompez de poste — je vous le passe.

— ....Allo.......
— *B.N.P. j'écoute.*
— *Bonjour madame, je voudrais parler à Hervé Leclerc.*
— ....C'est de la part de qui.......
— *De la part de son frère.*
— *Ne quittez pas,* ....Je vous le passe.......
— *Merci Madame — Allô Hervé ?*
— ....Qui demandez-vous....... ?
— *Hervé Leclerc.*
— ....Vous vous trompez de poste.... *Monsieur, je vous repasse le standard*
— *Merci.*
— ....Je vous en prie.......

4. WRITE THE CORRECT FORM :

CORRECT FORM

Cette candidate est **ambitieux/ambitieuse.** . . . .
J'habite un **bel/beau** *appartement.* . . . .
Il s'intéresse aux **nouvels/nouvelles** *technologies.* . . . .
Il a un curriculum vitae **intéressant/intéressante.** . . . .
Dans cette boutique, les vendeuses sont très **gentils/gentilles.** . . . .
Pour déjeuner, je connais une très **bon/bonne** *adresse.* . . . .
J'aime beaucoup les **vieils/vieilles** *rues de Paris.* . . . .

5. MAKE PAIRS OF OPPOSITES

1. *sympathique*
2. *gros*
3. *gentil*
4. *grand*
5. *en retard*
6. *chaud*
7. *âgé*
8. *détester*

A. *aimer*
B. *froid*
C. *petit*
D. *en avance*
E. *jeune*
F. *mince*
G. *antipathique*
H. *méchant*

6. « SAVOIR » OR « CONNAÎTRE » ?

Est-ce que vous **connaissez/savez** *le jeune homme qui est près du bar ?* . . . .

Il **sait/connaît** *que vous êtes canadienne.*
. . . .

Nous ne **connaissons/savons** *pas les États-Unis*
. . . .

Francis Duplord, est-ce que tu le **connais/sais** *?* . . . .

Est-ce que vous **savez/connaissez** *où se trouve la rue Blanche ?* . . . .

Je ne **sais/connais** *pas faire du ski* . . . .
. . . .

7. WRITE THE CORRECT PRONOUN IN THE BLANKS :

Comment .... appelez-vous ?
Est-ce qu'il .... intéresse à l'informatique ?
Le soir on ne .... couche pas tôt.
Je .... présente : Hubert Duval.
Vous ne pouvez pas .... tromper.
En été est-ce que tu .... baignes dans le lac ?
Nous .... occupons de cette affaire tout de suite.
Le matin elle .... lève à 7 heures.

(Check your answers on page 39 of your booklet)

Mr. MARTIN AND MONSIEUR DANIEL

The next morning's post brought another letter in the fine spidery hand. This time, it had no stamp or postmark, and had clearly been hand delivered. I ripped open the envelope with trembling hands and read :

Cher Monsieur,
Je regrette beaucoup le contretemps de hier soir. J'ai la mauvaise habitude d'être souvent en retard.

J'ai une nouvelle proposition à vous faire. Je dois repartir pour Paris cet après-midi. Il m'est impossible de rester ici un jour de plus. Si vous souhaitez me rencontrer, venez donc me retrouver à Paris ! Adressez-vous au guichet d'Air France à l'aéroport de Heathrow. L'hôtesse a votre billet. Le départ est à 9 heures demain matin (le 16 janvier). Vous avez toute la journée pour faire vos bagages, et moi j'ai quelques heures pour préparer votre arrivée. A l'aéroport de Paris-Charles de Gaulle, prenez un taxi et rendez-vous au 16 rue Las Cases dans le 7ᵉ arrondissement. Si je ne suis pas là, demandez les clés de l'appartement de Monsieur Daniel à la concierge. Elle s'appelle Madame Truand. Ouvrez la porte, et faites comme chez vous !
A bientôt.
Amicalement,
Martin Daniel

I would go and face Martin Daniel. I would find out what he wanted from me, and then demand that he leave me alone. Since I didn't want to tell anyone where I was going, I called my secretary and told her I had to make an unexpected trip out of town and would be back in a few days. I hung up before she had a chance to ask me if I had a number where she could reach me. If anything important came up, she would just have to deal with it.

That evening I packed my bag and went to bed early. I wanted to be fresh and alert for my Paris confrontation. I had a hard time falling asleep : I kept seeing sinister-looking figures in black macs hovering in the dark. Finally I got my imagination to stop running wild, and slept.

At the Air France ticket desk at Heathrow the next morning I was given my ticket by a charming young woman. She smiled as if she knew me and said, *« Voilà votre billet, Monsieur, comme d'habitude. Votre séjour à Londres a-t-il été agréable ?*

« Oui, merci, Mademoiselle », I replied without thinking, and without quite understanding the word *« séjour »*.

« Votre vol a 20 minutes de retard à cause du brouillard ici à Londres, vous avez donc le temps d'aller boire un café. L'embarquement est dans 45 minutes, porte numéro 35. Bon voyage ! » she said with a smile.

« Merci beaucoup, Mademoiselle, vous êtes très aimable », I said returning her smile.

She burst out laughing and said, *« Vous imitez bien les Anglais. Vous avez tout à fait leur accent ! Mais il ne faut pas le faire : ce n'est pas très gentil ! »*

I realized then that she thought I was Martin Daniel. Was this character forever to dog my footsteps ? I was beginning to feel quite fed up.

* * *

« Mesdames, Mesdemoiselles, Messieurs, nous allons atterrir dans quelques minutes à l'aéroport Paris-Charles de Gaulle. La température extérieure est de 6° Celsius. Il est 9 heures et 17 minutes, heure locale. Le Commandant Lorre et son équipage vous remercient d'avoir choisi Air France et espèrent vous revoir très prochainement sur nos lignes. »

As the plane came down to land I could think of nothing but Martin Daniel, and the confrontation that awaited me. As soon as I got through customs, I rushed over to the taxi rank and climbed into a taxi.

« Vous allez où, Monsieur ? » asked the driver.

« 16 rue Las Cases, dans le septième », I announced.

« Bien, Monsieur », he said. *« C'est un hôtel ? »*

« Non. Non. Je vais chez un ami », I replied, surprising myself at thus labelling Martin Daniel. But I suppose that by now he had become more than a passing acquaintance. And I certainly hoped he wasn't an enemy.

« Voilà, Monsieur, rue Las Cases, numéro seize. Cela vous fait cent dix francs », said the driver. I paid him, and walked into the building. The entrance was dark and grim-looking — even after I'd found the light switch.

The concierge lived in a tiny apartment leading off the entrance. It was as poorly lit as the entrance and smelled of cabbage soup.

« Mme Truand ? » I enquired.

« Ah, bonjour. C'est vous Monsieur Daniel ? Voici les clés. Attendez, j'ai du courrier pour vous », she said, handing me a few official-looking letters, probably bills, addressed to Martin Daniel.

« Bon, au revoir. Je ferme car il fait froid dans l'escalier et je ne veux pas refroidir ma loge. »

With that, she closed the door, and I was left standing in front of a hand-scrawled list of tenants. *« M. Martin Daniel, 3e étage, gauche »*, I read. I walked up the spiralling staircase to the third floor (actually the fourth, since the French call the first floor the *« rez-de-chaussée »*) and let myself in.

The apartment seemed terribly familiar, but I didn't have time to analyze its familiarity, for, just as I walked in, the telephone began to ring. It took me a moment to find it. I finally uncovered it from under a pile of newspapers.

« Allô ? » I said.

« Martin ? » a female voice asked.

« Lui-même », I replied before I could stop myself.

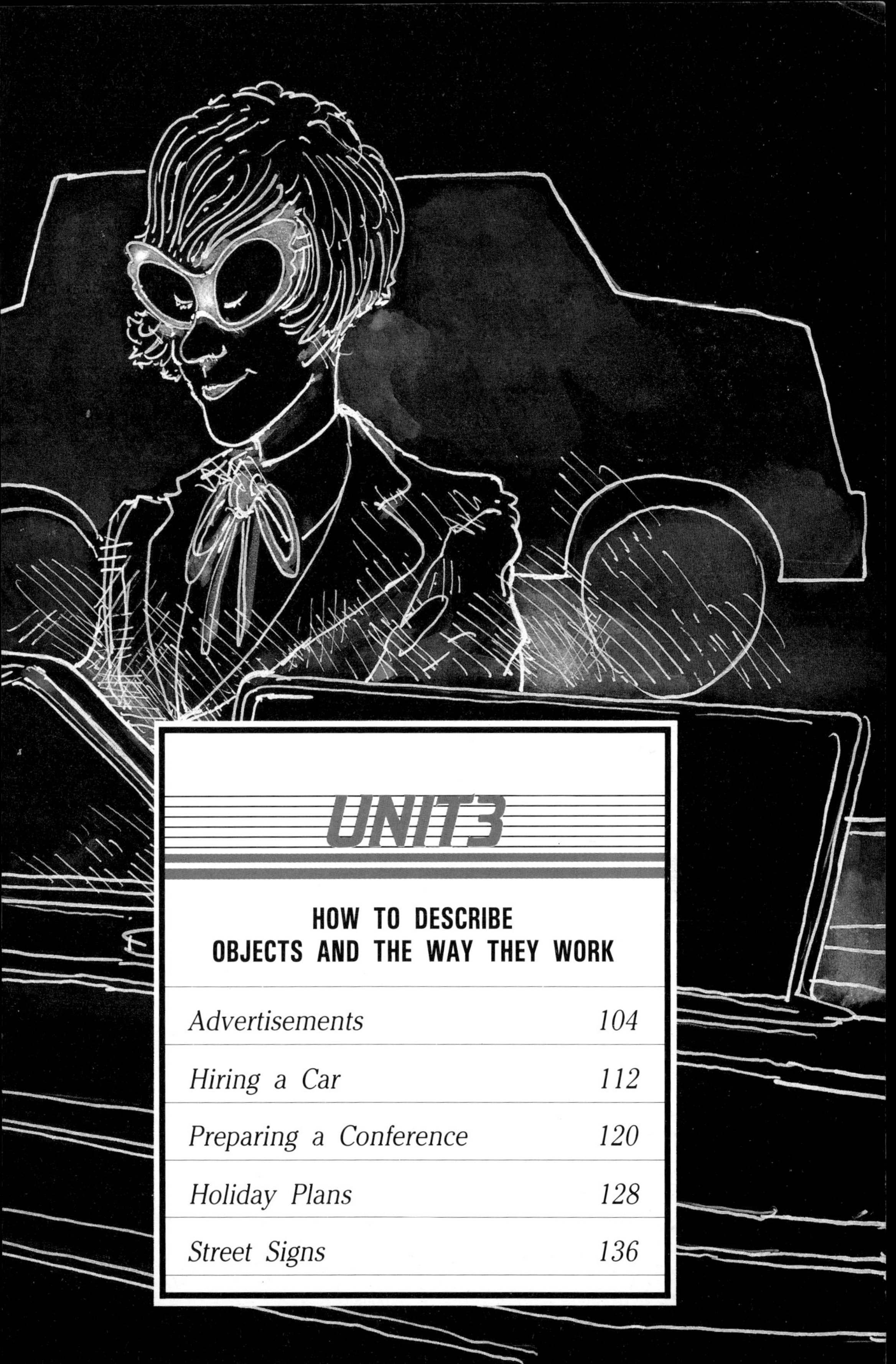

UNIT 3

HOW TO DESCRIBE OBJECTS AND THE WAY THEY WORK

3.1 CONTACTS

Listen

PUBLICITÉS

A la radio, une veille de week-end

« Samedi, temps instable toute la journée sur les Pyrénées, le Nord, le Nord-Est et les Alpes. Partout ailleurs le ciel restera bleu.
Dimanche, il fera beau : la journée sera ensoleillée sur l'ensemble du pays mais dans l'Ouest le ciel deviendra gris en fin de soirée. »

Mon premier est long et cylindrique
Mon deuxième est rouge, noir ou doré
Mon troisième a une plume en or ou en métal argenté
Mon quatrième est le messager de vos pensées
MON TOUT : CHARADE, le stylo fin et racé que vous n'allez plus quitter

Et maintenant une page de publicité :

Je ne suis pas fort
Je ne suis pas grand
Je ne suis pas brun
Je n'ai pas les yeux bleus
Je ne ressemble pas à Alain Delon
Mais je suis l'homme que les femmes s'arrachent
Je suis l'homme qu'elles aiment
Mon arme : l'eau de toilette de la séduction absolue : Goëland III

C'est la plus rapide
La plus jolie
La plus élégante
Elle a un charme fou
LA PETITE POMME 007
La nouvelle calculatrice de poche
Que vous allez acheter
Que vous devez acheter !

Le travail, c'est la santé
mais pour la conserver
il faut être installé FUTURA
Vous allez moderniser votre bureau ?
Alors choisissez FUTURA !
FUTURA, un mobilier conçu pour le confort et l'efficacité
FUTURA, des bureaux, des sièges, des rayonnages en bois massif et en métal chromé
FUTURA, les prix les plus bas pour les meubles les mieux adaptés
FUTURA, le mobilier que vous allez choisir !

Listen and repeat
(You may look at the translation on page 19 in the booklet.)

Publicités et carte météo
N.B. Darty est un magasin d'électroménager

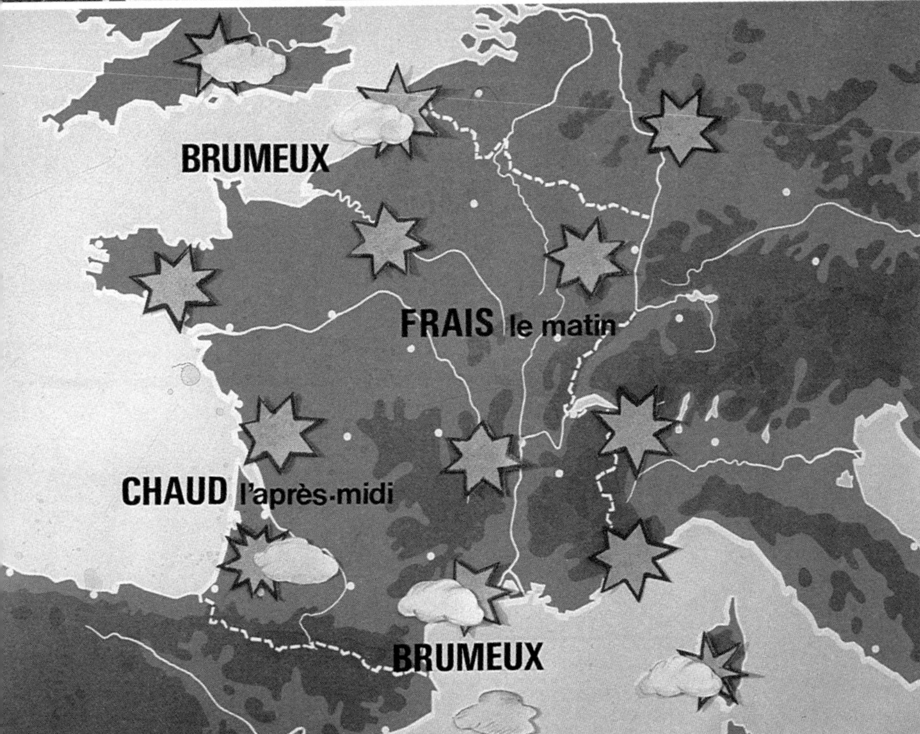

3.1 WORDS

NOUNS

publicité (F) — advertising, advertisement
veille (F) — the day before
ciel (M) — sky
ouest (M) — west
eau de toilette (F) — toilet water
séduction (F) — seductiveness
pomme (F) — apple
calculatrice (F) — calculator
plume (F) — pen
métal (M) — metal
pensée (F) — thought
stylo (M) — pen
santé (F) — health
mobilier (M) — furniture
efficacité (F) — efficiency
siège (M) — seat
bois (M) — wood
papier (M) — paper
or (M) — gold
argent (M) — silver
couleur (F) — colour

---

plastique (M) — plastic
verre (M) — glass
cuir (M) — leather
crayon (M) — pencil
gomme (F) — eraser
bureau (M) — desk
étagère (F) — shelf
machine à écrire (F) — typewriter
photocopieuse (F) — photocopying machine
chaise (F) — chair
fauteuil (M) — armchair
bibliothèque (F) — bookcase (also, library)

ADJECTIVES

instable — unstable
ensoleilié(e) — sunny
rapide — fast
élégant(e) — elegant
fou (folle) — crazy, mad
long(ue) — long
cylindrique — cylindrical
doré(e) — gold-plated
argenté(e) — silver-plated
massif(ve) — solid
chromé(e) — chrome-plated
bas(se) — low

---

haut(e) — high
large — wide
court(e) — short
lent(e) — slow
bleu(e) — blue
blanc(he) — white
rouge — red
vert(e) — green
jaune — yellow
orange — orange
noir(e) — black
gris(e) — grey
beige — beige
violet(te) — purple
rose — pink
brun(e), marron — brown
cher(ère) — expensive, dear

VERBS

rester — to remain, to stay
devenir — to become
ressembler à — to resemble, to look like
s'arracher — to fight over
quitter — to leave
conserver — to keep
moderniser — to modernize

HOW TO SAY IT

1. DESCRIBING THINGS

Material

Les éléments sont en bois massif — The components are solid wood
Il a une plume en or — He has a gold pen
C'est du métal argenté — It is silver-plated

Colour, shape and size

C'est un stylo noir — It is a black pen
C'est un stylo fin — It is a fine point
La calculatrice est petite — The calculator is small

2. ASKING ABOUT THINGS

Qu'est-ce que c'est ? — What is it ?
C'est un stylo ? — Is it a pen ?
C'est en quoi ? — What is it made of ?
C'est du métal ? — Is it made of metal ?
C'est comment ? — What's it like ?
C'est cylindrique ? — Is it cylindrical ?

3. COMPARISON OF THINGS AND PEOPLE

Cette calculatrice est la plus rapide — This calculator is the fastest
Je suis le plus fort — I am the strongest
Ce sont les meubles les mieux adaptés — These are the most suitable pieces of furniture

4. COMPARING PEOPLE'S APPEARANCES

Je ne ressemble pas à Alain Delon — I don't look like Alain Delon
On dirait Catherine Deneuve — She looks just like Catherine Deneuve

3.1 ORAL PRACTICE

1.
GRAMMAR : SEE PAGE 41

SAYING WHAT THINGS ARE MADE OF :

Listen :

(Stylo) (or)

— Mon stylo est en or.

(chaise) (métal chromé)

— Ma chaise est en métal chromé.

NOW, SAY WHAT THE FOLLOWING THINGS ARE MADE OF

(Stylo) (or) — (chaise) (métal chromé) — (calculatrice) (plastique) — (table) (verre) — (briquet) (argent) — (fauteuil) (cuir) — (bibliothèque) (bois)

2.
GRAMMAR : SEE PAGE 47

VERB PRACTICE : THE FUTURE FORMS

Listen :

(Vous déjeunez maintenant ?)

— Non, je déjeunerai plus tard.

(Il travaille maintenant ?)

— Non, il travaillera plus tard.

NOW, SAY THAT THE FOLLOWING THINGS WILL HAPPEN LATER

(Vous déjeunez maintenant ?) — (Il travaille maintenant ?) — (Je téléphone maintenant ?) — (Elles choisissent maintenant ?) — (Vous sortez maintenant ?) — (J'écris maintenant ?) — (Ils partent maintenant ?)

3.
GRAMMAR : SEE PAGE 48

VERB PRACTICE : FUTURE INTENTIONS AND IMMEDIATE FUTURE

Listen :

(Est-ce qu'il pleut ?)

— Est-ce qu'il va pleuvoir ?

(Est-ce qu'elles partent ?)

— Est-ce qu'elles vont partir ?

NOW, CHANGE THE FOLLOWING QUESTIONS ABOUT THE PRESENT INTO QUESTIONS ABOUT THE IMMEDIATE FUTURE

(Est-ce qu'il pleut ?) — (Est-ce qu'elles partent ?) — (Est-ce qu'il neige ?) — (Est-ce que tu viens ?) — (Est-ce que vous allez au cocktail ?) — (Est-ce que vous prenez rendez-vous ?) — (Est-ce qu'ils choisissent un nouveau directeur ?)

4.
GRAMMAR : SEE PAGE 45

SUPERLATIVES

Listen :

(Cette femme est élégante ?)

— Oui, c'est la plus élégante.

(Ces enfants sont beaux ?)

— Oui, ce sont les plus beaux.

NOW, ANSWER THESE QUESTIONS USING THE SUPERLATIVE

(Cette femme est élégante ?) — (Ces enfants sont beaux ?) — (Ces meubles sont chers ?) — (Cette voiture est rapide ?) — (Ces voitures sont modernes ?) — (Ce vendeur est dynamique ?) — (Cet homme est fort ?)

5.
GRAMMAR : SEE PAGE 48

VERB PRACTICE : IRREGULAR FUTURE FORMS

Listen :

(Cette semaine il fait chaud)

(La semaine prochaine/froid)

— La semaine prochaine il fera froid.

(Cette année je vais au Sénégal)

(L'année prochaine/en Suède)

— L'année prochaine j'irai en Suède.

NOW, SAY WHAT WILL HAPPEN IN THE FUTURE

(Cette semaine il fait chaud) (la semaine prochaine/froid) — (Cette année je vais au Sénégal) (l'année prochaine/en Suède) — (Cette fois-ci nous prenons le train) (la prochaine fois/l'avion) — (Ce mois-ci je suis à Paris) (le mois prochain/à Hong Kong) — (Aujourd'hui il y a du vent) (demain/de la neige) — (Cette fois-ci il faut téléphoner) (la prochaine fois/écrire)

6.
GRAMMAR : SEE PAGE 43

PRONOUN PRACTICE : THE RELATIVE PRONOUN « QUE »

Listen :

(Je vais acheter cette calculatrice)

— Regardez la calculatrice que je vais acheter.

NOW, DRAW ATTENTION TO THE FOLLOWING USING « REGARDEZ... QUE »

(Je vais acheter cette calculatrice) — (Nous prendrons ces sièges) — (Il va moderniser ces bureaux) — (Elle veut me donner ce stylo) — (Elle va m'acheter cette eau de toilette) — (Je veux ce mobilier)

RADIO AND TV, A CONTROVERSIAL EXPLOSION

After years of state-run television and tightly controlled radio, France has undergone a media explosion. The result is that it has recently acquired more radio stations and television channels (including cable channels) than in the preceding decades. But not everyone is happy with the current variety — many listeners and viewers complain that quantity does not mean quality. Ignoring the controversy (which is likely to grow as the explosion continues in the next few years), here's a rapid guide to the new and not-so-new channels on your TV set and on the countless overlapping stations on your radio.

TELEVISION : *France now has five television channels which may be viewed without paying for a special subscription. The new ones are all private (and consequently have lots of advertising) and there is a trend to privatize the older state-run channels. One of the private channels, TV6, specializes in rock videos (often British or American), so you can always relax by listening to rock groups. If your television set is equipped with an unscrambler, you can watch Canal Plus, a paying station showing many recent films.*

All feature the usual cocktail of news programmes, made-for-television films, game shows, French and foreign soap operas and films. If you're tired of working on your French and want a quiet evening in front of the box, remember that all foreign films and programmes (including "Benny Hill", "Starsky and Hutch", "Dynasty" and "Dallas") that are shown during prime time are dubbed in French. However, late-night films (10.30 or 11.00 p.m.) every Friday and Sunday are in their original language (often English) with French subtitles.

So if you can't cope with Jean Gabin's tough-guy accent or John Wayne speaking fluent French, try switching to the film in VO ("version originale" as opposed to VF, or "version française").

The best French advertisements, even if you can't understand them perfectly, are worth watching ; they are often humorous in the best tongue-in chook Gallic tradition and their generous budgets lure many internationally famous film directors. Advertising remains a major bone of contention between the state-run and the privately-owned channels. Although money from advertising partially finances the state-run channels, ads may only be shown between programmes and no film is ever interrupted with commercials. The private channels, however, are not subject to such rules, and programmes and films may be interrupted as often as every 15 minutes.

RADIO : *For a taste of French radio, switch to the FM metre band of your radio and listen to countless stations, each with its own kind of music. The FM band was formerly the home of the* radios libres, *"pirate" stations which have since been legitimized. They used to have to fight for their space on the air. Now, although each one has been allotted its space and times, they still jostle each other on the band. The rich ones, such as the highly-popular disco music station NRJ, can be heard over a large spectrum. The poorer ones broadcast locally (sometimes to only one arrondissement of Paris) and they are easily elbowed off the air.*

Here, again, if you're tired of making the mental effort to tune in to French and you find that you've suddenly become homesick for the chimes of Big Ben, you can tune in to BBC Radio 4 (in the north of France) or to the more elusive BBC World Service. Some local stations broadcast in English and retransmit the BBC World Service news programme (such as Radio Coast on the Côte d'Azur). Happy listening and viewing ! □

Listen **Complainte du progrès**

Boris Vian

Autrefois pour faire sa cour
On parlait d'amour
Pour mieux prouver son ardeur
On offrait son cœur
Maintenant c'est plus pareil
Ça change ça change
Pour séduire le cher ange,
On lui glisse à l'oreille
Ah Gudule, viens m'embrasser
Et je te donnerai
Un frigidaire, un joli scooter
Un atomizer et du Dunlopillo
Une cuisinière avec un four en verre
Des tas de couverts et des pelles à gâteau
Un tourniquette pour faire la vinaigrette
Un bel aérateur pour bouffer les odeurs
Des draps qui chauffent,
Un pistolet à gauffres
Un avion pour deux
Et nous serons heureux
Autrefois s'il arrivait
Que l'on se querelle
L'air lugubre on s'en allait
En laissant la vaisselle
Maintenant que voulez-vous
La vie est si chère
On dit rentre chez ta mère
Et on se garde tout
Ah Gudule, excuse-toi
Ou je reprends tout ça...

The Lament of Progress

In the old days, when you courted, you spoke of love
To show your ardour, you offered you heart
Now, everything's changed
If you want to seduce your loved one, you have to whisper in her ear
Oh, Gudule, come and kiss me and I'll give you
A fridge, a pretty scooter,
An atomizer and a Sleeprest mattress
A cooker and a glass-door oven
Loads of silverware and cake slices
A beater to make vinaigrette
A beautiful extractor to sniff out odours
Electric sheets, a waffle-maker
An aeroplane for two, and then we'll be happy
In the old days, you sometimes fought, and off you went with a gloomy look, leaving the dishes behind
Now, what can I say ? The cost of living is so high
So you shout, Go back to mother, Gudule, and you keep everything for yourself
Say you're sorry, Gudule, or I'll take everything back...
(Complete song on page 20)

Listen to the song, "La Complainte du Progrès", and look at the translation on the facing page. Then do the crossword puzzle below. It shouldn't be too hard: you'll find many of the words in the song.

Across

1. *It cools and preserves.*
7. *A girl is one, but a boy isn't.*
8. *It's pretty (at least in the song!) and it gets you round town.*
11. *« Rentre chez ta mère et ... père. »*
12. *« ... lit ». Find the correct definite article.*
13. *February 14th is famous for this.*
15. *« ... est heureux. »*
16. *When number 13 across goes wrong, these sometimes get broken.*
19. *« ... es belle. »*
21. *Without this, you wouldn't have any dinner.*

Down

1. *You cook cakes in this.*
2. *Corsica (la Corse) is one.*
3. *Add this to "possible" and you get its opposite. (Just like in English!)*
4. *This is a fast way to travel.*
5. *In French, this rhymes with "beautiful".*
6. *You say: « à Bordeaux » but « ... France ».*
8. *Under.*
9. *Abbreviation for "Centre national de recherche scientifique" (important French research centre).*
10. *A musical note. (This is easy! It's the same in English.)*
11. *« Ah ... Gudule ... Excuse-... »*
13. *With.*
14. *« C'est mon armoire, et ... cuillère. »*
15. *« ... arrivait. »*
17. *Famous volcano in Sicily.*
18. *« On ... dit au cher ange. »*
20. *Iron.*
22. *« ... cœur. » Find the correct indefinite article.*
23. *If.*
24. *And.*

(See solutions on page 20)

Listen

LOCATION DE VOITURE

À Toulouse, dans une agence de la société Europcar

M. Peterkin : *Je suis M. Peterkin de la société IPK. Ma secrétaire vous a envoyé un télex pour la location d'une voiture.*

L'employé : *C'est exact. Bonjour M. Peterkin. Nous vous avons réservé une Peugeot 505 SR. Ce modèle vous convient ?*

M. Peterkin : *Oui, c'est très bien.*

L'employé : *Voulez-vous signer ce formulaire, s'il vous plaît ?... Merci. Vous avez une assurance tous risques.*

M. Peterkin : *Parfait.*

L'employé : *Votre permis de conduire, je vous prie.*

M. Peterkin : *Le voilà.*

L'employé : *Et j'aurais besoin aussi de votre passeport.*

M. Peterkin : *Oui. Tiens ! Je ne le trouve pas. Je l'ai pris pourtant... Ah, le voilà!*

L'employé : *Si vous voulez bien me suivre jusqu'au parking, je vais vous donner votre voiture. Voilà les clés.*

M. Peterkin : *Trois clés ?*

L'employé : *Oui, la grande sert à ouvrir les portières et le coffre ; la moyenne, c'est la clé de contact et la petite, c'est pour le bouchon du réservoir d'essence.*

M. Peterkin : *Au fait, qu'est-ce que je prends comme essence ? De l'ordinaire ou du super ?*

L'employé : *Du super !*

L'employé : *Tenez, c'est la voiture blanche, là-bas, devant la pompe à essence...*

. . . .

M. Peterkin : *Il y a 4 ou 5 vitesses ?*

L'employé : *5 vitesses.*

M. Peterkin : *Et ce petit bouton noir à gauche, il sert à quoi ?*

L'employé : *C'est pour les essuie-glaces, vous le tournez de gauche à droite.*

M. Peterkin : *D'accord. Et l'interrupteur rouge ici, qu'est-ce que c'est ?*

L'employé : *C'est l'interrupteur de dégivrage de la vitre arrière.*

M. Peterkin : *Et pour les phares, ça marche comment ?*

L'employé : *Vous tournez la manette qui est à gauche du volant.*

M. Peterkin : *Bon, ça va. Je peux la laisser demain soir à Grenoble ?*

L'employé : *Bien sûr ! A côté de l'agence, vous avez une station Shell ouverte toute la nuit. Vous pouvez laisser les clés au pompiste.*

M. Peterkin : *Entendu !*

L'employé : *Vous réglez maintenant ?*

M. Peterkin : *Oui. Je peux régler avec la carte « Diners club » ?*

L'employé : *Si vous voulez.*

Listen and repeat
(You may look at the translation on page 21 in the booklet.)

1. Peugeot 505
2. Place du Capitol, à Toulouse
3. Vue de Grenoble et des Alpes
4. Station service
5. Panneaux d'autoroute

3.2 WORDS

location (F) — rental
voiture (F) — car
formulaire (M) — form
assurance (F) — insurance
permis de conduire (M) — driving license
passeport (M) — passport
parking (M) — car park, parking lot
clé (de contact) (F) — (ignition) key
portière (F) — car door
bouchon (M) — cap (of petrol tank)
réservoir (M) — (petrol-)tank
essence (F) — petrol, gas
essence ordinaire (F) — standard grade petrol
essence super (F) — high grade petrol
pompe à essence (F) — petrol pump
vitesse (F) — gear
bouton (M) — button, switch
essuie-glace (M) — windscreen wiper
interrupteur (M) — switch
dégivrage (M) — demister
vitre (F) — car window
phare (M) — headlight
manette (F) — lever
volant (M) — steering wheel
station (service) (F) — service station
pompiste (M) — garage attendant
ceinture de sécurité (F) — safety belt
carte grise (F) — car registration papers
véhicule (M) — vehicle
automobiliste (M ou F) — driver
conducteur(trice) — driver
porte (F) — door
fenêtre (F) — window

louer — to rent
envoyer — to send
convenir — to suit
avoir besoin — to need
ouvrir — to open
régler — to pay
démarrer — to start
accélérer — to accelerate
ralentir — to slow down
freiner — to brake
s'arrêter — to stop
allumer — to turn on
éteindre — to turn off
avancer — to go forwards
reculer — to back up
fermer — to close, to shut
payer — to pay
rouler — to drive

c'est exact — that's right, that's correct
tous risques (assurance) — comprehensive (insurance)
parfait — perfect
au fait — by the way
mettre le contact — to start (a car)
mettre la radio — to turn/switch on the radio
mettre le chauffage — to turn/switch on the heating
mettre les essuie-glaces — to turn/switch on the windscreen wipers
être en panne — to break down
faire marche arrière — to go into reverse
faire le plein d'essence — to fill up (the petrol tank)
couper le contact — to switch off the ignition

HOW TO SAY IT

1. POINTING TO THINGS

Voilà les clés — Here are your keys
Ce petit bouton noir... — This little black button...
C'est la voiture blanche, là-bas — It's the white car over there
La grande clé sert à ouvrir les portières — The big key opens the car doors

2. FUNCTIONS – SAYING WHAT SOMETHING IS FOR

Cette clé sert à ouvrir les portières — This key opens the car doors
La petite, c'est pour le bouchon du réservoir d'essence — The little one is for the petrol cap
La moyenne, c'est la clé de contact — The middle-sized one is the ignition key
Cet interrupteur, il est utilisé pour le dégivrage — This switch is for the demister
Cet interrupteur, on l'utilise pour le dégivrage — This switch is for the demister
Avec cette clé, on ouvre le bouchon du réservoir — You unlock the petrol cap with this key

3. ASKING WHAT SOMETHING IS FOR OR HOW IT WORKS

Ça sert à quoi ? — What's this for ?
À quoi est-ce que ça (cela) sert ? — What's this for ?
Ça marche comment ?
Comment est-ce que ça (cela) marche ? — How does it work ?

4. POLITE REQUESTS

Voulez-vous signer ce formulaire, s'il vous plaît ? — Would you sign this form, please ?
Si vous voulez bien me suivre jusqu'au parking — If you would just follow me to the car park
J'aurais besoin aussi de votre passeport — I'll also need your passport
Je vous demanderais de me donner votre passeport, s'il vous plaît — May I have your passport, please ?

5. ASKING WHAT IS POSSIBLE

Je peux laisser la voiture à Grenoble ? — May I leave the car in Grenoble ?
Il est possible de régler avec une carte de crédit ? — May I pay with a credit card ?

6. ANSWERING "NO"

C'est impossible — It is not possible
Vous ne pouvez pas — You cannot
Non, je regrette — No, I'm sorry
Non, je suis désolé(e) — No, I'm sorry

3.2 ORAL PRACTICE

1. GRAMMAR : SEE PAGE 47

« SERVIR À » : SAYING WHAT THINGS ARE FOR

Listen :

(Avec cette clé on ouvre les portières ?)
— Oui, elle sert à ouvrir les portières.

NOW, CONFIRM WHAT THE FOLLOWING THINGS ARE USED FOR

(Avec cette clé on ouvre les portières ?) — (Avec ce bouchon on ferme le réservoir ?) — (Avec cette clé on met le contact ?) — (Avec ce bouton on met le chauffage ?) — (Avec cette manette on allume les phares ?) — (Avec cette clé on coupe le contact ?)

2. GRAMMAR : SEE PAGE 42

PRONOUN PRACTICE : PRONOUNS AS DIRECT OBJECTS

Listen :

(Vous donnez les clés au pompiste ?)
— Oui, je les donne au pompiste.
(Il a son passeport ?)
— Oui, il l'a.

NOW, ANSWER THE FOLLOWING QUESTIONS IN THE AFFIRMATIVE, REPLACING THE NOUNS WITH THE APPROPRIATE PRONOUNS

(Vous donnez les clés au pompiste ?) — (Il a son passeport ?) — (Vous laissez la voiture à Grenoble ?) — (Vous fermez le bouchon du réservoir avec cette clé ?) — (Elle a son permis de conduire ?) — (Vous ouvrez les portières avec cette clé ?) — (Il allume le chauffage ?)

3. GRAMMAR : SEE PAGE 41

PRONOUN PRACTICE : DIRECT OBJECT PRONOUNS IN NEGATIVE SENTENCES

Listen :

(Vous ne trouvez pas votre passeport ?)
— Non, je ne le trouve pas.

NOW, ANSWER THE FOLLOWING QUESTIONS IN THE NEGATIVE FORM, REPLACING THE NOUNS WITH THE APPROPRIATE PRONOUN

(Vous ne trouvez pas votre passeport ?) — (Vous ne prenez pas cette voiture ?) — (Il n'a pas son permis de conduire ?) — (Vous ne connaissez pas la 505 ?) — (Vous n'avez pas les clés ?) — (Il n'allume pas ses phares ?) — (Vous n'aimez pas ce modèle ?)

4. GRAMMAR : SEE PAGE 42

PRONOUN PRACTICE : PERSONAL PRONOUNS AS DIRECT OBJECTS

Listen :

(Il t'emmène au garage ?)
— Oui, il m'emmène au garage.

NOW, ANSWER IN THE AFFIRMATIVE, USING THE APPROPRIATE PERSONAL PRONOUN

(Il t'emmène au garage ?) — (Je vous laisse à l'agence ?) — (Tu m'attends ?) — (Il me cherche ?) — (Il me paye en espèces ?) — (Jacques et Micheline, ils vous suivent ?)

5. GRAMMAR : SEE PAGE 41

PRONOUN PRACTICE : PERSONAL PRONOUNS AS DIRECT OBJECTS IN NEGATIVE SENTENCES

Listen :

(Je vous laisse à Grenoble)
— Je ne vous laisse pas à Grenoble.

NOW, PUT THE FOLLOWING AFFIRMATIVE SENTENCES IN THE NEGATIVE FORM

(Je vous laisse à Grenoble) — (Il m'emmène à Toulouse) — (Vous me payez par chèque) — (Je vous attends) — (Elle te cherche) — (Ils nous appellent souvent) — (Nous te suivons)

6. SEE PAGE 112

QUESTIONS ABOUT TYPE : « WHAT KIND OF... »

Listen :

(Je prends de l'essence)
— Qu'est-ce que vous prenez comme essence ?

NOW, LISTEN TO THE FOLLOWING STATEMENTS AND ASK QUESTIONS USING « COMME »

(Je prends de l'essence) — (Il vend des voitures) — (Elle veut une assurance) — (Il a une carte de crédit) — (Je loue une voiture) — (Il y a plusieurs modèles)

ON THE ROAD

s a nervous driver and an even more ervous passenger, my first piece of dvice about driving in France is: Don't". My more mobile friends tell e there is nothing to it, and they vax eloquent about the excitement of veaving in and out of the screeching, onking traffic. To me, it has about s much appeal as a bullfight, and ooks just as deadly.

irst, there is the speed. An initiation de into Paris along the lethal ring oad (périphérique) can resemble a peeded-up silent movie. Except it's ot that silent. Klaxons Rule O.K., and vhen in doubt — honk. If you can eep your sang-froid through the peed and the noise, your next test of strength is the dreaded priorité à droite (give way to the right) rule. I have never quite understood it. All I know is that as you speed down a busy, apparently main road, countless little beaten-up Renaults will come veering in from side streets on the right, and collision seems imminent. But it's all just a battle of nerves, really. Someone always gives way at the last minute. Well, usually. If you look at the fronts of many Parisian cars, they seem to carry the tell-tale dent that speaks of their own particular Waterloo.

If you feel sluggish (unlikely!) and want that extra shot of adrenalin, nothing works as well as a drive around the Arc de Triomphe. I dare anyone to try it at rush hour in a small Fiat and come out feeling sleepy. Rule Number One at this, and other celebrated Parisian roundabouts, is very simple: it's "Chacun pour soi" (every man for himself). The bigger your car, the better your chances. I often think one of the most satisfying experiences would be to drive through the frenetic, narrow streets of the Latin Quarter in a high-speed tank.

BUMPER TO BUMPER Then there are the delights of Parisian parking. If you are very lucky, you'll find that perfect little place (a near impossibility on a Saturday night) only to find, as you come out of your restaurant or cinema, that two other cars have sandwiched you firmly bumper-to-bumper. Do not despair. It's time to employ the Parisian Bump Method. It's very simple — you just ease forward and back gently bashing the two cars in question. Foreigners often stop in amazement at the simple practicality of the method. It may seem a little brutal, but "When in France . . ." etc.

But, if you've survived, maybe even enjoyed, the bullfight mentality of the cities, nothing is lovelier than to drive through the apple orchards and cornfields of Normandy, or cruise along the coast road on the Riviera, maybe driving inland for a chilled glass of white wine in the shady square of a Provençal village.

Just one last word of warning. If you think Parisian traffic is frightening, everything on four wheels gets faster and — how to put it? — more "dynamic" as you go south, with tempers warming in the Mediterranean sun, and hand gestures becoming more graphic. Still, this is all really Second Degree Stuff. After all, there's always Italy . . . □

3.2 TAKE A BREAK

N° 1 Listen

Listen to the people on the cassette describing the objects they would like to rent. Then look at the illustrations below and write the number of the person you think is speaking in the box next to the corresponding image.

N° 2

Identify the following road signs from the list below, putting the correct numbers in the appropriate boxes.

1. *passage à niveau*

2. *circulation à sens unique*

3. *circulation dans les 2 sens*

4. *fin de limitation de vitesse à 60 km/h*

5. *croisement*

6. *chaussée rétrécie*

7. *cédez le passage*

8. *virage à droite*

9. *route prioritaire*

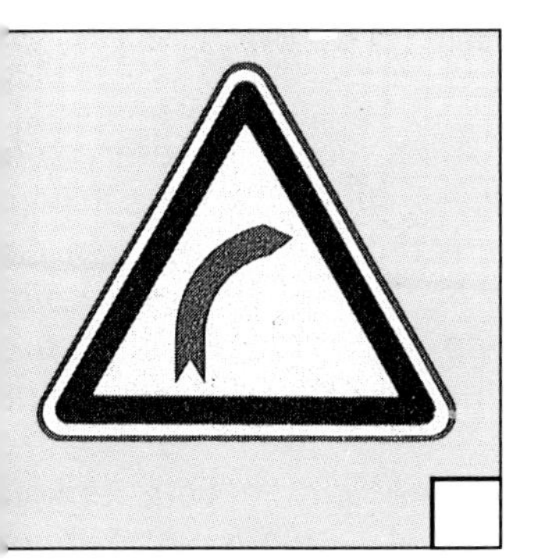

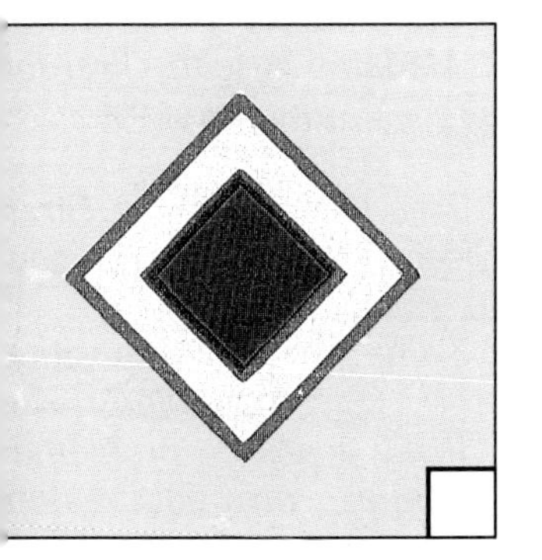

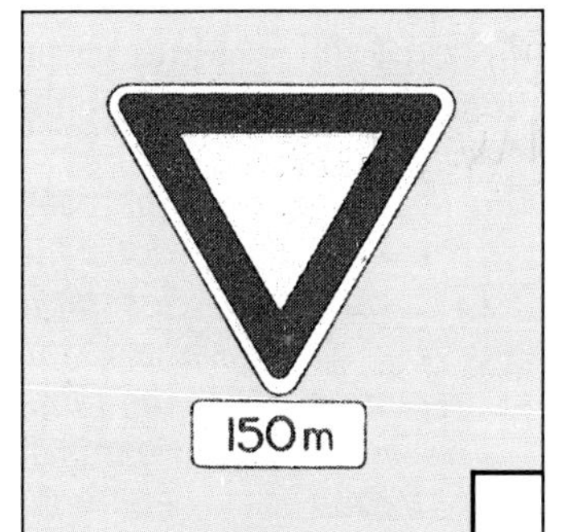

(See solutions on page 22)

Listen

LA PRÉPARATION D'UN CONGRÈS

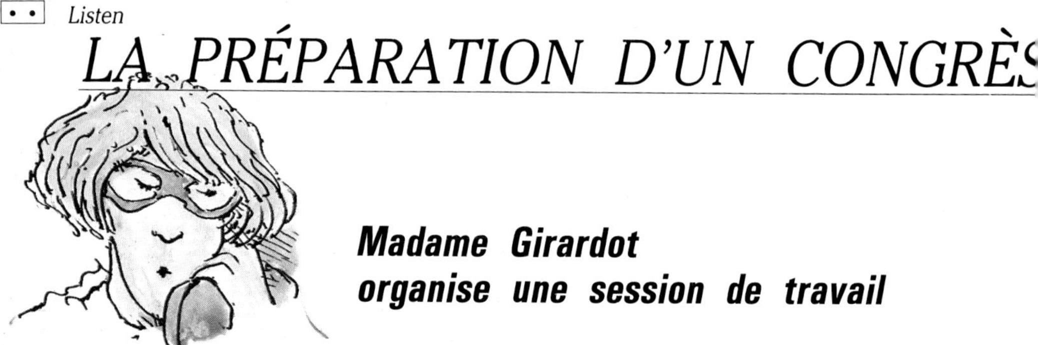

Madame Girardot organise une session de travail

L'organisateur : *Novotel, bonjour.*

Mme Girardot : *Bonjour Monsieur, je vous téléphone pour la réservation d'un salon ; je voudrais organiser une session de travail de trois jours, pour 70 personnes, les 20, 21 et 22 octobre. Est-ce que vous avez une salle disponible à ces dates ?*

L'organisateur : *Un instant, je vous prie, je regarde... j'ai le salon bleu qui est rectangulaire. Il fait 170 m²; c'est la taille idéale pour 70 personnes.*

Mme Girardot : *Et combien coûte la location de ce salon ?*

L'organisateur : *Il fait 4 000 F TTC sans repas.*

Mme Girardot : *On ne peut pas déjeuner sur place ?*

L'organisateur : *Si, vous avez des menus « journées d'étude » qui sont servis dans un salon contigu.*

Mme Girardot : *Vous pouvez me donner les prix ?*

L'organisateur : *Bien sûr. Nos menus sont à 150 F par personne (taxe et service compris).*

Mme Girardot : *Pour l'hébergement, est-ce que vous auriez 40 chambres pour les 3 nuits des 20, 21 et 22 ?*

L'organisateur : *Une minute, s'il vous plaît... Je regarde les réservations... Oui, je les ai.*

Mme Girardot : *Alors, vous me réservez le salon bleu et les 40 chambres, s'il vous plaît ; ma secrétaire vous confirmera par télex ; pour les repas, je verrai plus tard... Est-ce que vous pourriez m'envoyer une documentation avec un plan d'accès ?*

L'organisateur : *Bien sûr, je vous envoie notre brochure et j'attends votre télex. Vous pouvez me donner votre nom ?*

Mme Girardot : *Madame Arlette Girardot des laboratoires Mardomme.*

L'organisateur : *Très bien, Madame Girardot. Quelle disposition voulez-vous pour les tables du salon ?*

Mme Girardot : *J'aimerais une disposition de tables en U. C'est possible ?*

L'organisateur : *Il n'y a pas de problème et vous souhaitez un équipement audiovisuel ?*

Mme Girardot : *Euh... un magnétoscope, un écran, un projecteur de diapositives et si possible, deux micros.*

L'organisateur : *L'écran et les micros sont inclus dans le prix de la location, mais le magnétoscope et le projecteur sont facturés 800 F par jour.*

Mme Girardot : *Très bien, c'est entendu.*

Listen and repeat
(You may look at the translation on page 22 in the booklet.)

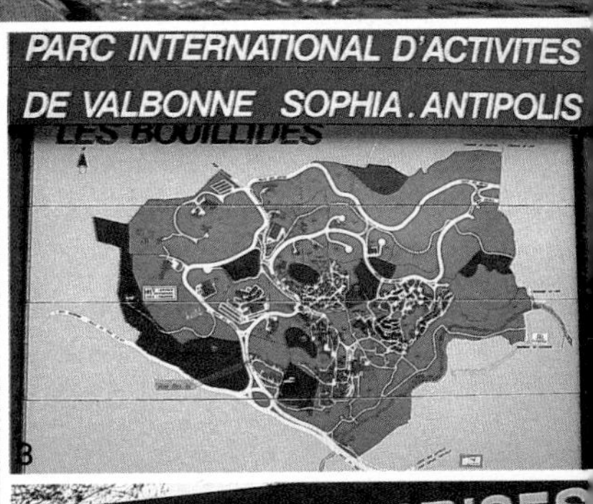

1. Côte d'Azur
2. Village d'entreprises et centre de congrès de Sophia Antipolis
3. Plan du village

3.3 WORDS

NOUNS

préparation (F) — groundwork, preparation
congrès (M) — congress
session (F) — session
travail (M) — work
salle (F) — (conference) room
salon (M) — room
repas (M) — meal
taille (F) — size
taxe (F) — tax
TTC -toutes taxes comprises- (F) — tax included
menu (M) — set meal ***(1)***
hébergement (M) — accommodation
documentation (F) — written information
plan d'accès (M) — street map
brochure (F) — brochure
équipement (M) — equipment, facilities
magnétoscope (M) — VCR, video cassette recorder
écran (M) — screen
projecteur (M) — projector
diapositive (F) — slide, transparency
micro (M) — microphone

---

prix (M) — price
tarif (M) — price
disque (M) — record
magnétophone (M) — tape recorder
prise (F) — socket
pièce (F) — room
renseignement (M) — information

ADJECTIVES

disponible — free, available
idéal(e) — ideal
compris(e) — included, inclusive
contigu(ë) — adjacent
inclus(e) — included, inclusive
rond(e) — round
oval(e) — oval
carré(e) — square
rectangulaire — rectangular

organiser — to organize
coûter — to cost
confirmer — to confirm
souhaiter — to wish
facturer — to invoice
télexer — to telex
recevoir — to receive
adresser — to send

je vous prie — please
sur place — on the premises, on the sport, there
une minute — just a moment

REMEMBER... REMEMBER... REMEMBER... REMEMBER... REMEMBER

(1) *« Menu » in English corresponds to « la carte » in French (« Je voudrais voir la carte, s.v.p. »). In French « un menu » is a set meal at a fixed price : « Nous prenons le menu à 50 francs. » —* ***(2)*** *If renting or buying a flat in France, you will often find the surface area measured in square metres. —* ***(3)*** *The habit of answering « si » to give an affirmative answer to a negative question is difficult to acquire.*

HOW TO SAY IT

1. GIVING DIMENSIONS AND PRICES

Il fait 170 mètres carrés (m²) — It's 170 square metres ***(2)***
C'est un salon de 170 mètres carrés (m²) — The room measures 170 square metres
Ce salon fait 4 000 F T.T.C. — This room costs 4,000 Francs, tax-included
Le menu est à 150 F — The set lunch is 150 Francs
Le projecteur est facturé 800 F par jour — There is a charge of 800 Francs a day for the projector
La chambre coûte 250 F par jour — The (bed-) room costs 250 Francs a day

2. ASKING ABOUT DIMENSIONS, PRICE AND AVAILABILITY

Il fait combien de long ? — How long is it ?
Combien coûte la location ? — How much is the rental ?
Les chambres sont à quel prix ? — How much are the rooms ?
Le menu est à combien ? — How much is the set lunch ?
Est-ce que vous auriez une salle disponible ? — Would you have a room free ?
Est-ce qu'il y a un magnétoscope ? — Is there a VCR ?

3. ANSWERING "YES" TO AFFIRMATIVE AND NEGATIVE QUESTIONS

(Est-ce que vous pourriez m'envoyer une documentation ?) — (Could you send me some information, please ?)

Oui — Yes
Bien sûr — Of course
D'accord — All right
C'est entendu — Right
Oui, c'est possible — Yes, I can
Il n'y a pas de problème — No problem
Tout à fait — Certainly

(On ne peut pas déjeuner sur place ?) — (Can't we eat there ?)
Si ! — Yes ***(3)***
Si, bien sûr ! — Yes, of course ***(3)***

4. ASKING WHAT SOMEONE WANTS

Quelle disposition voulez-vous ? — How would you like to arrange the seating ?
Vous souhaitez un magnétoscope ? — Would you like a VCR ?
Vous désirez une grande salle ? — Would you like a big room ?

5. SAYING WHAT YOU WOULD LIKE

J'aimerais une disposition de tables en U — I would like the tables in a U-shape
Je voudrais une salle avec un écran — I would like a room with a screen
Je souhaiterais avoir deux micros — I would like to have two microphones
Je désirerais deux projecteurs — I would like two projectors

3.3 ORAL PRACTICE

1. SEE PAGE 122

TALKING ABOUT SHAPE, SURFACE AREA AND PRICES :

Listen :

(Salon bleu/rectangulaire/100 m²/1 000 F)
— Le salon bleu est rectangulaire, il fait 100 m² et coûte 1 000 F.

NOW, DESCRIBE THE FOLLOWING ROOMS

(Salon bleu/rectangulaire/100 m²/1 000 F) — (Salon orange/rond/150 m²/1 500 F) — (Salon jaune/ovale/100 m²/1 000 F) — (Salon blanc/rectangulaire/250 m²/2 500 F)

2. GRAMMAR : SEE PAGE 42

PRONOUN PRACTICE : THE INDIRECT OBJECT PRONOUNS « LUI » AND « LEUR »

Listen :

(Il téléphone à son client ?)
— Oui, il lui téléphone.
(Le directeur écrit aux employés ?)
— Oui, il leur écrit.

NOW, ANSWER THE FOLLOWING QUESTIONS IN THE AFFIRMATIVE WITH « LUI » OR « LEUR »

(Il téléphone à son client ?)— (Le directeur écrit aux employés ?) — (La secrétaire dit bonjour à ses collègues ?) — (Le responsable donne les nouveaux tarifs à ses clients ?) — (Pierre demande des renseignements à la réceptionniste ?) — (La vendeuse confirme par télex à l'acheteur ?)

3. GRAMMAR : SEE PAGE 42

PRONOUN PRACTICE : THE INDIRECT OBJECT PRONOUNS « ME », « TE », « NOUS » AND « VOUS »

Listen :

(Vous me téléphonez à 11 heures ?)
— Oui, je vous téléphone à 11 heures.
(Tu m'écris la semaine prochaine ?)
— Oui, je t'écris la semaine prochaine.

NOW, ANSWER THESE QUESTIONS IN THE AFFIRMATIVE, USING THE APPROPRIATE PRONOUNS

(Vous me téléphonez à 11 heures ?) — (Tu m'écris la semaine prochaine ?) — (Monsieur Dumont, je vous adresse le télex ?) — (Mesdames, je vous envoie la brochure ?) — (Il te dit bonjour ?) — (Madame, nous vous confirmons la réservation ?)

4. GRAMMAR : SEE PAGE 41

PRONOUN PRACTICE : INDIRECT OBJECT PRO NOUNS IN NEGATIVE SENTENCES

Listen :

(Elle lui envoie la brochure)
— Elle ne lui envoie pas la brochure.
(Je vous réserve le salon F)
— Je ne vous réserve pas le salon F.

NOW, PUT THESE SENTENCES IN THE NEGATIVE FORM

(Elle lui envoie la brochure) — (Je vous réserve le salo F) — (Il lui téléphone) — (Je leur confirme par téle — (Vous me donnez votre clé) — (Il nous facture le magnétoscopes)

5. GRAMMAR : SEE PAGE 42

PRONOUN PRACTICE : PRONOUNS AS DIREC AND INDIRECT OBJECTS

Listen :

(Je vais parler aux ingénieurs)
— Je vais leur parler.
(Il va inviter les responsables)
— Il va les inviter.

NOW, REPLACE THE DIRECT OR INDIRECT OBJECT IN TH FOLLOWING SENTENCES WITH THE APPROPRIAT PRONOUN

(Je vais parler aux ingénieurs) — (Il va inviter les res ponsables) — (Nous allons essayer cette calculatric — (Je vais téléphoner au comptable) — (Vous allez ache ter cette machine) — (Nous allons écrire à ces jeune filles) — (Elle va donner sa carte de visite)

6. GRAMMAR : SEE PAGE 48

PRONOUN PRACTICE : DIFFERENT WAYS O ASKING FOR THINGS POLITELY

Listen :

(Je voudrais un plan d'accès)
— Est-ce que vous pourriez me donner u plan d'accès ?

NOW, ASK FOR THE FOLLOWING THINGS USING THE MO POLITE FORM

(Je voudrais un plan d'accès) — (Nous voudrions un ren seignement) — (Le client voudrait une carte de visit — (Les représentants voudraient votre nom) — (Je vou drais le prix du salon F) — (Le directeur voudrait so billet d'avion) — (Nous voudrions l'adresse de l'hôte

BUSINESS MEETINGS

French business meeting has little n common with an Anglo-Saxon one. Vhere the British and the Americans ove to follow formal procedures, the rench love to improvise. In Britain nd the States those attending a neeting are expected to follow cerain rules of meeting etiquette, and here may even be a moderator to nsure that no one speaks out of turn r interrupts, that the agenda is kept o, that committees and subommittees are formed and minutes f the meeting taken. At a French neeting there will be an agenda 'ordre du jour), but it may or may ot be followed, and meeting etiuette is much freer. The French are pparently too individualistic to bow own to a series of rules telling them ow to express themselves. In a ountry where conversation is regardd as a fine art and where people pend hours chatting in cafés, it is ot surprising that all rules governing elf-expression should be rejected as nnecessarily repressive.

THREE, A MAGIC FIGURE *The foreigner attending a meeting in France may be surprised to find that all the speakers break down everything they have to say into three categories. There are never two or four problems to be examined, never five explanations for a sudden drop or rise in sales. Everything — just as in fairy tales — seems to revolve around the magic figure of three. The reason is simple enough. All French schoolchildren are taught that, in a rational, Cartesian approach to experience, things break down into* première, deuxième, troisième.

Another thing that may surprise the foreigner at a French meeting is the way everyone talks at the same time. The stigma that is attached to interrupting others in many parts of the world does not seem to exist in France. Television talk shows are known to degenerate into verbal free-for-alls, where he or she who talks loudest talks longest.

Because meeting etiquette is so loose, it would seem that French meetings are not very productive. This is not entirely the case, for if the content often gets lost in various shouting matches, there are other things to look out for in a meeting. How the various participants present themselves and how they perform are key factors to watch for. Rivalries and alliances can be made and unmade at a meeting that seemed otherwise totally unproductive. It is after the meeting, over a cup of coffee or during a brief encounter in the corridor, that the real decisions are reached.

Meetings, originally regarded as an Anglo-Saxon import (the expression le meeting *has almost supplanted the French term* la réunion*), are now an integral part of French business life. To such an extent, in fact, that some wit has said the major ill of the French business world is not the trade deficit but* la "réunionite". □

3.3 TAKE A BREAK

Listen

Listen to the people describing the places they would like to rent or buy. Then put the number of each sentence in the box beside the appropriate place.

Across

1. *Rent this in France. In Hollywood, you'd probably be out in the open making movies.*

4. *Put these in verse, but don't write a long poem or you could find yourself in debt.*

6. *Put on your best one, Madame, if you're dining out at the Closerie des Lilas.*

7. *If you're on this in English, all's equal. In French, it's each man for himself. (................. personne)*

8. *I'll give it to you in French, if you give it to them. Je le .... donne.*

9. *« ..... Alpes sont très belles. »*

Down

1. *Rent, don't buy.*

2. *Places for sweet dreams, especially in a nice château.*

3. *Oh, you tardy souls. If you're always late, you'll get the sack.*

5. *Project all your slides on to this, and when you're fed up, go to the cinema.*

8. *This is a very straightforward article, but not very feminine.*

You'll find 12 things in the television set that you'd need for a conference. Circle the words (all in French, of course) which are written vertically, horizontally, diagonally, backwards or forwards. Use the English words below to help you.

computer — screen — mike — projector — switch — blackboard — table — paper — pens — room — conference room — equipment

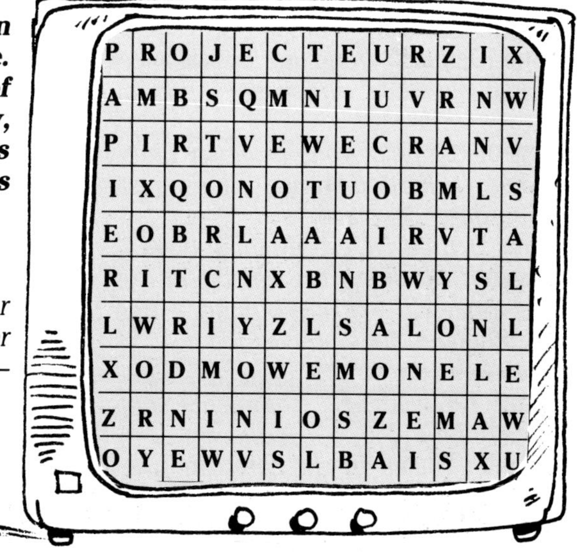

(See solutions on page 24)

3.4 CONTACTS

[• •] *Listen*

PROJETS DE VACANCES

Dans une agence de voyages Mme Delmas se renseigne sur les possibilités de séjour aux Antilles

Mme Delmas : *Bonjour Monsieur.*

L'agent : *Bonjour Madame, je peux vous renseigner ?*

Mme Delmas : *Oui, je voudrais aller en vacances aux Antilles.*

L'agent : *En voyage organisé ?*

Mme Delmas : *Non, pas de voyage organisé ; je préférerais aller à l'hôtel... ou louer une maison.*

L'agent : *Vous êtes combien ?*

Mme Delmas : *Quatre : mon mari, mes deux enfants et moi-même.*

L'agent : *Vos enfants ont quel âge ?*

Mme Delmas : *14 et 16 ans.*

L'agent : *Et vous voulez partir quand ?*

Mme Delmas : *Pendant les vacances de Pâques, deux semaines si possible.*

L'agent : *Je peux vous proposer l'hôtel du Parc à Fort-de-France ; il est juste en bordure de plage.*

Mme Delmas : *C'est un bon hôtel ?*

L'agent : *Oh oui, il est très bien ; c'est un 4 étoiles. Il y a une piscine et une discothèque. Vous pouvez jouer au tennis et faire du cheval.*

Mme Delmas : *Et comment sont les chambres ?*

L'agent : *Toutes les chambres ont une salle de bains ; elles sont toutes climatisées, elles donnent sur la mer. Elles sont assez grandes et, bien entendu, vous avez le téléphone et la télévision.*

Mme Delmas : *Ah oui... Très bien ! Et qu'est-ce que vous avez comme location ?*

L'agent : *Nous avons une maison de campagne qui se trouve en plein milieu d'un jardin tropical. Elle se compose d'un séjour, d'une chambre double avec salle de bains et de deux chambres simples ; la cuisine est entièrement équipée : réfrigérateur, congélateur, cuisinière électrique... Elle est à 10 km à l'est de Pointe-à-Pitre et à 5 km d'une très belle plage de sable fin où on peut faire de la voile.*

Mme Delmas : *Oui, c'est bien... mais... trop loin de la mer !*

L'agent : *Mais c'est tranquille. Sinon nous en avons une autre qui est située à proximité de Fort-de-France ; celle-là est à deux pas des plages, elle n'a que deux chambres. L'aéroport est à côté, il y a du bruit et donc ce n'est pas cher.*

Mme Delmas : *Je suppose que celle de Pointe-à-Pitre est très chère.*

L'agent : *Assez, oui !*

Mme Delmas : *Bon, je vais réfléchir...*

[• •] Listen and repeat
(You may look at the translation on page 24 in the booklet.)

1. Agence de voyages
2.-5. Marchés antillais
3. Brochure publicitaire
4. Plage à la Martinique

3.4 WORDS

projet (M) — plan
vacances (F) — holiday ***(1)***
voyage organisé (M) — package tour
mari (M) — husband
plage (F) — beach
quatre étoiles (M) — four-star
discothèque (F) — discotheque
piscine (F) — swimming pool
salle de bains (F) — bathroom
toilettes (F) — W.C.
séjour (M) — living-room
mer (F) — sea
maison de campagne (F) — country house
jardin (M) — garden
sable (M) — sand
cuisine (F) — kitchen
réfrigérateur (M) — refrigerator
congélateur (M) — freezer
placard (M) — cupboard, closet
cuisinière (F) — cooker
aéroport (M) — airport
jour férié (M) — holiday ***(1)***
baignoire (F) — bathtub
douche (F) — shower
centre (M) — centre

climatisé(e) — air-conditioned
tropical(e) — tropical
équipé(e) — equipped
électrique — electric, electrical
tranquille — quiet, calm
bruyant(e) — noisy
privé(e) — private

renseigner — to inform, to give information
louer — to hire, rent
donner sur — to look over, to face (of rooms)
réfléchir — to think something over
compter — to count
nager — to swim

en bordure de — on the edge of
loin de — far from
près de — close to, near
à proximité de — near to
à deux pas de — right next to (two steps away)
faire de la voile — to sail
faire de la planche à voile — to wind surf
se composer de — to consist of, to be made up of
au bord de — next to
a côté de — next to
en face de — facing

---

passer des vacances — to spend holidays
passer un jour/une nuit/une heure — to spend a day/a night/an hour
prendre des vacances — to take holidays
prendre un jour de congé — to take a day off ***(1)***
être en vacances — to be on holiday
avoir l'intention (de) — to mean to, to intend to
avoir envie (de) — to want to

REMEMBER... REMEMBER... REMEMBER... REMEMBER... REMEMBER

(1) *« Vacances » means a long holiday ; « jour férié » is a public holiday ; « jour de congé » is a day off.*

HOW TO SAY IT

1. SAYING WHAT YOU WANT TO DO

Je voudrais aller aux Antilles — I'd like to go to the West Indies
J'ai l'intention de louer une maison — I want to rent a house
J'aimerais partir pendant les vacances de Pâques — I'd like to leave during the Easter holidays
Je compte faire du cheval — I hope to do some riding
J'ai envie de prendre deux semaines de vacances — I feel like taking two weeks holiday

2. SAYING WHAT YOU PREFER OR WOULD PREFER

Je préférerais aller à l'hôtel — I'd rather go to the hotel
Je préfère louer une maison — I'd rather rent a house
J'aimerais mieux être au bord de la mer — I'd rather be by the sea
J'aime mieux jouer au tennis — I prefer playing tennis

3. DESCRIBING A PLACE

La maison se trouve au milieu d'un jardin — The house is in the middle of a garden
Elle est à 10 km à l'est de Pointe-à-Pitre — It is 10 kilometres to the east of Pointe-à-Pitre
Elle est située à proximité de Fort-de-France — It's near Fort-de-France
Il y a une piscine — There is a swimming pool
Vous avez le téléphone et la télévision — There is a phone and a television
Elle se compose d'un séjour et d'une chambre double — It's got a living-room and a double bedroom

4. GIVING OPINIONS

Il est très bien / *C'est très bien* — It's very good
Ce n'est pas mal — It's not bad
Ce n'est pas bien — It's not very nice

5. ASKING FOR INFORMATION

C'est un bon hôtel ? — Is it a good hotel ?
Comment sont les chambres ? — What are the rooms like ?
Qu'est-ce que vous avez comme location ? — What sort of rooms do you have for rent ?
Est-ce qu'il y a une piscine ? — Does the hotel have a swimming pool ?
Combien coûte la location ? — How much is it ?

3.4 ORAL PRACTICE

1. GRAMMAR : SEE PAGE 44

SAYING WHERE IT IS :

Listen :

(Loin)
— L'hôtel est loin de la plage.
(à 4 km)
— L'hôtel est à 4 km de la plage.

NOW, SAY WHERE THE HOTEL IS IN RELATION TO THE BEACH

(Loin) — (à 4 km) — (à deux pas) — (à proximité) — (au sud) — (près) — (à l'est) — (à 10 mn à pied) — (à côté) — (en face)

2. GRAMMAR : SEE PAGE 43

DESCRIBING A HOTEL

Listen :

(Hôtel 4 étoiles — 60 chambres — plage 2 km)
— C'est un hôtel 4 étoiles de 60 chambres, qui se trouve à 2 km de la plage.

NOW, DESCRIBE THE FOLLOWING HOTELS

(Hôtel 4 étoiles) — (60 chambres) — (plage 2 km) — (Hôtel 3 étoiles) — (40 chambres) — (aéroport 15 mn) — (Hôtel 4 étoiles) — (25 chambres) — (plage en face) — (Hôtel 2 étoiles) — (32 chambres) — (centre ville 5 mn)

3. GRAMMAR : SEE PAGE 46

ASKING PEOPLE TO REPEAT INFORMATION

Listen :

(Mon fils a 15 ans)
— Votre fils a quel âge ?
(La chambre fait 350 F)
— La chambre fait combien ?

NOW, ASK PEOPLE TO REPEAT WHAT THEY HAVE SAID, USING THE APPROPRIATE QUESTION WORD

(Mon fils a 15 ans) — (La chambre fait 350 F) — (Je pars le 17 décembre) — (Ils sont cinq) — (Les chambres sont très confortables) — (Elle va à Singapour) — (Je viens de Rome) — (Il est six heures et demie) — (Nous cherchons M. Lefranc)

4. GRAMMAR : SEE PAGE 42

PRONOUN PRACTICE : DEMONSTRATIVE PRONOUNS

Listen :

(La maison de Pointe-à-Pitre fait 5 500 F la semaine)
— Et celle de Fort-de-France ?

NOW, ASK QUESTIONS ABOUT THE FACILITIES IN FORT-DE-FRANCE USING « CELUI », « CELLE », « CEUX » OU « CELLES »

(La maison de Pointe-à-Pitre fait 5 500 F la semaine) — (L'hôtel de Pointe-à-Pitre a une piscine privée) — (Les plages de Pointe-à-Pitre sont très belles) — (Les restaurants de Pointe-à-Pitre sont excellents) — (La cuisine de Pointe-à-Pitre est très bonne) — (L'aéroport de Pointe-à-Pitre est loin du centre)

5. GRAMMAR : SEE PAGE 45

PRONOUN PRACTICE : « BON » AND « BIEN »

Listen :

(Vous jouez au tennis)
— Vous jouez bien au tennis.
(C'est un hôtel)
— C'est un bon hôtel.

NOW, ADD « BON » OR « BIEN » TO THE FOLLOWING SENTENCES

(Vous jouez au tennis) — (C'est un hôtel) — (Il ne travaille pas) — (Vous trouverez beaucoup de restaurants) — (J'ai vu un film) — (Il n'y a pas de discothèque) — (Il comprend le français)

6. GRAMMAR : SEE PAGE 43

PRONOUN PRACTICE : THE RELATIVE PRONOUN « OÙ »

Listen :

(Je suis dans cet hôtel)
— Voilà l'hôtel où je suis.

NOW, USE « VOILÀ... OÙ» TO POINT OUT THE PLACES MENTIONED

(Je suis dans cet hôtel) — (Les enfants font de la voile dans ce club) — (Il déjeune dans ce restaurant) — (Nous passons nos vacances dans ce pays) — (Vous achetez vos billets dans cette agence) — (Je passe mes nuits dans cette discothèque)

HOLIDAYS

f you want to do business in France n August, forget it. This is the sacred month, when Paris and other big ities put up their shutters and take art in the annual migration — La rance est en vacances. The obvious dvantage for the foreign traveller is hat, unless you love the "sardine yndrome", all you have to do is go n holiday in June or September: ou'll have lower prices, better serice, and a healthy space between ou and your white/red/brown neighbour on the beach. And do go on oliday in France: it probably offers he most varied countryside, climate nd cuisine in Europe. Boiling beaches, risp mountain air, rolling valleys, châeaux and simple rural inns — you'll find them all in France. Here is a mini-guide to just a few of the regional delights.

PROVENCE: *Green and golden country dotted with black cypresses and silver olive trees. Stay in one of the tiny medieval "perched villages", full of fountains and flowers. Head for the fashionable French Riviera (Côte-d'Azur) for the sea air, but be prepared for concrete hotel complexes, crowds and high prices. If you are in a group of four or more, the most economical accommodation is a rented villa, either on the coast or a few miles inland.*

THE ATLANTIC COAST FROM NANTES TO BIARRITZ: *France's most beautiful sandy beaches are along this long stretch of coast. The weather here is warmer and sunnier than in Brittany and the beaches are larger, less crowded, and sandier than on the Côte d'Azur (in fact, much of the sand on the rocky Mediterranean beaches was carried, by truck, from the southwestern Atlantic coast).*

THE ALPS: *The obvious Mecca for ski-worshippers, but also an excellent summer spot for hikers who want to discover a region at their own pace. Lots of delightful villages, with inns and hotels at reasonable prices.*

CORSICA: *It's been called the "rough diamond" of the Mediterranean. It lives up to its name, with wild mountains, waterfalls, and dozens of deserted beaches for those who like to get away from it all. A car is essential to hunt out the real beauty spots — but only for non-dizzy drivers: the roads often give aerial views of the island for those brave enough to look down, and down, and down ...*

BRITTANY: *Small fishing villages, long sandy beaches, rocky coves, and lots of crêpes (fine pancakes) and cider. Good weather is definitely not guaranteed, but, if you like wind and waves, you'll love this wild, unspoilt Celtic corner of France.*

CENTRAL FRANCE: *Various regions — the Dordogne, Auvergne, Burgundy and many more — offer the best view of an old, rural way of life that has long disappeared in other Northern European countries. A good way is to drive from village to village, staying in inns (auberges) or small, family-run hotels; or you can stay put and rent a self-catering gîte, a very inexpensive cottage or farmhouse situated in a natural beauty spot. You'll get to know the villagers, and sample the local cuisine. There's no better way into the heart of France.*

3.4 TAKE A BREAK

N° 1 — Listen

Listen to the people on the cassette describing the sort of holidays they like, then match the people with the brochures of the holidays each one will go on.

N° 2

Look at the messages on the postcards below and fill in the missing words from the following list:

gens, nous, mer, piscine, jouer, fait, étoiles, courts, ne, venir, hôtel, faire, plage, suis.

(See solutions on page 25-26)

3.5 CONTACTS

Listen

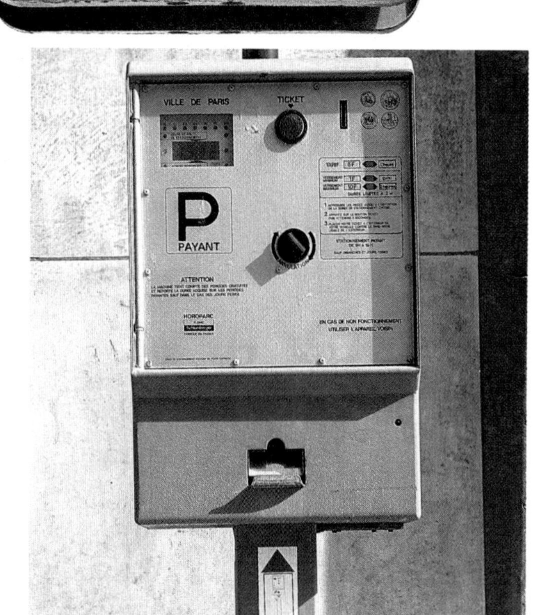

ÉCRITS DE LA RUE

Modes d'emploi

Parcmètre

Insérez la monnaie jusqu'à l'obtention du temps de stationnement désiré.
Appuyez sur le bouton « ticket ». Prenez votre ticket et affichez-le (lisible de l'extérieur) derrière le pare-brise de votre voiture.
En cas de panne, prenez votre ticket à l'autre horodateur ou adressez-vous au 46.30.54.27.
Tarif : 1 heure - 5 francs
2 heures - 10 francs
Temps de stationnement maximum autorisé : 2 heures.
Cet appareil n'accepte que les pièces de 1 F, 2 F, 5 F, 10 F.

Photo d'identité

Pour faire une photo d'identité :

- *Dégagez le rideau du fond.*
- *Réglez le siège pour que votre visage se reflète dans la glace, voyant vert allumé, introduisez votre monnaie 10 F, 5 F.*
- *Appuyez.*

Cabine téléphonique

Cette cabine peut être appelée à ce numéro : 48.80.30.21
tarif : *1re impulsion, 1 F*
tarif réduit : *voir le tableau*
pour les numéros : *consulter l'annuaire*
renseignements : *12*
service d'urgence : *18*
pompiers : *18*
police : *17*
SAMU : *45.67.50.50.*

En cas de dérangement, signalez-le en appelant le 13 à partir d'un autre poste ; la communication est gratuite.

Cet appareil fonctionne uniquement avec une télécarte.
Vous devez d'abord introduire la carte et, seulement ensuite, composer le numéro de votre correspondant.
La télécarte est en vente dans les agences commerciales des Télécommunications, dans les bureaux de poste ainsi que dans les bureaux de tabac.

Comment téléphoner

- *Pour Paris/région parisienne, il faut faire le numéro à 8 chiffres de votre correspondant*
- *Pour la province, il faut faire le 16, puis le numéro à 8 chiffres de votre correspondant*
- *International avec la télécarte*

Introduire la télécarte, composer le 19, l'indicatif du pays et le numéro de votre correspondant.
Pour avoir le numéro d'un correspondant, appeler l'opérateur : 19 33 + indicatif du pays

Sur l'appareil

DÉCROCHEZ
INTRODUIRE LA CARTE OU
FAIRE LE NUMÉRO D'URGENCE
FERMEZ LE VOLET, S'IL VOUS PLAÎT
CRÉDIT 30,80 F
NUMÉROTEZ
PATIENTEZ S'IL VOUS PLAÎT
NUMÉRO APPELÉ...
CRÉDIT 21 F
RACCROCHEZ
RETIREZ VOTRE CARTE

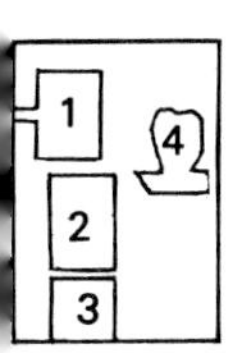

1.-2. Parcmètres
3. Photomaton
4. Agents de police « contractuelles »

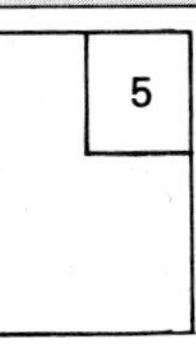

5. Cabine téléphonique

3.5 WORDS

mode d'emploi (M) — instructions
parcmètre (M) — parking-meter
monnaie (F) — change **(1)**
stationnement (M) — parking
extérieur (M) — outside, exterior
pare-brise (M) — windscreen
appareil (M) — instrument, machine
pièce (F) — coin **(1)**
cabine (F) — phone-box, booth
télécarte (F) — telephone card
carte (F) — card
télécommunication (F) — telecom
bureau de tabac (M) — tobacconist's
bureau de poste (M) — post office
étranger (M) — abroad
indicatif (M) — dialling code
photo d'identité (F) — passport photo
voyant (M) — light, indication
argent (M) — money **(1)**
urgence (F) — emergengy
volet (M) — shutter, lid
annuaire (M) — telephone book
pompiers (M) — firemen
police (F) — police
communication (F) — telephone call

lisible — legible
allumé(e) — lit up, switched on
autorisé(e) — authorized
éteint(e) — switched off
gratuit(e) — free
payant(e) — paying
réduit(e) — reduced

insérer — to insert, to put in
appuyer (sur)— to press, to push
afficher — to display
s'adresser — to go to someone (for informatio
fonctionner — to work (machines)
introduire — to insert
retirer — to withdraw
pousser — to push
régler — to adjust
tirer — to pull
toucher — to touch
oublier — to forget
faire (un numéro de téléphone) — to dia
composer (un numéro de téléphone) — t
dial
garder — to keep
utiliser — to use
se souvenir (de) — to remember
se rappeler — to remember
numéroter — to dial
consulter — to look up
signaler — to tell (the operator)
patienter — to hold the line, to hang on

en panne — out of order
faire l'appoint — to give the exact change
être autorisé — to have permission
être permis — to be allowed
être défendu — to be forbidden
en vente — on sale
(ne pas) marcher — (not) to work
rendre la monnaie — to give change
en dérangement — out of order

HOW TO SAY IT

1. GIVING INSTRUCTIONS

Insérer la monnaie — Insert the coin
Vous devez d'abord introduire la carte — You have to insert the card first
Il faut faire le 16 — You have to dial 16
Réglez le siège — Adjust the seat
Pour avoir le numéro d'un correspondant, appeler l'opérateur — To get a telephone number, call the operator
Si vous voulez l'international, faites le 19 — Dial 19 if you want to make an international call
Pour avoir la province, vous n'avez qu'à faire le 16 — If you want to call the provinces, just dial 16

2. WHAT IF... ?

En cas de panne, prendre votre ticket à l'autre horodateur — In case of malfunction, obtain your ticket from another distributor
Si l'appareil ne fonctionne pas, appeler le 12 — If the phone is not working, dial 12

3. SAYING THAT SOMETHING IS NOT WORKING

Cet appareil est en panne — This machine is out of order
L'horodateur ne fonctionne pas — The distributor is not working
Le téléphone ne marche pas — The phone is not working

4. GIVING A SERIES OF INSTRUCTIONS

D'abord... / *Tout d'abord* / *Premièrement...* — First of all,...
... et puis — ... and then
... puis / *... ensuite* — ... then
... après — after(wards)
... deuxièmement — secondly
Enfin... — Finally,...
Pour finir... — And in conclusion...

REMEMBER... REMEMBER... REMEMBER... REMEMBER... REMEMBER

(1) *« Monnaie » means change (and not money) ; « une pièce de monnaie » is a coin (« pièce » is also a room), « argent » is money (also silver).*

3.5 ORAL PRACTICE

1. GRAMMAR : SEE PAGE 47

GIVING INSTRUCTIONS : « IL FAUT.. »

Listen :

(Introduisez votre carte !)
— Il faut introduire votre carte.

NOW, REPEAT THE FOLLOWING INSTRUCTIONS USING « IL FAUT » AND THE INFINITIVE

(Introduisez votre carte !) — (Faites le numéro de votre correspondant !) — (Mettez deux pièces de 1 franc) — (Faites l'appoint !) — (Prenez votre ticket à l'autre distributeur !) — (Adressez-vous aux renseignements) — (Consultez l'annuaire !)

2. GRAMMAR : SEE PAGE 47

GIVING INSTRUCTIONS : THE IMPERATIVE FORM

Listen :

(J'appelle l'opérateur ?)
— Oui, appelez-le.

NOW, ANSWER IN THE AFFIRMATIVE USING THE IMPERATIVE FORM

(J'appelle l'opérateur ?) — (J'introduis les pièces ?) — (Je retire la carte ?) — (Je garde les tickets ?) — (Je prends la photo ?) — (Je fais le 16 ?) — (Je laisse la monnaie ?)

3. GRAMMAR : SEE PAGE 45

ONLY : « NE... QUE »

Listen :

(Ce téléphone fonctionne seulement avec une télécarte)
— Ce téléphone ne fonctionne qu'avec une télécarte.

NOW, TRANSFORM THE FOLLOWING SENTENCES USING « NE... QUE »

(Ce téléphone fonctionne seulement avec une télécarte) — (Cet appareil accepte seulement les pièces de 1 F) — (Cette voiture roule seulement avec du super) — (Le stationnement est autorisé seulement le dimanche) — (Le numéro fait seulement huit chiffres)

4. GRAMMAR : SEE PAGE 47

GIVING NEGATIVE INSTRUCTIONS

Listen :

(Je règle le siège ?)
— Non, ne le réglez pas maintenant.
(J'introduis ma carte ?)
— Non, ne l'introduisez pas maintenant.

NOW, ANSWER IN THE NEGATIVE USING THE IMPERATIVE FORM :

(Je règle le siège ?) — (J'introduis ma carte ?) — (Je mets la pièce ?) — (Je fais les huit chiffres ?) — (Je tire le rideau ?) — (Je compose le numéro ?) — (Je prends les billets ?)

5. GRAMMAR : SEE PAGE 47

VERB PRACTICE : REFLEXIVE VERBS IN THE IMPERATIVE

Listen :

(Ne vous adressez pas à ce bureau)
— Mais si, adressez-vous à ce bureau !

NOW, GIVE COUNTER-INSTRUCTIONS

(Ne vous adressez pas à ce bureau) — (Ne vous asseyez pas sur ce siège) — (Ne vous présentez pas à la réception) — (Ne vous levez pas tôt) — (Ne vous baignez pas ici)

6. GRAMMAR : SEE PAGE 42

PRONOUN PRACTICE : DIRECT OBJECT PRONOUNS

Listen :

(J'introduis la monnaie ?)
— Oui, vous devez l'introduire.

NOW, ASK QUESTIONS USING THE VERB « DEVOIR » AND REPLACING THE NOUNS WITH THE APPROPRIATE PRONOUNS

(J'introduis la monnaie ?) — (Il affiche son ticket ?) — (Elle compose le 19 ?) — (Je mets les pièces ?) — (Elle retire la télécarte ?) — (Je fais les huit chiffres ?)

HOW TO USE IT

*You're in France, you've tasted the food, drunk the wine, seen some of the sights, and, as a carefree foreigner, you've invested in a gadget — some technical trinket, a Gallic toy. You open the box, look at the instructions and . . . horror. You can't understand a word. What do you do ? My advice is : nothing. Unless you want to set fire to the hotel room or blow up your friend's apartment, the best course is to panic and go straight back to the shop and ask them to show you how the thing works. Instruction manuals (*modes d'emploi*) are full of horrible technical terms and unless you are very machine-minded, you'd be better off waiting for an expert. For those stubborn pioneering individuals who believe in the ultimate challenge, here are a few hints :*

If you get anything from a common cold to an upset stomach, you're going to be given a box with a harmless piece of paper telling you what to take, when and where . . . in French. If the medicine comes in a long and cylindrical form do not swallow *it. The French have a mania for suppositories — medically, they're supposed to be much better for you — but many a foreigner must have got rid of his 'flu in a simple and effective way — by choking himself to death. So do beware. If in doubt, talk to a pharmacist : they're very well informed about all possible bugs and drugs, and can often give you as much advice as a doctor.*

FAMOUS LAST WORDS

Although most of the instructions will be totally incomprehensible, there are a few universal key words (remember them well, as you prepare to plug in the hair dryer — they might be the last words you ever learn !). Allumer *= to switch on ;* éteindre *= to switch off ;* appuyer *= to push ;* bouton, touche *= button or switch ;* brancher *= to plug in ;* vérifier *= to check ;* régler *= to adjust, fix ;* utiliser *= to use. Those words, combined with such welcome international commands as "STOP" and "GO" might help avoid imminent disaster, but don't blame me if you end up throwing the new toy out of the window in frustration.* □

Listen ***Les amoureux des bancs publics***

Georges Brassens

Les gens qui voient de travers pensent que les bancs verts qu'on voit sur les trottoirs
Sont faits pour les impotents ou les ventripotents
Mais c'est une absurdité car à la vérité ils sont là c'est notoire
Pour accueillir quelque temps les amours débutants
Les amoureux qui se bécotent sur les bancs publics (ter)
En se foutant pas mal du regard oblique des passants honnêtes
Les amoureux qui se bécotent sur les bancs publics (ter)
En se disant des je t'aime pathétiques ont des petites gueules bien sympathiques
Ils se tiennent par la main parlent du lendemain du papier bleu d'azur
Que revêtiront les murs de leur chambre à coucher
Ils se voient déjà doucement, elle cousant lui fumant dans un bien-être sûr
Et choisissent les prénoms de leur premier bébé
Les amoureux...
Quand la sainte famille machin croise sur son chemin deux de ces malappris
Elle leur décoche hardiment des propos venimeux
N'empêche que toute la famille, le père, la mère, la fille, le fils, le Saint-Esprit
Voudraient bien de temps en temps pouvoir se conduire comme eux
Les amoureux...

Park Bench Lovers

Some people are under the false impression that the green benches in parks and in the street
Were put there for invalids or for the old and grey
But that's ridiculous because as everyone knows
Their purpose is to welcome incipient loves
Lovers who kiss and embrace on park benches
Ignoring the sideways glances of honest passersby
Lovers who kiss and embrace on park benches
While whispering sweet nothings have nice kind faces
They hold hands, talk of the morrow when their bedrooms will be papered in azure blue
They see themselves as they will be then: she, sewing calmly, he, smoking, ensconced in their future happiness
They see themselves choosing a name for their first baby
Lovers . . .
When a respectable family crosses the path of these badly behaved park bench lovers
It spits out a few unkind words
But the fact remains that the whole family, father, mother, son, daughter and the Holy Ghost
Would give their eye-teeth to be able, once in a while, to be like them
Lovers . . .

(Cont. on page 28)

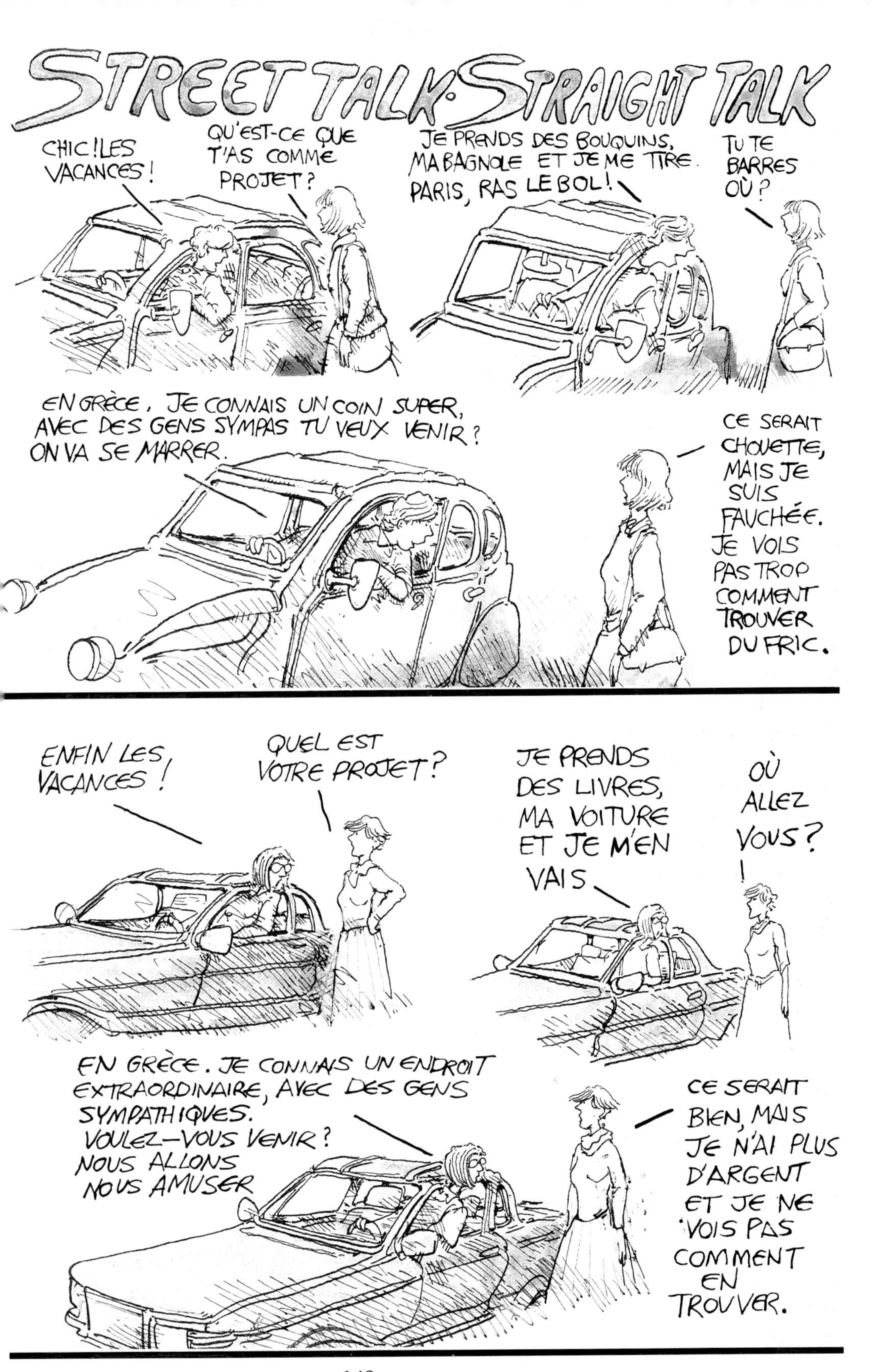
STREET TALK · STRAIGHT TALK
CHIC! LES VACANCES!
QU'EST-CE QUE T'AS COMME PROJET?
JE PRENDS DES BOUQUINS, MA BAGNOLE ET JE ME TIRE. PARIS, RAS LE BOL!
TU TE BARRES OÙ?
EN GRÈCE. JE CONNAIS UN COIN SUPER, AVEC DES GENS SYMPAS TU VEUX VENIR? ON VA SE MARRER.
CE SERAIT CHOUETTE, MAIS JE SUIS FAUCHÉE. JE VOIS PAS TROP COMMENT TROUVER DU FRIC.
ENFIN LES VACANCES!
QUEL EST VOTRE PROJET?
JE PRENDS DES LIVRES, MA VOITURE ET JE M'EN VAIS
OÙ ALLEZ VOUS?
EN GRÈCE. JE CONNAIS UN ENDROIT EXTRAORDINAIRE, AVEC DES GENS SYMPATHIQUES. VOULEZ-VOUS VENIR? NOUS ALLONS NOUS AMUSER
CE SERAIT BIEN, MAIS JE N'AI PLUS D'ARGENT ET JE NE VOIS PAS COMMENT EN TROUVER.

3 WRITTEN PRACTICE

3.1

COMPLETE. Put the verbs in brackets in the future: *Dimanche je (aller) .... à la campagne. — Demain nous (être) .... à Londres — Est-ce que vous (avoir) .... le temps? Ils (venir) .... plus tard — Ils ne (savoir) .... pas répondre — Je ne (pouvoir) .... pas parler.*

TRANSLATE: *Demain il y aura du soleil, mais il ne fera pas chaud — L'hiver il fait jour tard et il fait nuit tôt — Aujourd'hui il fait froid, il pleut et il y a du vent : quel sale temps !*
My boss looks like Paul Newman, but he doesn't look at me — Nathalie has got brown hair.

3.2

COMPLETE with le, la, l', les: *Vous avez votre assurance? Non je ne .... ai pas — Cette voiture, je ne peux pas .... conduire — Il cherche ses papiers mais il ne .... trouve pas — Et ce bouton? Vous .... tournez de gauche à droite.*

TRANSLATE: *Je vous donne les clés, laissez-les au pompiste — A quoi sert le petit bouton noir qui est à droite du volant? Comment marchent les essuie-glaces? Est-ce que cette voiture vous convient?*
This key is for the ignition — I'd like high grade petrol — Would you please give me your passport? How does the demister work? What's this little red button for?

3.3

COMPLETE with the appropriate interrogative word: *.................. vous appelez-vous? — .... âge avez-vous? .... vous faites? Je suis ingénieur — .... coûte votre magnétoscope? .... parlez-vous? À ma collègue — .... va-t-il? À un congrès — .... partez-vous? Demain — .... habites-tu en banlieue? Parce que j'aime le calme.*

TRANSLATE: *Je vous téléphone pour réserver des chambres — Est-ce que vous auriez un salon disponible pour le 3 décembre? — Vous me réservez le magnétoscope? C'est entendu.*
How much is the set lunch? It is 200 F — The room is 20 m² — How long is it? How much does it cost to rent the car for three days? Could you book me a table for 30 people? Without any problem.

3.4

COMPLETE with au, la, à, du, de la, de l', des: *L'hôtel n'est pas loin .... plages — Fort-de-France est .... sud .... île — Les restaurants sont .... milieu .... parc — Les chambres donnent sur .... mer — Le village est .... 4 km .... plage.*

TRANSLATE: *Qu'est-ce que vous avez comme brochure sur les États-Unis? — Je compte partir au mois de juin — Pendant les vacances j'ai envie d'aller en Inde — J'irai en avion jusqu'à Delhi.*
This hotel is a 10-minute walk from the beach — I intend to go skiing during the Chrismas holidays — I'd rather go to the seaside this summer — He wants to go riding — She will be on holiday on July 31st.

3.5

COMPLETE with derrière, à, dans, pour, avec, sur: *Insérer la monnaie .... l'appareil et appuyez .... le bouton — .... Paris vous devez faire un numéro .... huit chiffres — On peut téléphoner .... une télécarte — Mettez votre ticket .... le pare-brise.*

TRANSLATE: *Pour changer de l'argent, allez à la BNP qui se trouve avenue de l'Opéra — Cette machine ne rend pas la monnaie — Introduisez votre carte dans l'appareil mais n'oubliez pas de la retirer.*
If the telephone is out of order, call 45.51.05.78 — To buy your ticket, go to the airport — Insert 1 or 2 F coins only — To call Paris, dial 16-4 — To call abroad you have to dial 19.

(Check your answers on page 39 of your booklet)

IMPROVE

CARS

voiture (F) — car
'oit (M) — roof
volant (M) — steering wheel
siège (M) — seat
portière (F) — car door
tableau de bord (M) — dashboard
klaxon (M) — horn
clignotant (M) — indicator
rétroviseur (M) — rearview mirror
banquette (F) — back seat
evier de vitesse (M) — gear lever
'rein à main (M) — hand brake
essuie-glaces (MPL) — windscreen wiper
chauffage (M) — heater
pare-brise (M) — windscreen
vitre (F) — car window
vitre-arrière (F) — near window
voyant (M) — (dashboard) light
capot (M) — bonnet, hood
coffre (M) — boot, trunk
aile (F) — wing
roue (F) — wheel
pneu (M) — tyre
chambre à air (F) — inner tube
roue de secours (F) — spare wheel
cric (M) — jack
pot d'échappement (M) — exhaust pipe
plaque d'immatriculation (F) — number plate
pédale (F) — pedal
pare-chocs (M) — shock absorbers
phare (M) — headlight
anti-brouillard (M) — fog light
moteur (M) — engine
batterie (F) — battery
radiateur (M) — radiator
réservoir d'essence (M) — petrol tank
bougie (F) — spark plug
ceinture de sécurité (F) — safety belt
boîte de vitesse (F) — gear box
ventilateur (M) — ventilator
fusible (M) — fuse
carburateur (M) — carburettor
embrayage (M) — clutch
direction (F) — steering
allumage (M) — ignition

SPORT AND HOLIDAY ACTIVITIES

gymnase (M) — gymnasium
stade (M) — stadium
court de tennis (M) — tennis court
terrain de sport (M) — sports ground
football (M) — football, soccer
rugby (M) — rugby
natation (F) — swimming
équitation (le cheval) (F) — horse-riding
ski nautique (M) — water-skiing
voile (F) — sailing
planche à voile (F) — wind-surfing
golf (M) — golf
vélo (M) — cycling
escrime (M) — fencing
judo (M) — judo
gymnastique (F) — gymastics
danse (F) — dancing
yoga (M) — yoga
escalade (F) — rock climbing
cartes (F) — cards
échecs (M) — chess
dames (F) — draughts, checkers
bridge (M) — bridge
randonnée (F) — hiking
pêche (F) — fishing
lecture (F) — reading
dessin (M) — drawing
peinture (F) — painting
poterie (F) — pottery
musique (F) — music
jouer d'un instrument — to play an instrument
violon (M) — violin
piano (M) — piano
guitare (F) — guitar
saxophone (M) — saxophone
flûte (F) — flute
batterie (F) — drums

3. TEST YOURSELF

1. FILL IN THE BLANKS WITH « LE, LA, LES, L', VOUS, NOUS, TE, ME, T', M' »

Où est la clé de la voiture ? Je ne .... trouve pas.
Est-ce que je peux .... payer avec la carte bleue, s'il vous plaît ?
Ces candidats sont intéressants : je dois .... rencontrer demain.
Je crois que c'est ici : vous pouvez .... laisser au coin de la rue, s'il vous plaît
Je n'achète pas cette maison : je ne .... aime pas.
Je .... suis ? Oui, tu me suis.
Si vous avez un passeport, prenez ....
Je ne comprends pas comment marche le clignotant — est-ce que vous pouvez .... aider, s'il vous plaît ?
Mademoiselle, nous attendons depuis une demi-heure, est-ce que le directeur v. .... recevoir bientôt ?
Chéri, je .... appelle dès que j'arrive.

2. WRITE THE CORRECT FORM :

CORRECT FORM

La semaine prochaine le temps sera/seront *doux* ....
On laissera/laisseront *la voiture à Lyon* ....
Il y aura/auront *des nuages au sud* ....
Pour aller à Athènes nous prendrez/prendrons *l'avion* ....
Tu finiras/finira *ce travail jeudi prochain* ....
Les enfants ferons/feront *du ski* ....
Dans un mois vous viendrez/viendrai *me voir* ....
Je pourrai/pourrez *prendre les billets mardi* ....
Ils auront/sauront *froid* ....

3. MAKE PAIRS OF OPPOSITES

1. *long*	A. *gris*
2. *rapide*	B. *reculer*
3. *ancien*	C. *derrière*
4. *bas*	D. *retirer*
5. *ensoleillé*	E. *moderne*
6. *être en panne*	F. *court*
7. *introduire*	G. *s'arrêter*
8. *devant*	H. *lent*
9. *démarrer*	I. *haut*
10. *avancer*	J. *marcher*

4. CROSS OUT THE INCORRECT REPLIES

l est grand ? beaucoup/très/pas beaucoup.
/ous faites du sport ? très/pas beaucoup/beaucoup.
l pleut chez vous ? beaucoup/un peu/très.
/ous aimez le café ? pas beaucoup/très/beaucoup.
ia voiture marche bien ? très/un peu/pas beaucoup.
Cet hôtel est confortable ? beaucoup/pas beaucoup/très/pas très.
On mange bien ici ? beaucoup/pas beaucoup/très.
l y a du soleil à Strasbourg ? beaucoup/très peu/très/pas très.
Elle a du charme ? très/beaucoup/peu/pas beaucoup.

5. FILL IN THE BLANKS WITH THE APPROPRIATE WORD FROM THE LIST:

hares — régler — choisir — réfléchir — permis de conduire — ressembler — faire le plein — indicatif — volant — bruit.

l est comme moi : il me ....
l y a plusieurs couleurs, vous pouvez ....
e n'ai plus d'essence, je dois ....
Pour tourner, j'utilise le ....
Après le 19 on fait l' .... *du pays.*
L'aéroport est à côté, alors il y a du ....
Pour conduire il vous faut le ....
Avant d'acheter ce mobilier, je voudrais ....
Quand je conduis la nuit, je dois allumer les ....
Est-ce que je peux .... *par chèque ?*

6. FILL IN THE BLANKS WITH « CE, CETTE, CET, CES, CELUI, CELLE, CEUX, CELLES »

Ne prenez pas .... voiture, prenez .... de gauche.
.... hôtels sont bien, mais .... de Fort-de-France sont mieux.
J'aime beaucoup .... plages mais je préfère .... de Pointe-à-Pitre.
Quel salon voulez-vous ? Réservez-moi .... qui fait 300 m².
.... appareil est en panne.
Vous voulez .... chambres ? Non, je voudrais .... du premier étage.
Ce sont vos billets ? Non, ce sont .... des enfants.
Montrez-moi .... modèle et .... qui est à côté.
Je connais les enfants de Véronique mais pas .... de Cécile.
Vous devez prendre .... avion.

(Check your answers on page 39 of your booklet)

Mr. MARTIN AND MONSIEUR DANIEL

artin, comment vas-tu ? Ça fait plusieur jours que j'essaie de te joindre, mais tu n'es jamais là. Qu'est-ce que tu fais ? On peut se voir ? » the mysterious female caller aske in a breathless, throaty voice.

« *Je rentre à l'instant de Londres* » I replied. « *Ah, très bien. On peut déjeune ensemble si tu veux. On se retrouve à 1 heures à notre petit restaurant habituel ?*

« *Lequel ?* » I asked in a noncommitta voice.

« *Qu'est-ce qui se passe ? Tu as perdu la mémoire à Londres ? Au Petit Parc rue Vavin, à Montparnasse. Bon, il faut que je file. A tout à l'heure. Au revoir.* »

I didn't even know her name, but if she thought I was Martin Daniel, I could be sure she woul recognize me. And if my host couldn't be bothered to be at home when I arrived, I wasn't going to fee guilty about going out with his girlfriend — for I assumed that's who the mysterious caller was. Throug her I would be able to find out more about « *Monsieur Daniel* », who already seemed to know every-thing there was to know about me.

I unpacked some clothes and put them away in the closet. It was filled rather untidily with sweat ers, shirts, and some suits and jeans hanging on wire hangers. But what immediately caught my eye wa a black raincoat — the same one I'd seen in the ornate Belle Epoque mirror in London. I hung up m dirty old tan raincoat and put on the black one. Then I went out.

The early morning mist had cleared and a pale January sun was shining over Paris. I stopped a a newspaper kiosk and bought a map of the city.

« *Un plan de Paris, s'il vous plaît, Madame* », I said to the frozen-looking woman behin a pile of newspapers and magazines. She was wearing a thick woollen scarf around her neck and fingerles gloves.

« *Il fait froid aujourd'hui* », I said, glancing at her reddened fingers.

« *Ah, oui, Monsieur, et puis ici il y a plein de courants d'air. Voilà, Monsieur ça vous fait vingt-neuf francs.* »

« *Merci, Madame, et au revoir.* »

« *Au revoir, Monsieur, et bonne journée.* »

It was already 12 o'clock so I looked up Rue Vavin on the map and started walking there. I arrived at the Petit Parc at ten to one. I was expecting to be recognized at the restaurant but I wasn't quite prepared for the warm welcome I got. Martin Daniel was certainly a popular fellow.

« Bonjour Monsieur Daniel. Ça fait un moment qu'on ne vous a pas vu. Vous allez bien ? »

« Très bien, merci. Je voudrais une table pour deux personnes, s'il vous plaît. J'attends Mademoiselle... » I left the name hanging, hoping that he would fill it in.

« Ah, oui, Mademoiselle Spinelli va être contente. Elle qui adore les huîtres ! Nous avons d'excellentes huîtres de Bretagne aujourd'hui. Asseyez-vous, Monsieur, je vous apporte l'apéritif. Un kir royal, comme d'habitude ? »

« Oui, merci. »

As I sat there sipping the delicious "kir royal" (which I discovered to be champagne with a sweet berry liqueur), I thought that it wasn't so unpleasant being Martin Daniel. Here I was, in a strange city, being warmly greeted everywhere as a generous patron, and meeting a woman for lunch who sounded quite impatient to see *me*.

A few moments later, Mademoiselle Spinelli walked into the restaurant. I knew she was Mademoiselle Spinelli the moment she said *« bonjour »* to the waiter. I recognized the deep throaty voice.

« Salut, Martin », she said.

« Salut, ma belle », I replied without — and I'm sure of this — a trace of an accent.

« Alors, tu n'embrasses plus ta petite Sonia ? »

"Sonia, what a lovely name," I thought, and kissed her. The scent she wore seemed very familiar, but I couldn't quite place it. It reminded me vaguely of lime and cinnamon. The waiter brought her a "kir royal" and handed us the menu. Then he said, *« Comme plats du jour nous avons des blancs de poulet à la sauce de cresson, du bœuf gros sel, et la lotte au poivre vert. Et pour commencer je vous recommande des huîtres. »*

« Je prendrai une demi-douzaine d'huîtres et la lotte », said Sonia.

« Et la même chose pour moi », I said.

« Et comme boisson ? » asked the waiter.

« Un Sancerre blanc », I said, surprising myself at my knowledge of wines.

When lunch was over, the waiter brought the bill. I was going to reach into the pocket of my tweed jacket to pull out the French Francs I'd bought the day before at my London bank, when my eye caught the corner of what looked like a cheque book protruding from the black raincoat on the chair next to me. I pulled it out and examined it : it read *« Martin Daniel, 16 rue Las Cases, 75007 Paris »*. And then I did something I didn't think I would ever do : I wrote out and signed a cheque. I'm normally a scrupulously honest person, and this was forgery — forgery liable to land me in some French prison — but somehow I couldn't stop myself. Then, before I tore out the cheque, I noticed something strange. The signature was in the same spidery hand that I was accustomed to seeing on Martin Daniel's letters. I grabbed the bill and started writing meaningless sentences on the back. They all came out in the same spidery hand. I couldn't seem to write anything in my own round English hand. Sonia was looking at me with raised eyebrows.

« Qu'est-ce que tu fais ? » she asked.

« Oh, rien », I said. *« On me dit toujours que mon écriture n'est pas très lisible. Alors, j'essaie de voir. J'écris sans réfléchir. »*

« Ah, c'est de l'écriture automatique ! Il paraît qu'on dévoile des choses importantes et très profondes quand on écrit sans réfléchir. Montre-moi. Tiens, c'est drôle. C'est écrit "mon nom est Martin Daniel". C'est tout à fait évident, et pas très profond », she said with a laugh.

TO BE CONTINUED...

UNIT 4

HOW TO ASK FOR INFORMATION AND EXPRESS OPINIONS

4.1 CONTACTS

Listen

UN DÉJEUNER D'AFFAIRES

Monsieur Lefort,
P.-D.G. d'une société d'électronique lyonnaise
a invité un client américain à déjeuner

Le maître d'hôtel : *Bonjour, Messieurs, vous avez réservé ?*

M. Lefort : *Oui, une table pour deux au nom de la société Ecel.*

Le maître d'hôtel : *Vous avez choisi, Messieurs ?*

M. Lefort : *Non, pas encore. Qu'est-ce qu'il y a dans votre salade terre et mer ?*

Le maître d'hôtel : *Du canard, des épinards, des truffes ; voilà pour la terre ! Et pour la mer, une coquille Saint-Jacques, un filet de sole, une langoustine ; le tout arrosé de vinaigre de framboise.*

M. Sullivan : *Ça a l'air délicieux. Je crois que je vais essayer.*

M. Lefort : *Parfait, alors... une salade terre et mer en entrée... Non, deux, je vais prendre la même chose.*

Le maître d'hôtel : *Et ensuite ?*

M. Lefort : *Qu'est-ce qu'on pourrait prendre ?*

Le maître d'hôtel : *Aujourd'hui, nous avons du bar à l'oseille.*

M. Sullivan : *Du bar à l'oseille ? Comment est-ce que ça se dit en anglais ?*

M. Lefort : *Je ne sais pas du tout ; le bar, c'est un poisson qu'on appelle aussi loup de mer ; c'est délicieux ! Et l'oseille, ça ressemble aux épinards mais c'est plus acide.*

M. Sullivan : *Bon, alors je vais goûter.*

M. Lefort : *Moi, je voudrais un filet de bœuf.*

Le maître d'hôtel : *Vous le voulez comment ?*

M. Lefort : *Saignant, s'il vous plaît.*

Le maître d'hôtel : *Vous prendrez un dessert ?*

M. Lefort : *Nous verrons après.*

Le maître d'hôtel : *Que désirez-vous boire ?*

M. Lefort : *Vous pouvez nous conseiller ?*

Le maître d'hôtel : *Oui, en vin blanc nous avons deux excellents vins, un Sancerre et un Châblis. Comme vin rouge, je vous recommande le Pommard, c'est notre meilleur Bourgogne.*

M. Lefort : *Alors, vous nous donnerez une bouteille de Sancerre et une demie de Pommard.*

Le maître d'hôtel : *Vous voulez un apéritif ?*

M. Sullivan : *Non merci, ce n'est pas la peine.*

Listen and repeat
(You may look at the translation on page 29 in the booklet.)

1. Carte de vins 2. Vue de Lyon
3. Restaurant lyonnais 4. Cave 5. Dégustation de vins

4.1 WORDS

salade (F) — salad
canard (M) — duck
épinards (M) — spinach
truffes (F) — truffle
filet (M) — fillet
vinaigre (M) — vinegar
entrée (F) — starter
poisson (M) — fish
bœuf (M) — beef
dessert (M) — dessert
cru (M) — a named vineyard
apéritif (M) — aperitif, pre-dinner drink
bouteille (F) — bottle
crème (F) — cream
spécialité (F) — speciality

---

huile (F) — oil
poulet (M) — chicken
viande (F) — meat
fromage (M) — cheese
beurre (M) — butter
pain (M) — bread
légume (M) — vegetable
frites (F) — chips
fruit (M) — fruit
gâteau (M) — cake
sel (M) — salt
sucre (M) — sugar
poivre (M) — pepper
moutarde (F) — mustard
addition (F) — bill
plat du jour (M) — speciality of the day
carafe d'eau (F) — jug of water
veau (M) — veal
tarte (M) — pie, tart

ADJECTIVES

délicieux(se) — delicious
acide — acid, sour
régional(e) — regional
mauvais(e) — bad

essayer — to try
appeler — to call
ressembler — to resemble, to look like
goûter — to taste
désirer — to want
conseiller — to advise, to give advice
recommander — to recommend
commander — to order

il y a — there is, there are
avoir l'air — to seem ***(1)***
ce n'est pas la peine — it's not necessary ***(2***
qu'est-ce que c'est ? — what's that ? what i
it ?
viande saignante — rare (of meat)
viande à point — medium rare
viande bien cuite — well done
viande bleue — very rare

REMEMBER... REMEMBER... REMEMBER... REMEMBER... REMEMBER

(1) *Apart from to seem, to appear, « avoir l'air » can be translated as to look or to sound, depending o which of the five senses perceives the information : Regardez ce gâteau ! Oui, il a l'air délicieux (it look delicious). J'ai bu du Chambertin 1961 hier. Ça a l'air délicieux (that sounds delicious).* — ***(2)*** *« C*

HOW TO SAY IT

1. ASKING SOMEONE WHAT HE WOULD LIKE TO EAT OR DRINK (IN A RESTAURANT)

Vous avez choisi ? — Are you ready to order ?
Vous prendrez un dessert ? — Are you having dessert ?
Vous voulez une entrée ? — Would you like a starter ?
Vous désirez ? / *Que désirez-vous ?* — What would you like ?
Que désirez-vous boire ? / *Comme boisson, qu'est-ce que je vous sers ?* — What would you like to drink ?

2. ASKING FOR ADVICE (IN A RESTAURANT)

Qu'est-ce qu'on pourrait prendre ? — What shall we have ?
Vous pouvez nous conseiller ? — Could you advise us ?
Qu'est-ce que vous nous conseillez ? / *Qu'est-ce que vous nous recommandez ?* — What do you recommend ?
Qu'est-ce que vous nous proposez ? — What do you suggest ?

3. ASKING FOR DETAILS ON A MENU

Qu'est-ce qu'il y a dans votre salade ? — What's in your salad ?
Qu'est-ce que c'est, le bar ? — What's a "bar" ?
C'est comment, la salade terre et mer ? — What's the "terre et mer" salad like ?
Comment est-ce que ça se dit en anglais ? — What do you call that in English ?

4. DESCRIBING FOOD

Ça ressemble aux épinards — It is like spinach
Ça a le goût de cassis — It tastes like blackcurrant

5. COMMENTING ON FOOD

C'est délicieux — It's delicious
C'est excellent — It's excellent
C'est très bon — It's very good
C'est mauvais — It's not very good

REMEMBER... REMEMBER... REMEMBER... REMEMBER... REMEMBER

n'est pas la peine » is a variation on « cela ne vaut pas la peine », signifying that something is not worth doing. It is often used to refuse an offer of help politely (you needn't bother).

4.1 ORAL PRACTICE

1. GRAMMAR : SEE PAGE 40

INDEFINITE QUANTITIES : SOME

Listen :

(Qu'est-ce qu'il y a dans votre salade ?) — (canard)
— Il y a du canard.

NOW, YOU DESCRIBE THE CONTENTS OF THE SALAD USING « DU », « DE LA », « DE L' » OR « DES », AS NECESSARY

(canard) — (épinards) — (truffes) — (fromage) — (crème) — (vinaigre) — (huile)

2. GRAMMAR : SEE PAGE 44

ASKING FOR SPECIFIC QUANTITIES

Listen :

(Vous voulez aussi de l'eau ?) — (une carafe)
— Oui, donnez-moi une carafe d'eau.

NOW, YOU ASK FOR THE FOLLOWING THINGS IN THE SPECIFIED QUANTITIES

(Vous voulez aussi de l'eau ? - une carafe) — (Vous voulez aussi du sancerre ? - une bouteille) — (Vous voulez aussi du vin ? - un litre) — (Vous voulez aussi de la bière ? - un verre) — (Vous voulez aussi du sucre ? - un kilo) — (Vous voulez aussi des allumettes ? - une boîte) — (Vous voulez aussi des cigarettes ? - un paquet)

3. GRAMMAR : SEE PAGE 40

ASKING FOR FOOD AND DRINK

Listen :

(pain)
— S'il vous plaît, est-ce que je pourrais avoir du pain ?

NOW, YOU ATTRACT THE WAITER'S ATTENTION AND ASK FOR THE FOLLOWING THINGS USING « UN », « UNE », « DES » OR « DU », « DE LA », « DE L' », AS APPROPRIATE

(pain) — (apéritif) — (moutarde) — (verre de vin) — (eau) — (frites) — (café crème) — (entrée) — (sel)

4. GRAMMAR : SEE PAGE 42

PRONOUN PRACTICE : ALTERNATIVE WAYS OF ASKING FOR THINGS

Listen :

(Je voudrais de la salade, s'il vous plaît
— Pour moi, de la salade, s'il vous plaît

NOW, YOU ASK FOR THE FOLLOWING THINGS USING « POUR » AND THE APPROPRIATE PRONOUN

(Je voudrais de la salade, s.v.p.) — (Catherine voudrait de l'eau, s.v.p.) — (Nous voudrions du pain s.v.p.) — (Patrick voudrait du fromage, s.v.p.) — (Les enfants voudraient un gâteau, s.v.p.) — (Claire et Sophie voudraient du vin rouge, s.v.p.)

5. GRAMMAR : SEE PAGE 40

SAYING WHAT YOU WOULD LIKE TO EAT

Listen :

(le bar - l'oseille)
— Pour moi, du bar à l'oseille.

NOW, YOU SAY WHAT YOU WOULD LIKE TO EAT

(Le bar - l'oseille) — (La tarte - les pommes) — (Le veau - la crème) — (Le canard - les olives) — (Le poulet - le vin blanc) — (Les épinards - le beurre

6. GRAMMAR : SEE PAGE 45

SUPERLATIVES : THE BEST

Listen :

(C'est un bon bordeaux ?)
— Oui Monsieur, c'est le meilleur bordeaux de notre carte.

NOW, YOU RECOMMEND THE ITEMS ON THE MENU USING « LE MEILLEUR », « LA MEILLEURE » OR « LES MEILLEURS »

(C'est un bon bordeaux ?) — (C'est une bonne salade ?) — (C'est un bon dessert ?) — (Ce sont de bons vins ?) — (C'est un bon apéritif ?) — (Ce sont de bonnes entrées ?)

BON APPÉTIT !”

he great French cook, Carême, lways insisted that the greatest nemy of good cooking was economy, nd that was why he liked working nly for Rothschild. The Troisgros rothers, who run an elite restaurant, ay they refuse even to think about noney, that it is incompatible with rt. Others have compared haute cui- ine with haute couture, both of vhich were not made for a world vhich wants to economize.

rench cooking is expensive because relies on only the best of products. allows for no cheating in its ingre- ients, which must be beautifully suc- ulent and ripe. This means accepting he limitations and variations imposed y each season. It is impossible to ffer the same dishes all year round. ach major item must retain its own avour, even when artistically blended vith a myriad of other spices and ngredients. French cooking relies on the freshness and variety of the produce available, which is why Lyons remains the country's gastronomic capital. It has the greatest variety of fresh produce at its doorstep. Paul Bocuse, one of France's greatest chefs, goes personally to the market every day, selecting the ingredients for the day's cooking. In Paris, such attention to detail is more difficult now that the great Parisian market, Les Halles, has been torn down and moved to Rungis on the outskirts ot town.

"NOUVELLE AND VIEILLE CUISINE" *French cooking, for long a bastion of tradition, was shaken a few years ago by the advent of* la nouvelle cuisine, *a style of cooking which is supposedly lighter than* la vieille cuisine, *with all its heavy cream-and-butter sauces. It is inspired by Japanese cooking with its emphasis on texture rather than aroma. "The largest cookery school is now in Japan, run in partnership with Bocuse," writes sociologist and historian Theodore Zeldin in his book,* The French. *"Bocuse was fascinated by the meticulous care of the Japanese in their cooking, their multiplicity of small quantities, their stress on presentation."*

Zeldin finds that "there are fashions in food as there are in clothes, and no style can be certain of continuing to please for ever. There are certainly those, like the Figaro's *food expert, James de Coquet, who claim that the purpose of cooking is to give a sense of security, and that change is the last thing needed; but against him people like Gault and Millau, who popularized the Nouvelle Cuisine, demand surprise and excitement."*

Of course, attitudes to food vary according to social class, and you will find this reflected in French restaurants. The upper classes often favour the small portions and "surprise" of the elegant nouvelle cuisine restaurants. The working class and the middle class believe that meals should be copious and filling. Desserts, they say, should comprise cheese and *a sweet and not cheese* or *a sweet. This heavier, peasant-style fare is usually served in small bistros and simple restaurants boasting checkered tablecloths. As a rule of thumb, you can usually expect the size of the bill to be in inverse proportion to the size of the portion on your plate. If you are served three salad leaves with four slices of kiwi, you can be sure the bill will be astronomical. But a giant* pot au feu *in a little neighbourhood bistro, washed down with a litre of red wine, will cost a modest price. But no matter what fare you go for, you will rarely be disappointed with what's on your plate in France. As Bocuse says, "Food is magic."* □

Listen **Que reste-t-il de nos amours ?**

Charles Trénet (Trénet-Chauliac)

Ce soir, le vent qui frappe à ma porte
Me parle des amours mortes, devant le feu qui s'éteint
Ce soir, c'est une chanson d'automne
Dans la maison qui frissonne et je pense aux jours lointains
Que reste-t-il de nos amours ?
Que reste-t-il de ces beaux jours ?
Une photo, vieille photo de ma jeunesse
Que reste-t-il des billets doux, des mois d'avril, des rendez-vous ?
Un souvenir qui me poursuit sans cesse
Bonheur fané, cheveux au vent
Baisers volés, rêve émouvant
Que reste-t-il de tout cela ? dites-le moi
Un petit village, un vieux clocher
Un paysage, si bien caché
Et dans un nuage, le cher visage de mon passé
Les mots, les mots tendres qu'on murmure
Les caresses les plus pures, les serments au fond des bois
Les fleurs, qu'on retrouve dans un livre
Dont le parfum nous enivre, se sont envolées, pourquoi ?
Que reste-t-il de nos amours ?
Que reste-t-il de ces beaux jours ?
Une photo...
... et dans un nuage le cher visage de mon passé

What Remains of Our Love

This evening, the wind that beats against my doo
Speaks to me of dead loves, before the dying embe
Tonight, I hear an autumn song
In the house that shivers, and I think of those byegone days
What remains of our love ?
What remains of those happy days ?
A photo, an old photo from my youth
What remains of our love letters, of past Aprils, o rendez-vous ?
A memory that never ceases to haunt me
Faded happiness, hair flowing in the wind
Stolen kisses, passionate dreams
What remains of all that, tell me
A little village, an old bell tower
In a hidden landscape
And in a cloud, a dear face from my youth
The words, the sweet words one whispers
The purest of caresses, and promises made in th woods
The pressed flowers one tumbles on between th pages of a book
Whose perfume goes to our head, have all flow away, why ?
What remains of our love ?
What remains of those happy days ?
A photo . . .
. . . and in a cloud, that dear face from my pas

Jean-Pierre is a young, inexperienced waiter, and today is his first day on he job at an elegant, very busy restaurant. Table number 5 was particulary lifficult : the four diners kept changing their minds — and their order — and talking too fast. Jean-Pierre thinks he has all the orders, but he doesn't emember what comes first. Can you help Jean-Pierre decide if something s a starter (entrée), main dish (plat), cheese (fromage), or sweet (dessert), so he can serve the dishes in the right order ? To make things more diffi- cult some of the diners have decided to skip some dishes. By the way, in France, cheese is always served before cake, ice cream or fruit.

gâteau au chocolat (2), magret de canard, potage maison, plateau de fromage (3), profi- terolles, salade de chèvre chaud (2), portion de brie, rillettes, daurade au four, brochette d'agneau, fraises des bois, foie de veau.

(See solutions on page 30)

4.2 CONTACTS

Listen

QUELQUES COURSES

1. A la pharmacie

Pharmacienne : *Bonjour Monsieur.*

Client : *Bonjour Madame, j'ai très mal à la tête, est-ce que vous avez de l'aspirine, s'il vous plaît ?*

Pharmacienne : *J'ai de l'Aspégic 500.*

Client : *C'est aussi bien que l'aspirine ?*

Pharmacienne : *C'est de l'aspirine mais c'est bien mieux que les cachets ; c'est plus concentré et comme c'est en poudre, ça agit plus rapidement. Voilà... vous en prendrez trois fois par jour dans un demi-verre d'eau. Ce sera tout ?*

Client : *J'ai mal à l'estomac, je ne digère pas bien.*

Pharmacienne : *Pour la digestion, j'ai soit des pastilles Rennie, soit du Normogastryl. Qu'est-ce que vous préférez ?*

Client : *Qu'est-ce qui est le plus efficace ?*

Pharmacienne : *C'est à peu près la même chose. Les deux sont assez efficaces.*

Client : *Alors donnez-moi des pastilles Rennie ; J'en prends combien ?*

Pharmacienne : *Prenez-en deux maintenant et deux autres dans quelques heures.*

2. Chez le marchand de journaux

Vendeur : *Monsieur, vous désirez ?*

Client : *Est-ce que vous avez le « Herald Tribune » ?*

Vendeur : *Ah non ! Je suis désolé mais nous ne l'avons plus.*

Client : *Alors donnez-moi des enveloppes, du papier à lettres et un carnet de timbres.*

Vendeur : *Je regrette Monsieur, mais nou n'avons pas de timbres, on n'en ven pas ici. Demandez au bureau de taba juste en face !*

Client : *Bon, je prends déjà le papier à le tres et des enveloppes. Vous m'en dor nez vingt s'il vous plaît. Vous faites de photocopies ?*

Vendeur : *Oui, bien sûr.*

Client : *Est-ce que vous pourriez me pho tocopier ce document, s'il vous plaît*

Vendeur : *Oui. En combien d'exemplaires*

Client : *Oh ! Faites-m'en quatre.*

Vendeur : *Voilà.*

Client : *Merci Monsieur ; au revoir.*

3. Au bureau de tabac

Buraliste : *Monsieur ?*

Client : *Est-ce que je pourrais avoir di timbres s'il vous plaît ?*

Buraliste : *A combien ?*

Client : *C'est pour des cartes postales, pou les États-Unis. Et je voudrais aussi de Royales.*

Buraliste : *Un paquet ?*

Client : *Non, donnez-m'en deux.*

Buraliste : *Voilà ...*

Client : *Merci !...*

Buraliste : *Monsieur... Monsieur !... Vou oubliez votre portefeuille !*

Client : *Non, il n'est pas à moi. J'ai l mien dans ma poche.*

Listen and repeat
(You may look at the translation on page 31 in th booklet.)

Pharmacie « ouverte » 2. Intérieur de vieille pharmacie
Papeterie ancienne 4. Intérieur d'un tabac-journaux
.-7. Enseignes

1 2 3 4 5 6 7

4.2 WORDS

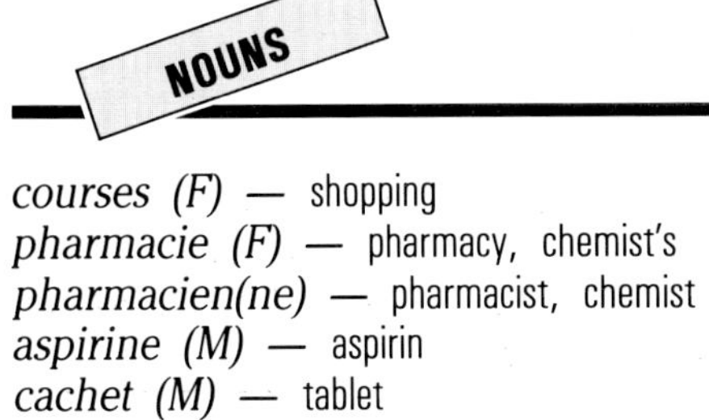

courses (F) — shopping
pharmacie (F) — pharmacy, chemist's
pharmacien(ne) — pharmacist, chemist
aspirine (M) — aspirin
cachet (M) — tablet
poudre (F) — powder
estomac (M) — stomach
digestion (F) — digestion
pastille (F) — pastille, lozenge
marchand(e) — shopkeeper
journal (M) — newspaper
enveloppe (F) — envelope
papier à lettres (M) — writing paper
lettre (F) — letter
carnet de timbres (M) — booklet of stamps
timbre (M) — stamp
photocopie (F) — photocopy
document (M) — document
exemplaire (M) — copy ***(1)***
carte postale (F) — post card
portefeuille (M) —wallet
poche (F) — pocket

---

médicament (M) — medicine
sirop (M) — syrup
rouge à lèvres (M) — lipstick
blondes (F) — light tobacco cigarettes
brunes (F) — dark tobacco cigarettes

savon (M) — soap
tube de dentifrice (M) — tube of toothpast
brosse à dents (F) — toothbrush
rasoir (M) — razor
lame de rasoir (F) — razor blade
crème à raser (F) — shaving soap

agir — to act, to work, to take effect
digérer — to digest
demander — to ask, to ask for
photocopier — to photocopy

avoir mal à — to have a pain, ache, to hu
trois fois par jour — three times a day
c'est tout — that's all

REMEMBER... REMEMBER... REMEMBER... REMEMBER... REMEMBER

(1) *The word « exemplaire » is used when referring to copies of things such as books, newspapers or rep duced documents, particularly when giving a number. The word « copie » exists in French, often design ing an imitation.* — ***(2)*** *« La crève » : familiar.*

HOW TO SAY IT

1. SAYING WHAT YOU WANT (IN A SHOP)

Est-ce que vous avez de l'aspirine, s'il vous plaît ? — Have you got any aspirin, please ?
Donnez-moi un carnet de timbres, s'il vous plaît — Give me a booklet of stamps, please
Est-ce que je pourrais avoir 10 timbres, s'il vous plaît ? — Could I have 10 stamps, please ?
Je voudrais aussi des Royales — I'd like some Royales too, please

2. MAKING COMPARISONS

C'est plus concentré (que l'aspirine) — It's stronger (than aspirin)
C'est aussi bien que l'aspirine — It's as good as aspirin
C'est bien mieux que les cachets — It's much better than the tablets
C'est à peu près la même chose — It's more or less the same thing

3. ASKING PRICES

Des timbres à combien ? — What price stamps do you want ?
Quel est le prix des cartes postales ? — How much are the postcards ?
Je vous dois combien ? — How much do I owe you ?
Ça fait combien ? — How much does that come to ?

4. APOLOGISING

Je suis désolé, mais nous n'avons plus « Le Monde » — I'm sorry, we've run out of "Le Monde"
Je regrette, Monsieur, mais je n'ai pas de timbres — I'm sorry sir, I haven't got any stamps
Excusez-moi, mais nous ne faisons pas de photocopies — I'm sorry, but we don't do photocopies

5. TALKING ABOUT YOUR STATE OF HEALTH

J'ai mal à la tête (au dos, aux dents...) — I've got a headache (backache, toothache...)
Je ne me sens pas bien / *Je ne suis pas bien* — I don't feel well
Je me sens mal — I don't feel (at all) well
Je ne suis pas en forme — I'm not feeling very well
J'ai la crève — I've got a bad cold ***(2)***
Je vais très bien — I'm feeling very well
Ça va bien — Everything's fine / I'm fine
Je suis en pleine forme — I feel great

Michael is a pillock!

4.2 ORAL PRACTICE

1. GRAMMAR : SEE PAGE 40

INDEFINITE QUANTITIES : « DU », « DE LA », « DES »

Listen :

(N'oublie pas l'aspirine !)
— C'est vrai ; donnez-moi de l'aspirine, s'il vous plaît.

NOW, ASK FOR THE FOLLOWING ITEMS USING « DU », « DE LA » OR « DES »

(N'oublie pas l'aspirine !) — (N'oublie pas les timbres) — (N'oublie pas le dentifrice !) — (N'oublie pas la crème à raser !) — (N'oublie pas les enveloppes !) — (N'oublie pas le savon !) — (N'oublie pas l'eau de Cologne !)

2. GRAMMAR : SEE PAGE 41

PRONOUN PRACTICE : « EN »

Listen :

(Est-ce que vous avez du sirop ?)
— Oui, j'en ai.
(Est-ce qu'il fume des blondes ?)
— Oui, il en fume.

NOW, GIVE SHORT AFFIRMATIVE ANSWERS TO THE FOLLOWING QUESTIONS, USING « EN »

(Est-ce que vous avez du sirop ?) — (Est-ce qu'il fume des blondes ?) — (Est-ce que vous prenez du café ?) — (Est-ce qu'elle fait des photocopies ?) — (Est-ce que vous vendez de la crème à raser ?) —

3. GRAMMAR : SEE PAGE 40

NEGATION : « NE...PAS » FOLLOWED BY « DE »

Listen :

(Vous avez des timbres ?)
— Non, nous n'avons pas de timbres.

NOW, ANSWER IN THE NEGATIVE FORM, USING « NE...PAS » + « DE/D' »

(Vous avez des timbres ?) — (Il boit du café ?) — (Vous achetez de l'eau de Cologne ?) — (Elle veut un apéritif ?) — (Vous vendez des cartes postales ?) — (Il prend un dessert ?) — (Elle demande des cigarettes ?)

4. GRAMMAR : SEE PAGE 41

PRONOUN PRACTICE : « EN » WITH NUMBER[S]

Listen :

(Vous prenez deux boîtes d'allumettes ?)
— Oui, j'en prends deux.
(Je fais une photocopie ?)
— Oui, vous en faites une.

NOW, ANSWER IN THE AFFIRMATIVE USING « EN » AN[D] CONFIRMING THE NUMBER

(Vous prenez deux boîtes d'allumettes ?) — (Je fai[s] une photocopie ?) — (Elle écrit trois cartes postales [?] — (Vous utilisez deux lames de rasoir ?) — (Tu ach[e]tes un carnet de timbres ?) — (Il demande cin[q] enveloppes ?)

5. GRAMMAR : SEE PAGE 41

EXPRESSING POSSESSION WITH « À »

Listen :

(C'est votre portefeuille ?)
— Non, il n'est pas à moi.
(Ce sont les cigarettes de Pauline ?)
— Non, elles ne sont pas à elle.

NOW, ANSWER THE FOLLOWING QUESTIONS IN TH[E] NEGATIVE USING « À » AND THE PRONOUN

(C'est votre portefeuille ?) — (Ce sont les cigarett[es] de Pauline ?) — (Ce sont tes enveloppes ?) — (C'e[st] le journal de Jean ?) — (Marie, Laura, ce sont v[os] timbres ?) — (Ce sont nos documents ?) — (C'est m[on] papier à lettres ?) — (Ce sont les cartes postales d[es] enfants ?) — (Ce sont les photocopies de Brigitte [et] Sylvie ?)

6. GRAMMAR : SEE PAGE 42

EXPRESSING POSSESSION : POSSESSIV[E] PRONOUNS

Listen :

(Ce briquet est à vous, Madame ?)
— Non, ce n'est pas le mien.
(Ces cartes postales sont à vous, Monsieur
— Non, ce ne sont pas les miennes.

NOW, ANSWER IN THE NEGATIVE FORM, USING TH[E] APPROPRIATE POSSESSIVE PRONOUN

(Ce briquet est à vous, Madame ?) — (Ces cartes po[s]tales sont à vous, Monsieur ?) — (Ces cigarettes so[nt] à eux ?) — (Ce rouge à lèvres est à elle ?) — (Ce jou[r]nal est à eux ?) — (Ces photocopies sont à moi ?) [—] (Ces documents sont à vous, Messieurs ?)

THE SHOP ON THE CORNER

As we have already mentioned, one ɔf the delights of France is the way that every excess, every vice, is cater-ed for instantly, abundantly and effi-iently. You just have to know where o go.

'LE TABAC" France is the smoker's aradise. Cigarettes are much cheap-r than in Britain or the U.S., and xtremely easy to obtain. Run out ? Just look for the red, diamond-shaped ign saying tabac : often tucked away n the corner of a crowded café, the abac (prononced "taba") can supply ou with about 300 brand names to elp you blacken your lungs. You can et light tobacco, filtered cigarettes es blondes) or, for those really intent n self-destruction, there are the amous dark Gauloises or Gitanes, which leave bits in your mouth, and ive you that early-morning rattle. If ou're hooked on cigars, pipes or even iddies, the tabac will meet your very need.

f you are more intent on ruining your eeth than your lungs, the tabac can upply you with a variety of sweets, hocolate and chewing gum.

or those who want to add gambling ɔ their list, you can do that at the tabac too. For a small sum, you can get your weekly lottery or loto ticket, which may enable you to invest in vices far more exotic than chewing gum. The chances of your winning are remote, but at least you'll be in good company — about six million French men and women lose on the loto every week.

If your only weakness is excessive communication, you'll still need the tabac as the most convenient source for stamps, pens and postcards, as well as telephone credit cards (télécartes), sold in some tabacs.

"LA PHARMACIE" If you've got bronchitis (too many brunes ?), indigestion (too much foie gras ?) or the eternal hangover (that one little cognac too many ?) head for the nearest pharmacie. Unless you are seriously ill, French pharmacists are well-equipped to advise you on which drug to take from their enormous panoply of products. A word of advice : French pharmaceutical products are, on the whole, much more expensive than those in Britain or the U.S., so do come stocked up with a good supply. If you are truly horrified by the price of a tube of toothpaste, try the local supermarket, where prices are generally much cheaper.

"LE TRAITEUR" These are the gourmet's delight. If you really want to satisfy the eye and whet the appetite, go straight to the traiteur (delicatessen). Here, the range of brightly coloured and brilliantly arranged salmon pâtés, coquilles Saint-Jacques and smoked hams and salads will set the taste buds spinning.

Almost as impressive are the fromageries (cheese shops) with about 200 varieties, and the wine shops, with anything from cheap plonk (and it really is cheap) to the distinguished dusty old bottles which you can only afford if you've just won the loto.

Most of the small shops keep civilised opening hours — 9.00 to 13.00 and 16.00 to 19.00, so you can fulfil your desires until late in the day.

For those night-owls who only get cravings when the stars come out, there are the Drugstores (about five of them in Paris) which sell anything from food to medicine to newspapers and cigarettes around the clock.

France leaves you no excuse for under-indulgence ! □

4.2 TAKE A BREAK

N° 1

Listen

Listen to the shoppers on your cassette. Can you guess where they are? Look at the shop signs below, and put the number corresponding to each shopper in the boxes next to the signs.

PAPETERIE

N° 2

Fill in the words from the clues below :

1. If you wander around France without these, you've had it !
2. The food is incredible. So is the bill. « Garçon ! L'...... s'il vous plaît »
3. If she's really ...... to you, you won't mind how ...... her tastes are.
4. These are all the things you bought the day you went berserk on the Faubourg Saint-Honoré.
5. Never forget to ask the price ! « Combien ça ......, s'il vous plaît ? »
6. O.K., so you're loaded. Nothing to worry about if you're that ......
7. If you can't remember n° 5, try this : « Je vous dois ......, s'il vous plaît ? »

Now look at the word in the diagonal if you want a nasty shock !

N° 3

Find the odd man out in each of the following lists. Then discover what all the other words in each list have in common by unscrambling the letters on the right.

a) Escalope, saumon, truite, coquille Saint Jacques, raie, daurade.

SOSOSPNI

b) Muscadet, Sancerre, Beaujolais, Chateaubriand, Champagne.

NIVS

c) Religieuse, financier, bavette, amandine, millefeuilles, tarte aux pommes.

SSEITPIEARS

d) Camembert, Brie, Cantal, Bleu d'Auvergne, Brouilly, Munster.

GOAEFMSR

(See solutions on page 32)

Listen

DANS UN GRAND MAGASIN

Monsieur Price fait des courses aux Galeries Lafayette

1. Au rayon « parfumerie »

La vendeuse : *Monsieur, je peux vous aider ?*

M. Price : *Oui, je voudrais du parfum. C'est pour offrir.*

La vendeuse : *C'est pour une jeune personne ou pour une dame ?*

M. Price : *Pour une jeune fille.*

La vendeuse : *J'ai de très bons parfums, mais pour une jeune fille, je vous conseille plutôt cette eau de toilette.*

M. Price : *Celle-ci ?*

La vendeuse : *Oui, elle est plus légère qu'un parfum. Tenez, si vous voulez bien essayer.*

M. Price : *Oui, vous avez raison, elle est assez légère, mais je ne l'aime pas tellement.*

La vendeuse : *Et celle-là ? Elle est très fraîche ! Tenez.*

M. Price : *Hum, ah oui, je préfère ; elle sent un peu le citron. Je trouve qu'elle est très agréable. Je la prends...*

La vendeuse : *Je vous fais un paquet-cadeau ?*

M. Price : *Oui, s'il vous plaît.*

2. Au rayon « femmes »

M. Price : *Bonjour Madame, j'aurais voulu un pull-over en cachemire ; bleu de préférence...*

La vendeuse : *Quelle taille ?*

M. Price : *Je crois que ma femme fait du 42 ; du 14 en Grande-Bretagne.*

La vendeuse : *C'est ça ; un instant...*

M. Price : *Ah, il est superbe... euh... il coûte combien ?*

La vendeuse : *1 200 francs.*

M. Price : *C'est cher ; vous n'auriez pas quelque chose de moins cher ?*

La vendeuse : *Si, j'ai celui-ci, mais il est en laine et angora ; au toucher c'est un peu comme le cachemire. Tenez, regardez, il est aussi doux que l'autre.*

M. Price : *Oui, on dirait vraiment du cachemire. Il vaut combien ?*

La vendeuse : *700 francs.*

M. Price : *Il est de bonne qualité ?*

La vendeuse : *Ah oui, il est inusable. Mais attention, il se lave à l'eau froide.*

M. Price : *Je le prends. S'il ne lui va pas, je pourrai l'échanger ?*

La vendeuse : *Bien entendu ! Mais n'oubliez pas le ticket de caisse.*

3. Au rayon « jouets »

M. Price : *Madame, s'il vous plaît, je cherche les modèles réduits.*

Une vendeuse : *Ils sont juste devant vous*

M. Price : *Ah oui, je n'avais pas vu. Excusez-moi ! Il n'y a pas de petites voitures françaises ?*

La vendeuse : *Attendez, je vais voir... Non il n'y en a plus ; tous les modèles que nous avons sont sur le rayon. Vous savez, avec les fêtes, nous en vendons beaucoup.*

M. Price : *Tant pis, je vous remercie.*

Listen and repeat
(You may look at the translation on page 32 in the booklet.)

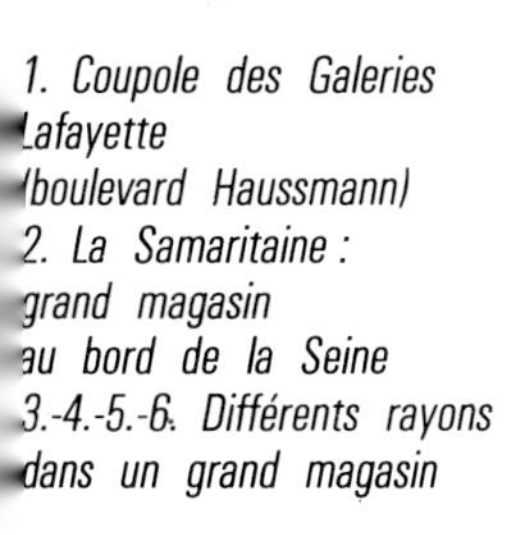

1. Coupole des Galeries Lafayette (boulevard Haussmann)
2. La Samaritaine : grand magasin au bord de la Seine
3.-4.-5.-6. Différents rayons dans un grand magasin

4.3 WORDS

grand magasin (M) — department store
magasin (M) — shop
rayon (M) — department
parfumerie (F) — perfume department, shop
parfum (M) — perfume
paquet (M) — packet
cadeau (M) — present, gift
vêtement (M) — article of clothing
pull-over (M) — pullover
cachemire (M) — cashmere
laine (F) — wool
angora (M) — angora
qualité (F) — quality
ticket de caisse (M) — receipt
caisse (F) — cashier's desk, cash register
jouet (M) — toy
modèle réduit (M) — scale model
rayon (M) — department
modèle (M) — model
fêtes (F) — holidays
manteau (M) — coat
robe (F) — dress
lunettes (F) — glasses
cravate (F) — tie
pantalon (M) — trousers
collants (M) — tights

léger(ère) — light
frais(fraîche) — fresh
agréable — pleasant
superbe — superb
doux(ce) — soft
inusable — long-lasting

---

lourd(e) — heavy
étroit(e) — narrow
long(ue) — long
habillé(e) — smart
sport — sportswear, casual (clothing)
classique — classic (clothing)
moderne — modern

aider — to help
offrir — to offer
essayer — to try on
sentir — to smell, to feel ***(1)***
valoir — to be worth
(se) laver — to wash
échanger — to exchange

---

rembourser — to reimburse

faire des courses — to shop, to go shopping
faire un paquet-cadeau — to gift wrap
faire du (taille) — to be (size)
aller (vêtement) — to go with (clothes), to fit (size) ***(2)***
on dirait du ... — it's just like...
tant pis — too bad

à la mode — in fashion

HOW TO SAY IT

1. SAYING WHAT YOU WANT (IN A SHOP)

Je voudrais du parfum — I'd like some perfume
J'aurais voulu un pull-over en cachemire — I was looking for a cashmere pullover
Est-ce que vous auriez du parfum ? — Have you got any perfume ?
Vous n'auriez pas quelque chose de moins cher ? — Have you got anything cheaper ?

2. LOCATING SOMETHING

Pardon, Monsieur, le rayon des jouets, s'il vous plaît ? — Excuse me, where's the toy department ?
Madame, je cherche les modèles réduits — Excuse me, I'm looking for the scale models

3. PRICES, SIZE AND QUALITY

L'eau de toilette sent un peu le citron — The toilet water smells a bit of lemon
On dirait vraiment du cachemire — It's really like cashmere
Au toucher, c'est un peu comme le cachemire — It feels a bit like cashmere
Ça vous fait penser au cachemire ? — It reminds you of cashmere ?
Il vaut 700 francs — It costs 700 Francs
Il coûte 1 200 francs — It costs 1,200 Francs
Il fait 1 200 francs — It costs 1,200 Francs
C'est du 42 — It's size 42
C'est un 44 — It's a size 44
C'est de la bonne qualité — It's good quality

4. GIVING ADVICE

Je vous conseille cette eau de toilette — I recommend this toilet water
Vous devriez prendre du cachemire — You should get cashmere
Il vaudrait mieux offrir une eau de toilette — I think toilet water would be a nicer present

REMEMBER... REMEMBER... REMEMBER... REMEMBER... REMEMBER

(1) *« sentir » is used for various senses. When it refers to smell it can be used both transitively and intransitively (sentir une rose, sentir bon). It can also be translated as to feel, but never in the sense of to touch. —* ***(2)*** *When « aller » refers to clothing, it can mean to go with, to fit, to suit.*

4.3 ORAL PRACTICE

1. GRAMMAR : SEE PAGE 42

PRONOUN PRACTICE : DEMONSTRATION PRONOUNS : « CELUI », « CELLE », « CEUX », « CELLES »

Listen :

(Vous prenez cette eau de toilette ?)
— Non, pas celle-là !
(Vous voulez ce pull ?)
— Non, pas celui-là !

NOW, REFUSE THE FOLLOWING ITEMS, USING « CELUI-LÀ », « CELLE-LÀ », « CEUX-LÀ » OR « CELLES-LÀ » AS NECESSARY

(Vous prenez cette eau de toilette ?) — (Vous voulez ce pull ?) — (Vous achetez ces jouets ?) — (Vous essayez ce manteau ?) — (Vous prenez cette robe ?) — (Vous voulez ces lunettes ?)

2. GRAMMAR : SEE PAGE 45

MAKING COMPARISONS : « AUSSI...QUE »

Listen :

(une eau de toilette) (légère)
— Cette eau de toilette est aussi légère que celle-là.

NOW, COMPARE TWO THINGS IN EACH EXAMPLE USING « AUSSI...QUE » AND THE APPROPRIATE DEMONSTRATIVE PRONOUN (« CELUI-LÀ », « CELLE-LÀ », « CEUX-LÀ », « CELLES-LÀ »)

(une eau de toilette) (légère) — (un parfum) (agréable) — (un pantalon) (chaud) — (des pulls) (doux) — (des lunettes) (jolies) — (une robe) (habillée) — (des collants) (chers) — (des manteaux) (longs)

3. GRAMMAR : SEE PAGE 45

MAKING COMPARISONS : « PLUS », « MOINS », « AUSSI »

Listen :

(pull bleu) (moins cher) (pull rouge)
— Le pull bleu est moins cher que le pull rouge.

NOW, YOU COMPARE THE TWO PULLOVERS USING « PLUS », « MOINS » OR « AUSSI » AS INDICATED

(pull bleu) (moins cher) (pull rouge) — (pull rouge) (plus grand) (pull bleu) — (pull vert) (aussi doux) (pull rouge) — (pull bleu) (plus chaud) (pull jaune) — (pull gris) (moins joli) (pull bleu)

4. GRAMMAR : SEE PAGE 41

PRONOUN PRACTICE : « EN »

Listen :

(Vous vendez beaucoup de cravates)
— Oui, j'en vends beaucoup.

NOW, ANSWER IN THE AFFIRMATIVE USING « EN » AND THE APPROPRIATE QUANTIFIER (« BEAUCOUP », « TROP », « ASSEZ » OR « PEU »)

(Vous vendez beaucoup de cravates) — (Il a peu de jouets) — (Vous achetez trop de vêtements) — (Il y a assez de modèles) — (Elle a peu de parfums) — (Vous offrez beaucoup de cadeaux ?)

5. GRAMMAR : SEE PAGE 45

NO MORE, NO LONGER : « NE...PLUS »

Listen :

(Il y a encore des petites voitures ?)
— Non, il n'y en a plus.

NOW, ANSWER IN THE NEGATIVE USING « NE...PLUS » AND THE PRONOUN « EN »

(Il y a encore des petites voitures ?) — (Ils ont encore des journaux anglais ?) — (Il y a encore des pulls bleus ?) — (Il prend encore des médicaments ?) — (Vous avez encore des timbres ?)

6. GRAMMAR : SEE PAGE 45

COMPARING QUANTITIES : « AUTANT DE », « PLUS DE », « MOINS DE »

Listen :

(Nous vendons du parfum) (plus)
— Nous vendons plus de parfum que l'année dernière.

NOW, CHANGE THESE SENTENCES USING « AUTANT DE », « MOINS DE » OR « PLUS DE » AS INDICATED

(Nous vendons du parfum) (plus) — (Nous vendons des modèles réduits) (autant) — (Nous vendons des vêtements) (moins) — (Nous vendons des jouets) (plus) — (Nous vendons des cravates) (moins) — (Nous vendons des robes) (autant)

SHOPPING

Traditionally a land of small shopkeepers and artisans, France now has some of the largest supermarkets in Europe (known as supermarchés *and* hypermarchés*) and the most fashionable department stores in the world (*grands magasins*).*

FRANCE'S SMALL SHOPS *They have been threatened with extinction for years, yet they hang on valiantly. In 1986, they still controlled 60 percent of the food trade (in complete contrast to the United States, where supermarkets have captured 75 percent of the market). On Saturday or Sunday mornings, French families still make their weekly foray to the local street market where fresh produce — often direct from the farm — can be purchased. The outdoor markets themselves are something of a feast, with marvellous displays of brightly coloured fruits and vegetables. When buying a cut of meat from the butcher or fresh fish from the fishmonger, all you have to do is ask for some cooking advice, and you will be showered with excellent recipes. Instead of being annoyed at being made to wait, the other customers in the queue will listen in rapt attention as if witnessing the description of some sacred ceremonial rite. In such an atmosphere, it is hard to believe that the supermarket will ever completely supplant the outdoor market.*

"LE GRAND MAGASIN" *Likewise, in spite of the variety and quality of the clothes, accessories, toiletries and even furniture found in the* grands magasins*, they are not likely to supplant the little boutiques and* parfumeries *that grace every neighbourhood. Often, the shopkeepers in these smaller shops are more attentive and helpful. They are trained people, usually endowed with impeccable taste : when they advise you to purchase a multi-coloured silk scarf to wear with the black coat you have just bought, they are not just trying to make an extra sale. The scarf probably adds that fashionable Parisian touch to the outfit, and you would be well advised to buy it. In the* grands magasins *you are left much more to your own devices : a positive point if you don't really know what you want and just wish to browse. In the small boutiques, browsing is usually discouraged, and you'll have a salesperson at your elbow saying, "*Je peux vous aider ?*" before you've had a chance to look at anything.*

Another advantage of the grands magasins*, such as* Printemps *or* Galeries Lafayette*, is that you can find literally anything in them. If you want to do some quick last minute shopping for friends and family back home, a couple of hours in one shop should leave you laden with gifts ranging from lingerie and perfume to toys, Lacoste shirts or anything else that catches your fancy.*

Some of the larger grands magasins *have a whole section devoted to designer clothes. There you will find expensive fashions normally not found on the mass-produced racks of the department stores.*

For all the advantages of the grands magasins*, if you have the time, don't miss a quick visit to some of the small shops. It is there — whether in exclusive clothing boutiques or local bakeries or cheese shops — that you will discover* la vieille France*, which some claim is rapidly disappearing, but which still looks very much alive.* □

N° 1

Listen

Listen to the people on the cassette giving clues to different words. Then, using the pictures to help you, unscramble the letters and write out the correct words.

IMBSTER — SQTEAPU — DAAXECU — TAUMENA — UOETJ

N° 2

Look at the objects and read the clues. Then fill in all the things you need for a good holiday. When you've done all that, you'll see another object appear in the column. If you didn't have these, and the sun was strong, you wouldn't even be able to read your list.

1. *If you're lying on a beach all day, you may want some of these.*
2. *Don't forget it gets cold at night !*
3. *There's nothing worse than hot feet.*
4. *This is just as useful for men with sunburn as for women going into mosques.*
5. *You'll want this if you like communicating.*
6. *This is a must if you want to find your way around.*
7. *This helps you go brown instead of red.*
8. *Without this, you won't even leave your own country.*
9. *These are essential for those who are pessimistic, or just plain prudent.*
10. *If you want proof that you've been away, you must take this with you.*
11. *Most of us look awful in them, but they leave your legs free.*
12. *This will keep your hair clean and shining.*
13. *If you're at all aquatic, this is the first thing on your list.*
14. *This anti-sunstroke device is ancient and effective.*
15. *Bung everything in this, and you're away !*
16. *Well, not quite. If you forget these, you may as well stay at home.*

(See solutions on page 34)

 *Listen*

LA DRAGUE

A la fermeture d'un Salon à Marseille (au stand MATRA)

Michel : *Excusez-moi, Mademoiselle, pourriez-vous me montrer vos nouveaux combinés téléphoniques, s'il vous plaît ?*

Véronique : *Oui, avec plaisir. Asseyez-vous, je vous prie ; voilà notre dernier modèle : le TM2, qui vient de sortir. Il a un grand succès, nous en avons déjà vendu beaucoup.*

Michel : *Et comment marche-t-il ?*

Véronique : *Oh ! C'est très simple : vous appuyez sur les touches correspondant au numéro que vous voulez faire ; le numéro s'affiche là, en bas, dans le carré noir.*

Michel : *Dites, il est 7 h 00 ; le Salon va fermer. Que diriez-vous d'aller prendre un verre sur le Vieux Port ?*

Véronique : *Mais je n'ai pas fini de vous expliquer...*

Michel : *Et puis on pourrait aller dîner ensemble, je vous emmènerai manger une bouillabaisse. Vous ne voulez pas dîner avec moi ? Je vous invite.*

Véronique : *Vous permettez que je continue ?*

Michel : *Euh... oui.*

Véronique : *Si personne ne répond, vous appuyez sur la touche mémoire.*

Michel : *Bon, j'achète votre TM2 si vous entrez votre numéro dans la mémoire.*

Véronique : *Pour le même prix, je suppose ?*

Michel : *Bien sûr, c'est juste pour essayer.*

Véronique : *Pour essayer quoi ?*

Listen and repeat
(You may look at the translation on page 34 in the booklet.)

Quelques mois plus tard...

LES MOTS SONT TROP PRÉCIEUX POUR LES CON

LES MOTS SONT TROP PRÉCIEUX POUR LES CONFIER A N'IMPORTE QUEL TÉLÉPHONE.
E QUEL TÉLÉPHONE.
Viens...
23 h 48.
J'ai composé son numéro sur l'écran digital de ma nuit blanche. Magiques : les chiffres se sont affichés sans faute dans le carré noir. Mais personne au bout du dring. J'ai mis son numéro en mémoire et j'ai appuyé sur rappel automatique. Au 15e rappel, il a enfin décroché. J'ai dit : "Viens...". Il a quand même mis 5 minutes et 10 secondes pour dire oui...
TM 2
J'arrive...
Réunion finie. Le numéro de Véronique sur le clavier magique. Clic, clac, merci Déclic. Personne... Pas de panique... ...Touche rappel automatique. Elle répond, endormie. Pardon pour le décalage horaire. Je prends le premier avion, j'arrive... Je t'aime.
DECLIC
MATRA
COMMUNICATION

1. Vieux Port, à Marseille

2. Publicité d'un appareil téléphonique

4.4 WORDS

drague (F) — flirting
fermeture (F) — closing time
salon (M) — show, trade fair
stand (M) — stand
combiné (téléphonique) (M) — receiver
succès (M) — success
touche (F) — key
carré (M) — square
mémoire (F) — memory
écran digital (M) — digital screen
nuit blanche (F) — a sleepless night
rappel (M) — call back
seconde (F) — second
clavier (M) — key board
décalage (horaire) (M) — time lag
mot (M) — word

---

ouverture (F) — opening time
foire (F) — trade fair
exposition (F) — exhibition
inauguration (F) — inauguration
ordinateur (M) — computer
micro (ordinateur) (M) — micro(-computer)
mini (ordinateur) (M) — mini(-computer)
hôtesse (F) — hostess
visiteur(euse) — visitor
exposant (M) — exhibitor

simple — simple
précieux(se) — precious
digital(e) — digital
magique — magic
automatique — automatic
endormi(e) — asleep

draguer — to flirt
montrer — to show
appuyer — to press
(s')afficher — to display
finir — to finish
expliquer — to explain
permettre — to allow, to let
continuer — to continue
répondre — to answer
entrer (en mémoire) — to enter (into a computer's memory)
supposer — to suppose
confier — to trust to, to entrust with
mettre (temps) — to take (time) ***(1)***
inviter — to invite
exposer — to exhibit
commencer — to begin
se promener — to go for a walk

avoir du succès —to be a success
au bout du fil — on the phone, at the other end of the line
mettre un numéro en mémoire — to enter a number on to the computer's memory
pas de panique — don't panic, no cause for panic

HOW TO SAY IT

1. INVITING PEOPLE OUT

Que diriez-vous d'aller prendre un verre sur le Vieux Port ? — What about having a drink in the old port ?
On pourrait dîner ensemble — We could have dinner together
Je vous emmène manger une bouillabaisse — I'll take you out for a bouillabaisse
Je vous propose d'aller prendre un verre — Let's have a drink
Si on allait dîner ensemble ?
Je vous invite à dîner
Vous voulez bien dîner avec moi ? — Why don't we have dinner together ?

2. ACCEPTING AN INVITATION

Oui, avec plaisir — Yes, that would be nice
Volontiers ! — Yes, certainly
D'accord ! — All right
Je veux bien — Yes, I'd love to
Pourquoi pas ? — Why not ?

3. DECLINING AN INVITATION

Je suis désolé, mais je suis pris — I'm sorry, but I'm not free
C'est très gentil, mais je ne peux pas — That's very kind of you but I can't
Je regrette, mais je dois rentrer — I'm sorry, but I have to go home
Non, je ne peux pas
Excusez-moi, mais je n'ai pas le temps — No, I can't

4. HOW TO HOLD THE FLOOR (IN A MEETING)

Vous permettez que je continue — May I carry on ?
Je peux continuer ? — May I continue ?
Je n'ai pas fini de vous expliquer — I haven't finished explaining it to you
Laissez-moi finir !
Laissez-moi terminer ! — Let me finish what I have to say !

REMEMBER... REMEMBER... REMEMBER... REMEMBER... REMEMBER

(1) *« Mettre du temps » means I/you/he/she etc. take x amount of time to do something : il met deux heures pour aller à son travail (he takes two hours to commute to work).*

4.4 ORAL PRACTICE

1.	GRAMMAR : SEE PAGE 47

MAKING SUGGESTIONS : « QUE DIRIEZ-VOUS DE... ? »

Listen :

(On va au restaurant ?)
— Que diriez-vous d'aller au restaurant ?

NOW, SUGGEST THE FOLLOWING ACTIVITIES USING « QUE DIRIEZ-VOUS DE... ? »

(On va au restaurant ?) — (On prend un verre ?) — (On sort ce soir ?) — (On va dans une boîte de nuit ?) — (On invite des clients ?) — (On réserve une table au Crazy Horse ?)

2.	GRAMMAR : SEE PAGE 48

SAYING THAT SOMETHING HAS BEEN DONE

Listen :

(composer le numéro) (je)
— C'est fait. J'ai composé le numéro.

NOW, SAY THAT YOU HAVE DONE THE FOLLOWING, USING « C'EST FAIT » AND PUTTING THE VERB INTO THE « PASSÉ COMPOSÉ »

(composer le numéro) (je) — (appuyer sur rappel) (nous) — (faire le 16) (André) — (décrocher le combiné) (vous) — (mettre le numéro en mémoire) (Martine et Françoise) — (acheter une télécarte) (tu)

3.	GRAMMAR : SEE PAGE 48

THE « PASSÉ COMPOSÉ » WITH VERBS OF MOVEMENT

Listen :

(Je vais au restaurant)
— Hier, je suis allé au restaurant.
(Nous sortons avec des amis)
— Hier, nous sommes sortis avec des amis.

NOW, STARTING WITH « HIER », PUT THE FOLLOWING SENTENCES INTO THE « PASSÉ COMPOSÉ », REMEMBERING TO USE THE VERB « ÊTRE » WITH VERBS OF MOVEMENT

(Je vais au restaurant) — (Nous sortons avec des amis) — (Vous arrivez en retard) — (Catherine rentre à huit heures) — (Nous restons toute la journée au bureau) — (Le directeur vient au Salon) — (Véronique et Michel partent pour Marseille) — (Vous tombez dans la piscine)

4.	GRAMMAR : SEE PAGE 48

VERB PRACTICE : THE PASSÉ COMPOSÉ WITH REFLEXIVE VERBS

Listen :

(Le numéro s'affiche dans le carré noir)
— Le numéro s'est affiché dans le carré noir.

NOW, PUT THESE SENTENCES IN THE PRESENT INTO THE « PASSÉ COMPOSÉ ». REMEMBER TO USE THE VERB « ÊTRE »

(Le numéro s'affiche dans le carré noir) — (Nous nous rencontrons sur le Vieux Port) — (Vous vous téléphonez au Salon) — (Véronique et Michel se présentent au directeur) — (Je m'arrête au stand MATRA) — (Nous nous asseyons près de la fenêtre)

5.	GRAMMAR : SEE PAGE 45

VERB PRACTICE : THE SIMPLE PAST (« PASSÉ COMPOSÉ ») + THE NEGATIVE FORM

Listen :

(Vous avez fini de lui expliquer ?)
— Non, je n'ai pas fini de lui expliquer.

NOW, ANSWER THESE QUESTIONS IN THE NEGATIVE

(Vous avez fini de lui expliquer ?) — (Il a mis le numéro en mémoire ?) — (Ils sont allés au Salon ?) — (Vous êtes sortis sur le port hier soir ?) — (Tu as appuyé sur la touche ?) — (Elle a mangé une bouillabaisse ?) — (Ils sont restés ensemble ?)

6.	GRAMMAR : SEE PAGE 47

PRONOUN PRACTICE : USING TWO VERBS

Listen :

(Vous avez fini d'expliquer à Michel ?)
— Non, je n'ai pas fini de lui expliquer.
(Vous avez fini de faire le numéro ?)
— Non, je n'ai pas fini de le faire.

NOW, REPLACE THE DIRECT OR INDIRECT OBJECT WITH THE APPROPRIATE PRONOUN

(Vous avez fini d'expliquer à Michel ?) — (Vous avez fini de faire le numéro ?) — (Vous avez fini de montrer les modèles ?) — (Vous avez fini de téléphoner à Stéphanie et Bernard ?) — (Vous avez fini de parler à l'hôtesse ?)

LA DRAGUE

he first French slang word most
eople learn is la drague. It's the uni-
ersal process whereby two people
et together. Of course, every country
s its own quaint little customs, and
e unschooled foreigner can find
m/herself in some very embarrassing
tuations if he/she is not au courant.
o, how does la drague work in
ance ? The answer is : very well.
s a country with a strong Latin
fluence, France still operates under
e precept, long defunct amongst
ore inhibited Anglo-Saxons, that the
lan must make a not-too-subtle
proach to drague the Woman.
/here ? Anywhere. Any woman (not
ecessarily young or beautiful) will find
at walking around Paris is quite a
ifferent experience from walking
round London or New York. She may get whistles, comments or just looks — but she'll be made very aware of the fact that she's a woman. If she walks slowly, hesitates, or looks lost, she may well find herself suddenly accompanied by a slightly-too-friendly dragueur. If he's charming, handsome and intelligent — fine. If he isn't, just quicken your pace, look straight in front of you, and ignore the pest who is whispering sweet nothings (or obscenities) in your ear. If this doesn't work, try the Garbo approach : look straight at him, and say "I want to be alone" ("Je voudrais être seule") or (I find this one works particularly well) "I'm married with seven children" ("Je suis mariée et j'ai sept enfants"). The thought of all those soiled nappies usually sends the dragueur scuttling into the nearest métro.

Of course, even in this "liberated" era, women rarely draguent the men. So what approach should the hopeful male take when faced with the doe-eyed beauty sitting alone in the café ? Don't say : "Habitez-vous chez vos parents ?" unless you think you could carry off the English equivalent of "Do you come here often ?" And don't be put off by her ice-cold, disdainful exterior. This is just a charming little French mannerism, particularly prevalent among les Parisiennes. Once you have proved your intelligence/wit/sense of humour and sensitivity, the lady will surely succumb. If she gets up and walks away, don't despair. There are fifty million people in France, and only twenty five million of them are men. □

Listen

The French at Home
What do the French do when they come home from work ? Take the following quiz, and then check your answers at the back of the book. Give yourself ten points for each right answer. If you score less than 50 points, your knowledge of the French is shaky — though it's nothing that a French holiday won't cure !

1. *Avant le dîner, quel pourcentage de Français lisent un journal ?*
a) 53 % b) 24 % c) 14 %

3. *Après le travail, quel pourcentage de Français passent un moment au café ?*
a) 12 % b) 2 % c) 1 %

2. *Après le travail, quel pourcentage de Français font du sport ?*
a) 8 % b) 5 % c) 2 %

4. *Avant le dîner, quel pourcentage de Français passent un moment avec leurs enfants ?*
a) 52 % b) 38 % c) 22 %

5. *Avant le dîner, quel pourcentage e Français se douchent ou prennent n bain ?*
) 12 % b) 9 % c) 3 %

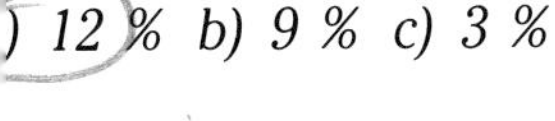

6. *Avant le dîner, quel pourcentage le Français écoutent de la musique ?*
a) 21 % b) 15 % c) 7 %

7. *Avant le dîner, quel pourcentage de Français vont voir des amis ?*
a) 17 % b) 6 % c) 2 %

8. *Avant le dîner, quel pourcentage de Français tricotent ou font de la couture ?*
a) 7 % b) 4 % c) 2 %

9. *Avant le dîner, quel pourcentage de Français lisent un livre ?*
a) 16 % b) 8 % c) 4 %

10. *Après le travail, quel pourcentage de Français regardent la télévision ?*
a) 43 % b) 32 % c) 26 %

(See solutions on page 36)

4.5 CONTACTS

Listen

BON VOYAGE

A Deauville

L'employé SNCF : *Monsieur ?*

Le voyageur : *J'aurais voulu aller au Mont Saint-Michel.*

L'employé SNCF : *Vous n'avez pas de chance, le train vient de partir.*

Le voyageur : *Et pour aller à Chenonceaux ?*

L'employé SNCF : *Chenonceaux ! Il faut que vous preniez un train pour Tours. Il y a un autorail qui fait la liaison. Vous voulez un billet de 1re ou de 2e classe ?*

Le voyageur : *Euh, 2e classe. Mais... il faut que j'aille ensuite en Provence.*

L'employé SNCF : *Quelle ville ?*

Le voyageur : *Arles.*

L'employé SNCF : *Alors, il faut que vous retourniez à Tours et que vous preniez le Tours-Bordeaux. A Bordeaux vous prendrez le train de nuit. Vous arriverez à Arles à 5 h 04.*

Le voyageur : *Bon d'accord. Je peux réserver une place ?*

L'employé SNCF : *Oui. Fumeurs ou non fumeurs ?*

Le voyageur : *Non-fumeurs, s'il vous plaît.*

L'employé SNCF : *Et pour le train de nuit, vous voulez une couchette ?*

Le voyageur : *Oui, je veux bien. En haut de préférence.*

L'employé SNCF : *J'ai peur que ce ne soit pas possible... Ah si ! Ça va. Tenez. Ce sera tout... ou vous voulez remonter jusqu'à Dijon ? C'est beau, la Bourgogne !*

Le voyageur : *Ah oui ! Excellente idée !*

1. Plage, à Deauville
2. Mont-Saint-Michel

3. Château de Chenonceaux
4. Orléans
5. Arènes, à Arles
6. Paysage en Bourgogne
7. Vieille porte de la ville, à Bordeaux

Le Mont-Saint-Michel

Situé en Normandie au milieu d'une baie de la Manche, le Mont-Saint-Michel est construit sur un îlot. Du VIIIe au XVIe siècle, des édifices romans et gothiques sont successivement bâtis : l'abbaye commencée au VIIIe siècle et continuée aux XIe et XIIe siècles est très bien fortifiée et n'a jamais été prise militairement ; c'est un chef-d'œuvre architectural surnommé « la merveille ».

Les châteaux de la Loire

Le Val de Loire est souvent appelé le « Jardin de la France ». C'est pourquoi, dès le XVe siècle, les rois de France et la noblesse ont voulu y habiter. Ils ont fait construire de magnifiques châteaux sur les bords de la Loire. Les plus célèbres sont : Amboise, Azay-le-Rideau, Blois, Chambord, Chenonceaux, Le Lude et Ussé.

Arles

Fondée par les Grecs, Arles est devenue une capitale romaine, puis un grand centre religieux au Moyen Age. Arles est située en Provence, sur le Rhône, au nord de la Camargue. Elle possède deux superbes antiquités gallo-romaines : les arènes et le théâtre antique. On y trouve également deux chefs-d'œuvre de l'art roman provençal : le portail et le cloître de l'église Saint-Trophime.
Van Gogh y a habité de 1888 à 1890.

Dijon

Dijon, ancienne capitale des Ducs de Bourgogne, est située à proximité de magnifiques vignobles.
C'est aussi une ville d'art célèbre ; on y visite le musée des Beaux-Arts, installé dans l'ancien palais des Ducs de Bourgogne (XIVe et XVe siècles) et l'église Notre-Dame, gothique du XIIIe siècle.
Une promenade dans les vieilles rues de la ville permet aux piétons d'admirer les maisons anciennes et les hôtels particuliers des XVe, XVIe et XVIIe siècles, ainsi que de goûter aux vins fameux de la région.

4.5 WORDS

voyageur(se) — traveller, passenger
train de nuit (M) — night train
place (F) — seat ***(1)***
fumeur (M) — smoking compartment
supplément (M) — surcharge
couchette (F) — couchette, berth (on a train)
voyage (M) — trip, journey
abbaye (F) — abbey
visiteur (euse) — visitor
château (M) — castle
roi/reine — king/queen
capitale (F) — capital city
spectateur (trice) — spectator
église (M) — church
vignoble (M) — vineyard
musée (M) — museum
piéton (M) — pedestrian
hôtel particulier (M) — private mansion ***(2)***
car (M) — bus, coach
promenade (F) — walk, stroll
vue (F) — view
fête (F) — festival
monument (M) — monument, historic building
chariot (M) — trolley
consigne (F) — left luggage
correspondance (F) — change
quai (M) — platform
aller-retour (M) — return
guichet (M) — ticket office
bagage (M) — luggage

compliqué(e) — complicated
religieux(se) — religious
magnifique — magnificent
célèbre — famous
romain(e) — Roman
antique — ancient
provençal(e) — provençal
ancien(ne) — former, old ***(3)***
fameux(se) — excellent (food)

programmer — to plan
retourner — to return
construire — to build, to construct
bâtir — to build
attirer — to attract
décorer — to decorate
entourer — to surround
visiter — to visit
devenir — to become
posséder — to possess
recevoir — to receive
installer — to install
admirer — to admire
terminer — to finish

---

composter — to punch a ticket ***(4)***
rater (le train) — to miss (a train)
avoir de la chance — to be lucky
ne pas avoir de chance — to be unlucky
avoir peur — to be afraid

HOW TO SAY IT

1. GIVING INSTRUCTIONS

Il faut prendre le train jusqu'à Nantes — You have to take the train to Nantes
Il faut que vous changiez à Rennes — You have to change at Rennes
Il suffit que vous retourniez à Tours — All you have to do is go back to Tours
A Bordeaux, vous prendrez le train de nuit — At Bordeaux, you take the night train

2. EXPRESSING OBLIGATION

Il faut que j'aille ensuite en Provence — After that I must go to Provence
Je dois aller à Bordeaux — I have to go to Bordeaux
Je suis obligé de rester à Tours — I have to stay in Tours

3. DESCRIBING A PLACE

Arles possède deux superbes antiquités — Arles has got two superb relics of ancient art
On y trouve deux chefs-d'œuvre de l'art roman — There are two masterpieces of Romanesque art there

4. EXPRESSING FEARS

J'ai peur que ce ne soit pas possible — I'm afraid that won't be possible
Je crains que ce soit impossible — I'm afraid that's impossible
J'ai peur d'être en retard — I'm afraid of being late

5. EXPRESSING SURPRISE

Ah oui ! / *Ah bon !* / *Comment !* — Oh !, Well !, What !
Ça alors ! / *Ça m'étonne !* — I'm amazed !
C'est incroyable ! — That's unbelievable

REMEMBER... REMEMBER... REMEMBER... REMEMBER... REMEMBER

***(1)** « Place » can mean seat, square or room. — **(2)** « Hôtel » in French does not only mean hotel in the English sense. It can also mean a privately owned mansion or a public building (such as l'hôtel de ville — the town hall). — **(3)** « Ancien » can mean both former and very old, depending on whether it is before or after the noun. Consequently « l'ancien président », means the former president, where as « des maisons anciennes » can be translated as very old houses. When referring to Ancient Greece or Rome, the correct expressions are « la Grèce antique » and « la Rome antique ». — **(4)** « Composter » : it's compulsary to do so ; if you forget to, you're liable to pay a fine.*

4.5 ORAL PRACTICE

1. GRAMMAR : SEE PAGE 48

VERB PRACTICE : THE SUBJUNCTIVE (REGULAR VERBS)

Listen :

(M. et Mme Thomas, vous achetez un billet ?)
— Oui, il faut que nous achetions un billet.

NOW, ANSWER THESE QUESTIONS IN THE AFFIRMATIVE, STARTING WITH « IL FAUT QUE », REMEMBERING TO USE THE SUBJUNCTIVE

(M. et Mme Thomas, vous achetez un billet ?) — (Je change à Rennes ?) — (Elle réserve pour ce train ?) — (Les Durand remontent jusqu'à Dijon ?) — (Je visite la Bourgogne ?) — (Hubert et Bernard, vous téléphonez pour réserver ?)

2. GRAMMAR : SEE PAGE 48

VERB PRACTICE : THE SUBJUNCTIVE (IRREGULAR VERBS)

Listen :

(Je dois aller en Provence)
— Il faut que j'aille en Provence.

NOW, TRANSFORM THE FOLLOWING SENTENCES REPLACING « DEVOIR » WITH « IL FAUT »

(Je dois aller en Provence) — (Il doit être à Dijon à six heures) — (Vous devez faire le voyage de nuit) — (Nous devons prendre la correspondance) — (Vous devez être à Bordeaux demain) — (Tu dois aller prendre les billets)

3. GRAMMAR : SEE PAGE 42

PRONOUN PRACTICE : OBJECT PRONOUNS

Listen :

(Vous me faites mon billet jusqu'à Tours ?)
— Oui, je vous le fais jusqu'à Tours.
(Il lui réserve la couchette ?)
— Oui, il la lui réserve.

NOW, ANSWER THESE QUESTIONS IN THE AFFIRMATIVE, SUBSTITUTING A PRONOUN FOR THE DIRECT OBJECT

(Vous me faites mon billet jusqu'à Tours ?) — (Il lui réserve la couchette ?) — (L'employé leur donne les renseignements ?) — (Vous nous préparez les réservations ?) — (Messieurs, il vous indique le numéro du train ?) — (Vous lui prenez sa place ?)

4. GRAMMAR : SEE PAGE 48

VERB PRACTICE : « VENIR DE » + INFINITIVE TO HAVE JUST DONE SOMETHING

Listen :

(Tu as pris les billets ?)
— Oui, je viens de prendre les billets.

NOW, ANSWER THE FOLLOWING QUESTIONS IN TH AFFIRMATIVE USING « VENIR DE »

(Tu as pris les billets ?) — (M. et Mme Vergely, vou avez réservé les places ?) — (Il a acheté le supplé ment ?) — (Ils ont fait les billets ?) — (Elle a téléphon à l'hôtel ?) — (Ils ont trouvé les réservations ?) – (Vous avez lu la brochure ?)

5. GRAMMAR : SEE PAGE 48

THE PASSIVE VOICE : THE PRESENT TENSE

Listen :

(Du VIIIe au XVIe, on bâtit des édifices)
— Des édifices sont bâtis du VIIIe au XVIe.

NOW, PUT THESE SENTENCES IN THE PASSIVE VOICE USING THE APPROPRIATE FORM OF THE VERB « ÊTRE »

(Du VIIIe au XVIe, on bâtit des édifices) — (Au 12e, on continue l'abbaye) — (On construit le théâtre au 1e siècle) — (On décore le château en 1520) — (On organise des fêtes en septembre) — (On commence les arènes en 46) — (On appelle cette région le « Jardin de la France »)

6. GRAMMAR : SEE PAGE 42

PRONOUN PRACTICE : « Y »

Listen :

(On trouve de belles antiquités à Arles ?)
— Oui, on y trouve de belles antiquités.

NOW, ANSWER THESE QUESTIONS IN THE AFFIRMATIVE USING THE PRONOUN « Y »

(On trouve de belles antiquités à Arles ?) — (Van Gogh a habité deux ans dans cette maison ?) — (On visite de beaux châteaux dans le Val de Loire ?) — (On a construit une abbaye sur le Mont-Saint-Michel ?) — (Il va souvent à Deauville ?) — (Elle est passée à Chenonceaux ?).

SHORT TRIPS OUT OF PARIS

If you're tired of Paris, you may not be tired of living — you may simply be hungering for some country or sea air. Even if you don't have much time and can't go off on an extended tour of France, you will be amazed by the varied countryside and the historical riches which are located only a short distance from Paris. And this is not exaggerated travelogue prose : France is known for its varied landscape — a boon to the harried visitor whose time is limited.

HALF-DAY AND DAY TRIPS If you haven't seen Chartres or Versailles, then brave the crowds and go. The simplicity and austerity of Chartres, its spire rising for miles out of the golden wheat fields, is an architectural joy and an essential complement to Paris's flamboyant Notre-Dame. The palace of Versailles and its rigorous gardens, ponds and fountains are of unequalled magnificence in France.

Besides Chartres and Versailles, Paris's immediate surroundings have much to offer : the palace of Vaux-le-Vicomte (on which many of the artists and craftsmen who built Versailles worked) ; the forest and palace of Fontainebleau, with the nearby artists' village of Barbizon ; Claude Monet's house and atelier at Giverny (where he painted his famous water lilies) ; Chantilly with its palace and forest (and cream) ; and La Malmaison, the residence of Napoleon and Josephine.

TWO- AND THREE-DAY TRIPS

If you have two or three days, the choices before you are vast. Are you in the mood for sea air and an incredible site ? Head for Brittany and the Mont Saint-Michel.

The best way to have the abbey (almost) to yourself is to sleep right on the Mont Saint-Michel . . . in a sleeping-bag, as there are very few rooms for rent ! Get up early and admire the site, with the sun rising over the horizon. During the busy spring and summer season, remember to book in advance in all of Brittany, as hotels fill rapidly.

A visit to the châteaux of the Loire is another trip you won't regret. Don't miss Chenonceaux, built right over the River Cher, and the animal park at Chambord. In the late spring and early summer, the countryside is at its best. Its rolling hills and peaceful flowered towns and villages have given the Loire Valley the apt name of the "Garden of France". As so many regions of France, the Loire Valley is known for its excellent foods and wines, so in between cultural visits, treat yourself to a delicious meal in a friendly country inn (where prices are generally lower and people friendlier than in busy Paris) or visit a wine cellar for some heady wine-tasting (driving is not recommended afterwards).

For more gastronomic and architectural pleasures visit Burgundy. Here, besides more wine-tasting in countless cellars, and meals, each more wonderful than the last, you can visit some of France's most beautiful romanesque architecture. Burgundy remains one of my favourite regions in France : the expressive sculptures of the cathedral at Autun, the well-preserved beauty of the Hospices de Beaune, the graceful whiteness of Vezelay, the rich greenery of the National Park of the Morvan all vie for the visitor's attention — followed by the cheering effects of a wonderful Burgundy wine.

Unless you have very little time, do try to squeeze in at least one trip outside Paris (or any other big city). Even if chlorophyll usually makes you choke, you'll have to admit that the French countryside is worth le déplacement (the journey).

4.5 TAKE A BREAK

Listen **_Un homme et une femme_**

Nicole Croisille et Pierre Barouh (Barouh-Lai)

Comme nos voix
Chantent tout bas
Nos cœurs y voient
Comme une chance, comme un espoir
Comme nos voix, nos cœurs y croient
Encore une fois, tout recommence
La vie repart
Combien de joies, bien des drames
Et voilà c'est une longue histoire
Un homme, une femme
Ont forgé la trame du hasard
Comme nos voix, nos cœurs y voient
Encore une fois, comme une chance
Comme un espoir
Comme nos voix, nos cœurs en joie
Ont fait le choix
D'une romance qui passait là
Chance qui passe là
Chance pour toi et moi
Toi et moi...

A Man and a Woman

As our voices
Are singing low
Our hearts can see
A glimmer on the horizon,
A ray of hope
Like our voices, our hearts believe
Once more, that it's all beginning again
Life is starting anew
So many joys, so much pain
It's a long story
A man, a woman
Have woven the cloth of chance
Like our voices, our hearts can see
Once more, a glimmer on the horizon
A ray of hope
Like our voices, our joyful hearts
Have chosen
A romance, that wandered by
A second chance
A ray of hope
For you and me
You and me . . .

STREET TALK · STRAIGHT TALK
ALORS, TA NOUVELLE BARAQUE?
VACHEMENT BIEN, MON VIEUX. Y'A PAS UN CHAT AUTOUR. JE SUIS PEINARD.
TU PEUX PAS SAVOIR!
TU TE RASES PAS?
TU RIGOLES! J'AI TOUT LE TEMPS DES COPAINS QUI VIENNENT SE METTRE AU VERT. C'EST LA BELLE VIE!
TU DÉBARQUES. Y A PLEIN DE PIEUS. ON VAS ÉCRASER UN MAX!
ET VOTRE NOUVELLE MAISON?
TRÈS BIEN, MON CHER. IL N'Y A PERSONNE AUX ALENTOURS. JE SUIS TRANQUILLE.
VOUS NE VOUS ENNUYEZ PAS?
MAIS NON J'AI DES AMIS QUI VIENNENT SE REPOSER. C'EST FANTASTIQUE!
BIEN SÛR. VOUS ARRIVEZ QUAND VOUS VOULEZ.
IL Y A BEAUCOUP DE LITS. NOUS ALLONS BIEN NOUS REPOSER.

4 WRITTEN PRACTICE

4.1

COMPLETE with un, une, le, la, du, de la, de l' : *Je voudrais .... fromage ; comment est .... camembert ? — Apportez-moi .... demi — J'aime beaucoup .... bière — Donnez-mo .... plat du jour et .... carafe d'eau — Dans cette sauce il y a .... huile, et .... vinaigre et de la moutarde.*

TRANSLATE : *Qu'est-ce que vous nous proposez comme entrée ? — Cette viande n'est pas assez cuite — Ce vin est mauvais, c'est du vinaigre — Vous aimez ce fromage ? Oui, il est délicieux.*
What do you call "entremet" in English ? What do you think of this dessert ? It's very good — May I have the bill, please ? This salad is better than the chef's salad — What's in your "aperitif maison" ?

4.2

COMPLETE with un, des, de, d', la, les : *Je voudrais .... rasoir — Je ne prends pas .... aspirine parce que je n'aime pas .... médicaments — Donnez-moi .... carte postale qui est derrière vous — Il a .... timbres à 2,50 F mais il n'a pas .... timbres à 4,20 F.*

TRANSLATE : *Vous pourriez me photocopier ces documents et m'en faire quatre exemplaires ? Vous voulez des timbres ? Oui donnez-m'en dix — Voilà de l'aspirine, vous en prendrez trois fois par jour.*
I've got a headache and a stomach ache — How much do I owe you for the medicine ? — The aspirin in powdered form is much better than the tablets — I'm sorry, we don't sell lipstick.

4.3

COMPLETE with il, elle, c' : *.................. est une robe blanche et .... est en laine — .... un parfum très léger et .... n'est pas très cher — .... est vendeur et .... est un très bon vendeur — .... est vendeuse au Printemps.*

TRANSLATE : *Je cherche le rayon parfumerie — Vous auriez des vêtements en laine ? — Ce savon sent l'orange — Vous n'auriez pas quelque chose de plus élégant ?*
It's really like wool — The coat costs 1,500 F — What's your size ? I'm size 42 — This dress fits me — You should go shopping today, as the shops will be closed tomorrow— If it's too small, can I change it ?

4.4

COMPLETE with bon, bien, meilleur, mieux : *L'hôtesse parle .... anglais que moi, pourtant je parle .... — C'est une .... voiture — J'achèterai le .... ordinateur.*

TRANSLATE : *Vous ne voulez pas venir au théâtre, je vous emmène ? Oui avec plaisir — J'ai envie d'aller au cinéma, tu viens ? Je suis désolée, mais je suis prise ce soir — Si on allait chez Jean-Baptiste ? What about going to the Opera tonight, and afterwards we could have supper on the "grands Boulevards" ? Why not ? He bought a new computer, and he didn't pay much for it — She went to the exhibition yesterday.*

4.5

COMPLETE. Put the verbs in brackets in the subjunctive : *Il faut que je (avoir) .... une place dans l'avion — Il faut qu'ils (être) .... à l'heure — Il vaudrait mieux qu'elle (aller) .... à la banque maintenant — J'aimerais que vous (faire) .... mon billet tout de suite.*

TRANSLATE : *Pour Chenonceaux, ce n'est pas direct, il faut changer — Ce soir je n'ai pas de train, je suis obligé de coucher à Caen — Nous allons prendre les billets tout de suite, si c'est possible.*
We must book the couchettes now — To book on the phone, you have to call the booking office at the station — I'm out of luck : I've just missed my train — I like the Loire valley very much.

(Check your answers on page 39 of your booklet)

IMPROVE

FOOD

aguette (F) — French loaf (of bread)
arte (F) — tart, pie
onbons (M) — sweets
iscuit (M) — biscuits
hocolat (M) — chocolate
lace (F) — ice cream
omme (F) — apple
range (F) — orange
anane (F) — banana
oire (F) — pear
aise (F) — strawberry
amboise (F) — raspberry
erise (F) — cherry
nandarine (F) — mandarin, orange
êche (F) — peach
bricot (M) — apricot
aisin (M) — grape
nanas (M) — pineapple
amplemousse (M) — grapefruit
oix (F) — nut
omme de terre (F) — potato
arotte (F) — carrot
hampignon (M) — mushroom
nelon (M) — melon
itron (M) — lemon
aricot vert (M) — French bean
hou (M) — cabbage
hou-fleur (M) — cauliflower
oncombre (M) — cucumber
aitue (F) — lettuce
ndive (F) — chicory
tomate (F) — tomato
poireau (M) — leek
petits pois (M) — peas
sole (F) — sole
maquereau (M) — mackerel
saumon (M) — salmon
thon (M) — tuna
entrecôte (F) — rib steak
rôti (M) — roast
veau (M) — veal
mouton (M) — mutton
escalope (F) — escalope (usually of veal)
poulet (M) — chicken
jambon (M) — ham
œuf (M) — egg
saucisson (M) — sausage
pâté (M) — pâté

CLOTHES

vêtements (M) — clothes
manteau (M) — coat
imperméable (M) — raincoat
blouson (M) — (lumber-) jacket
veste (F) — jacket
chapeau (M) — hat
écharpe (F) — scarf
foulard (M) — silk scarf
gants (M) — gloves
jean (M) — a pair of jeans
chemise (F) — shirt
chemisier (M) — shirt-style blouse
jupe (F) — skirt
bermuda (M) — bermuda short
survêtement (M) — overalls
maillot de bain (M) — bathing costume suit
lunettes (FPL) — glasses
lunettes de soleil (FPL) — sunglasses
cardigan (M) — cardigan
tailleur (M) — woman's suit
ensemble (M) — outfit
costume (M) — a man's suit
gilet (M) — waistcoat
ceinture (F) — belt
slip (M) — underpants
soutien-gorge (M) — brassière
combinaison (F) — slip
chemise de nuit (F) — nightdress
pyjama (M) — pyjamas
chaussettes (FPL) — socks
chaussures (FPL) — shoes
bottes (FPL) — boots
sandales (FPL) — sandals
tennis (FPL) — tennis shoes
sac (M) — bag
parapluie (M) — umbrella
mouchoir (M) — handkerchief
serviette (F) — briefcase
maquillage (M) — make-up
vernis à ongles (M) — nail varnish polish
bouton (M) — button
aiguille (F) — needle
fil (M) — thread
ciseaux (MPL) — scissors

4. TEST YOURSELF

1. FILL IN THE BLANKS WITH « LE, LA, LES, DU, DE LA, DE L', DES, DE, D' »

Le matin au petit,déjeuner je bois .... thé parce que je n'aime pas .... caf
Vous désirez ? Je voudrais .... eau, s'il vous plaît.
Excusez-moi, je n'ai plus .... parfum mais .... eau de toilette.
Donnez-moi .... allumettes, s'il vous plaît.
Je déteste .... laine, je préfère .... soie.
Est-ce que vous avez .... crème à raser ?
J'adore .... chaussettes en coton.
Il voudrait dix timbres à 2,20 F et un paquet .... enveloppes.
Voilà .... timbres, mais je n'ai plus .... allumettes.

2. FILL IN THE BLANKS WITH « ÊTRE » OR « AVOIR » :

J'................. déjeuné à midi et demi.
Hier soir nous .... sortis avec nos amis ; nous .... allés au Moulin Roug
Elle .... pris le train à la gare Montparnasse.
Est-ce que vous .... commandé les cafés ?
Vous .... arrivés en retard à cause de la pluie.
Tu n' .... jamais visité les châteaux de la Loire ?
Je .... venu vous voir ce matin, mais tu étais sorti.
Ce roi .... mort en 1715 et il .... habité Versailles.
Elle n' .... jamais montée en haut de la tour Eiffel.
Elles .... parties avant la fin du spectacle.

3. FILL IN THE BLANKS WITH THE APPROPRIATE WORD FROM THE LIST :

vignobles — place — consigne — célèbre — monuments — correspondance — construire — capita — châteaux — exposition — visiter — goûter.

Il faut changer à Strasbourg, mais il y a une .... sur le même quai.
Paris est la .... de la France.
Il y a une .... de peinture cubiste au Grand Palais.
Le Val de Loire est une région célèbre pour ses ....
En Bourgogne, on peut .... aux vins qui viennent des .... de la régio
Les rois de France ont fait .... beaucoup de résidences sur les bords de la Loir
Dans le sud de la France, il y a de nombreux .... gallo-romains.
Arles est une ville .... pour ses arènes.
Elle a laissé ses bagages à la .... puis elle est allée .... le théâtre antiqu
Je voudrais réserver une .... dans le TGV de 20 h 10.

4. FILL IN THE BLANKS WITH « LE, LA, L', LUI, LEUR, EN, Y »

Aude téléphone encore à Michel ? Oui, elle .... téléphone deux fois par jour : elle .... adore !
Vous connaissez Marseille ? Oui, j' .... suis déjà allé en 1985.
Il y a des langoustines, alors il va .... prendre.
Votre entrecôte, vous .... voulez saignante ?
Les comptables ? Je ne .... ai pas envoyé la facture.
Tiens, voilà un taxi, je vais .... prendre.
Elles aiment beaucoup la Provence, elles .... passent toutes leurs vacances.
Il ne boit pas de vin : il va .... goûter juste un peu.
La viande, nous .... mangeons bien cuite.

5. WRITE THE VERBS IN BRACKETS IN THE SUBJUNCTIVE FORM :

Il faut que nous **(partir)** .... *tout de suite.*
Il faut que vous **(prendre)** .... *ma voiture.*
Il vaudrait mieux qu'elle **(aller)** .... *au rayon des jouets.*
J'aimerais qu'elle **(faire)** .... *ce voyage avec moi.*
Je voudrais que nous **(réserver)** .... *les couchettes aujourd'hui.*
Il faut que vous **(visiter)** .... *les châteaux de la Loire.*
J'aimerais que vous **(pouvoir)** .... *tout voir.*
Nous voudrions qu'elle **(être)** .... *au salon tous les jours.*
Il faut que tu **(avoir)** .... *ton permis de conduire.*

6. FILL IN THE BLANKS WITH « BON, BIEN, MEILLEUR, MIEUX, LE PLUS, LA PLUS, LES PLUS »

Choisissez la voiture .... rapide.
Voici notre St-Émilion 76 : c'est notre .... Bordeaux.
Goûtez la tarte Tatin, c'est un très .... dessert.
Le lambswool c'est .... mais le cachemire c'est bien ....
Il prendra le pantalon .... cher.
Nous parlons .... espagnol.
Ces médicaments ne sont pas .... mais ce sont .... efficaces.

7. FIND THE VERB CORRESPONDING TO THE FOLLOWING NOUN :

réservation ....
fermeture ....
conseil ....
vendeuse ....
visiteur ....
jouet ....
appel ....
couchette ....
touche ....
promenade ....

(Check your answers on page 39 of your booklet)

Mr. MARTIN AND MONSIEUR DANIEL

Sonia was still laughing as we walked out of the restaurant. I liked her laugh almost as much as I liked her deep throaty voice. I decided I'd ask her to spend the afternoon with me and worry about the Martin Daniel mystery later.

« Qu'est-ce que tu fais cet après midi ? » I asked her as we stood in the busy street filled with lunch-time shoppers.

« Tu es vraiment très drôle. Tu ne penses qu'à t'amuser. Mais il faut que je travaille. D'ailleurs, je n'ai jamais compris comment tu peux te permettre de te balader toute la journée. À part tes voyages, je ne t'ai jamais vu travailler. Moi, j'ai un rendez-vous avec un client important à deux heures et demie. Il faut que je me dépêche. »

« Tu as encore dix minutes. Je t'accompagne », I said, ignoring her comments about my mysterious working habits. This Martin Daniel was quite a character. He obviously liked to have a good time and didn't have any serious money worries. I wouldn't be surprised if he was involved in some illegal line of work. His life was certainly very different from my own. I had to work hard for my living in an investment bank. The junior partners — and I was one of them — did all the work so that the big boys upstairs could take clients to lunch at the Savoy and roll back late in the afternoon, sleepy and flushed with wine.

Sonia and I walked together for a few blocks, until we reached the Tour Montparnasse. This, apparently, was where she worked. *« Bon, c'est là. »* she said. *« Au revoir. On se téléphone. »* She gave me a quick kiss and flew into the lift. I watched the numbers flash on as she went up. The lift stopped at the 23rd floor. I looked up the 23rd floor in the building directory in the lobby : *23e étage, M.A.R.C. Publicité, logos, images de marque, spécialiste du « corporate identity ».*

« Décidément, tout le monde a des soucis d'identité », I thought, and then stopped in my tracks. I was thinking in French, speaking French without trace of an accent and writing "automatically" in French. That was fine. But I had also adopted Martin Daniel's handwriting, and could no longer produce my own. I had an urgent need to get in touch with someone from my past — from Daniel Martin's life. I resolved to go back to the flat and call my secretary in London. She at least would remember who I really was.

I retraced my steps back to the flat, and let myself in. I was again struck by how familiar it looked. I couldn't recognize any individual object in the room, but the overall impression was one of *déjà vu*. I picked up the telephone directory and looked up the international code for calling London. I dialled the number and heard my secretary's familiar voice. I was never so happy to hear her.

"Hello ?" she said.

"Hello, Julia," I replied trying to sound cheerful. "How are you? How are things at the office ?"

"Who's calling, please ? Vous parlez français ?" I couldn't believe what she was saying. Had I suddenly developed a French accent in English ? Was I forgetting my own language, just as I had forgotten my own handwriting ? "Julia ! Julia ! This is Daniel calling. Daniel Martin. I'm calling from Paris. I told you yesterday I was going away on a short business trip . . . "

« Monsieur, je vous prie d'arrêter cette petite plaisanterie. Monsieur Martin m'a effectivement appelée hier pour me dire qu'il partait en voyage d'affaires, mais il n'est pas parti. Il a annulé son voyage et il se trouve, en ce moment même, dans son bureau. Sa porte est ouverte et je le vois de mon bureau. Vous voulez que je vous le passe ? »

So Julia too was part of the Martin Daniel conspiracy. *« Oui, passez-le-moi ».* I replied angrily.

A moment later a male voice said, "Hello ? Daniel Martin speaking. Who's calling, please ?"

"I'm Daniel Martin," I nearly screamed into the receiver. "Now, now, don't get excited," he said in a friendly tone. Then he lowered his voice and added, "Are you sure ? Isn't your name Martin Daniel ?" Before I could react his voice had returned to its friendly tone again, and I couldn't even be sure he had mentioned Martin Daniel. "I'm sorry, sir, but I believe you have the wrong number," he said, and hung up.

Je me suis assis sur le lit, et j'ai regardé le téléphone d'un air abruti pendant au moins dix minutes. Je crois que j'étais en état de choc. Daniel Martin avait, de toute évidence, et par des moyens mystérieux, pris mon identité — et il attendait que je prenne la sienne.

« Après tout, c'est moi qui suis le gagnant dans cette affaire. Il va se retrouver dans un bureau tous les jours ; il va travailler dur ! Le soir, il va rentrer dans un petit appartement où il ne recevra jamais d'appels de jeunes et jolies femmes. Pendant ce temps-là, je vais m'amuser à Paris ! » Rigolant comme un fou, je me suis dirigé vers la salle de bains pour prendre une douche et me préparer pour une belle soirée. Je voulais m'amuser. Je regardais dans la glace pour voir si je devais me raser. Le miroir me renvoyait uniquement une image de la salle de bains. J'ai bougé la tête de droite à gauche, et de gauche à droite, avec frénésie. Dans le miroir, il ne se passait rien.

PRACTICAL INFORMATION

The following section contains practical information for the visitor (useful addresses and telephone numbers, a map of the Paris métro and a map of France).

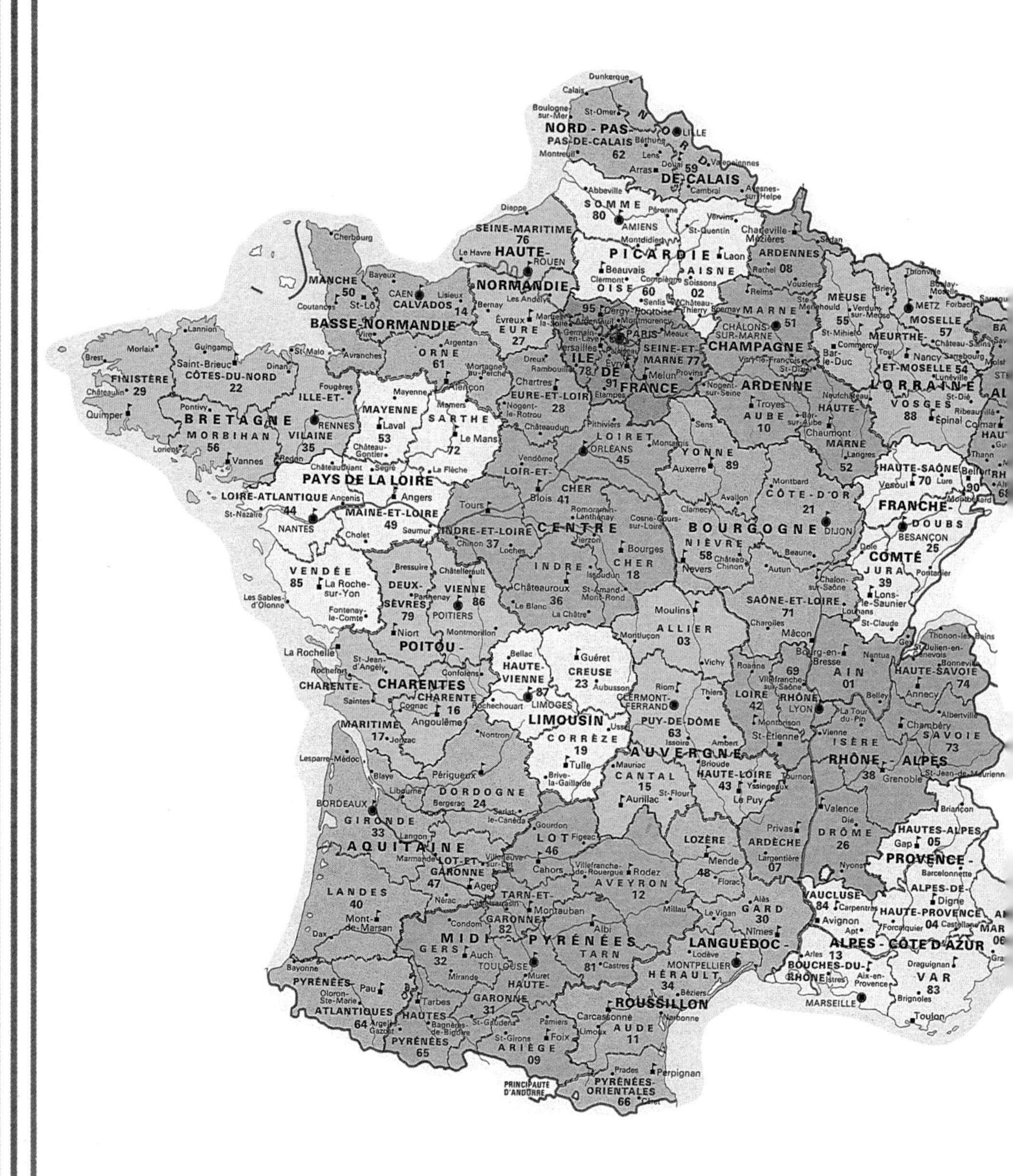
NORD - PAS-
DE-CALAIS
PAS-DE-CALAIS
62
NORD
59
LILLE
Dunkerque
Calais
Boulogne-sur-Mer
St-Omer
Arras
Douai
Lens
Valenciennes
Cambrai
Montreuil
SOMME
80
AMIENS
Abbeville
Péronne
PICARDIE
AISNE
02
Laon
St-Quentin
Soissons
OISE
60
Beauvais
Compiègne
Senlis
SEINE-MARITIME
76
HAUTE-
NORMANDIE
ROUEN
Dieppe
Le Havre
EURE
27
Évreux
Les Andelys
Bernay
MANCHE
50
St-Lô
Cherbourg
Coutances
Avranches
CALVADOS
14
CAEN
Bayeux
Lisieux
BASSE-NORMANDIE
ORNE
61
Alençon
Argentan
Vire
FINISTÈRE
29
Quimper
Brest
Morlaix
Châteaulin
CÔTES-DU-NORD
22
Saint-Brieuc
Guingamp
Lannion
Dinan
St-Malo
ILLE-ET-
VILAINE
35
RENNES
Fougères
Redon
BRETAGNE
MORBIHAN
56
Vannes
Lorient
Pontivy
MAYENNE
53
Laval
Mayenne
Château-Gontier
SARTHE
72
Le Mans
Mamers
La Flèche
PAYS DE LA LOIRE
LOIRE-ATLANTIQUE
44
NANTES
St-Nazaire
Ancenis
Châteaubriant
MAINE-ET-LOIRE
49
Angers
Saumur
Cholet
Segré
VENDÉE
85
La Roche-sur-Yon
Les Sables-d'Olonne
Fontenay-le-Comte
95
Cergy-Pontoise
78
Versailles
St-Germain-en-Laye
Rambouillet
Mantes-la-Jolie
91
Évry
Étampes
ILE
DE
FRANCE
PARIS
SEINE-ET-
MARNE 77
Melun
Meaux
Provins
EURE-ET-LOIR
28
Chartres
Dreux
Nogent-le-Rotrou
Châteaudun
LOIRET
45
ORLÉANS
Pithiviers
Montargis
LOIR-ET-
CHER
41
Blois
Vendôme
Romorantin-Lanthenay
INDRE-ET-LOIRE
37
Tours
Chinon
Loches
CENTRE
CHER
18
Bourges
Vierzon
St-Amand-Mont-Rond
INDRE
36
Châteauroux
Issoudun
Le Blanc
La Châtre
DEUX-
SÈVRES
79
Niort
Bressuire
Parthenay
VIENNE
86
POITIERS
Châtellerault
Montmorillon
POITOU -
CHARENTES
CHARENTE-
MARITIME
17
La Rochelle
Rochefort
Saintes
Jonzac
St-Jean-d'Angély
CHARENTE
16
Angoulême
Cognac
Confolens
HAUTE-
VIENNE
87
LIMOGES
Bellac
Rochechouart
CREUSE
23
Guéret
Aubusson
LIMOUSIN
CORRÈZE
19
Tulle
Ussel
Brive-la-Gaillarde
DORDOGNE
24
Périgueux
Bergerac
Sarlat-la-Canéda
Nontron
Ribérac
GIRONDE
33
BORDEAUX
Lesparre-Médoc
Blaye
Libourne
Langon
AQUITAINE
LANDES
40
Mont-de-Marsan
Dax
LOT-ET-
GARONNE
47
Agen
Marmande
Nérac
Villeneuve-sur-Lot
PYRÉNÉES-
ATLANTIQUES
64
Pau
Bayonne
Oloron-Ste-Marie
HAUTES-
PYRÉNÉES
65
Tarbes
Argelès-Gazost
Bagnères-de-Bigorre
GERS
32
Auch
Condom
Mirande
MIDI - PYRÉNÉES
TARN-ET-
GARONNE
82
Montauban
Castelsarrasin
HAUTE-
GARONNE
31
TOULOUSE
Muret
St-Gaudens
ARIÈGE
09
Foix
Pamiers
St-Girons
LOT
46
Cahors
Figeac
Gourdon
AVEYRON
12
Rodez
Villefranche-de-Rouergue
Millau
TARN
81
Albi
Castres
PRINCIPAUTÉ
D'ANDORRE
PYRÉNÉES-
ORIENTALES
66
Perpignan
Prades
Céret
AUDE
11
Carcassonne
Limoux
Narbonne
ROUSSILLON
HÉRAULT
34
MONTPELLIER
Béziers
Lodève
LANGUEDOC -
GARD
30
Nîmes
Alès
Le Vigan
LOZÈRE
48
Mende
Florac
CANTAL
15
Aurillac
Mauriac
St-Flour
AUVERGNE
PUY-DE-DÔME
63
CLERMONT-
FERRAND
Riom
Thiers
Issoire
Ambert
ALLIER
03
Moulins
Montluçon
Vichy
HAUTE-LOIRE
43
Le Puy
Yssingeaux
Brioude
LOIRE
42
St-Étienne
Roanne
Montbrison
RHÔNE
69
LYON
Villefranche-sur-Saône
ARDÈCHE
07
Privas
Largentière
DRÔME
26
Valence
Die
Nyons
ISÈRE
38
Grenoble
Vienne
La Tour-du-Pin
RHÔNE - ALPES
AIN
01
Bourg-en-Bresse
Nantua
Belley
Gex
SAVOIE
73
Chambéry
Albertville
St-Jean-de-Maurienne
HAUTE-SAVOIE
74
Annecy
Thonon-les-Bains
St-Julien-en-Genevois
Bonneville
HAUTES-ALPES
05
Gap
Briançon
ALPES-DE-
HAUTE-PROVENCE
04
Digne
Barcelonnette
Forcalquier
Castellane
PROVENCE -
ALPES - CÔTE D'AZUR
VAUCLUSE
84
Avignon
Carpentras
Apt
BOUCHES-DU-
RHÔNE
13
MARSEILLE
Arles
Aix-en-Provence
Istres
VAR
83
Toulon
Draguignan
Brignoles
YONNE
89
Auxerre
Sens
Avallon
NIÈVRE
58
Nevers
Clamecy
Cosne-Cours-sur-Loire
Château-Chinon
BOURGOGNE
CÔTE-D'OR
21
DIJON
Montbard
Beaune
SAÔNE-ET-LOIRE
71
Mâcon
Chalon-sur-Saône
Autun
Charolles
Louhans
JURA
39
Lons-le-Saunier
Dole
St-Claude
Pontarlier
FRANCHE-
COMTÉ
DOUBS
25
BESANÇON
HAUTE-SAÔNE
70
Vesoul
Lure
90
Belfort
ARDENNES
08
Charleville-Mézières
Sedan
Rethel
Vouziers
MARNE
51
CHÂLONS-SUR-MARNE
Reims
Épernay
Ste-Menehould
Vitry-le-François
CHAMPAGNE
ARDENNE
AUBE
10
Troyes
Bar-sur-Aube
Nogent-sur-Seine
HAUTE-
MARNE
52
Chaumont
Langres
St-Dizier
MEUSE
55
Bar-le-Duc
Verdun
Commercy
St-Mihiel
MOSELLE
57
METZ
Thionville
Forbach
Sarrebourg
MEURTHE-
ET-MOSELLE 54
Nancy
Toul
Lunéville
LORRAINE
VOSGES
88
Épinal
St-Dié
Neufchâteau
Colmar

LILLE
DEAUVILLE
PARIS
NANCY
STRASBOURG
MONT St MICHEL
QUIMPER
TOURS
DIJON
MOUTAR
LA ROCHELLE
VICHY
LIMOGES
LYON
GRENOBLE
BORDEAUX
AVIGNON
TOULOUSE
BAYONNE
MARSEILLE
PERPIGNAN
AJACCIO

ARRIVAL

Where to go when you first arrive ? The Paris Tourist Office, 127, av. des Champs-Elysées 8th. Tel. : 47.20.04.96 (métro Charles de Gaulle) will give you information on what's on, where to go, and what to do. Two weekly guides, Pariscope *and* Officiel des spectacles, *on sale at all news kiosks, will give you a complete listing of theatres, cinemas, restaurants, guided tours, etc.*

HOTELS

Where to stay ? The Paris Tourist Office, 127 av. des Champs-Elysées 8th, will reserve a room for you free of charge if you go in person. The following organizations will also book rooms free of charge if you call in advance :
Hotel Service. Tel. : 42.80.18.53. Paris Neotel. Tel. : 46.34.00.13. Phone Hotel. Tel. : 43.59.12.12. SOS Hotel. Tel. : 45.26.08.07.

CAFES

Which to choose ? For a thorough guide to cafes, opening hours, and specialities, get Gault-Millau's Le Guide de Paris *(in French) or* The Food Lover's Guide to Paris *by Patricia Wells (in English) available at the Paris Tourist Office. Other guides are available at W.H. Smiths and Sons, 248, rue de Rivoli 1st. Tel. : 42.60.37.97.*

Oh dear... the choice is vast! If you're really in the money try the Tour d'Argent *or* Maxim's. *For the thousands of other restaurants, ranging from the elegant to the homely, get Gault-Millau's* Guide de Paris. *If you want a quick guide to the cuisines of many countries, look in Pariscope, the weekly guide to what's on in Paris, on sale at news kiosks.*

Writers from Hemingway to Sartre ate here ara plaques with their names on their favourite Today, it's still a popular restaurant with publish located in the heart of the publishing quartier) won't see many impoverished writers here unless being taken out by their editors. A pianist pla jazz favourites in the evening. Prices expensive, exorbitant.
171 bd. de Montparnasse, Paris 14th. Tel : 43.26

One of the oldest and certainly one of th expensive restaurants in Paris, the Tour d'Argent *ably situated on the left bank, overlooking the ful and affluent île Saint-Louis. It was in th* d'Argent, *so the story goes, that Henry IV firs a fork. Now its more socially adept but equa clientele can feast on lobster poached in wild gus sauce and tender duck à la sauce béarna for 1,000 F or more per person (a cheaper fixed is available).*
15 Quai de la Tournelle, Paris 4th Tel : 43.54

For the tourist in a hurry: There are nu excursions, ranging from the Illuminations (110 F cruise along the Seine followed by a cabaret sh the Lido, Folies Bergère *or the* Moulin *(575-1,000 F) to a* Tour X *of "Forbidden Paris" (Information about all of these, and other tours, i able at the Paris Tourist Office.*
For the Culture Vulture: A detailed list of illum historical monuments can be obtained at the Info *tel. : 42.46.52.52.*
A nightly son et lumière is shown at Les In *(English version at 9.30 and 11.15 p.m. — in su only at the later time).*
For those who like to see and be seen: The "in at the moment (but fashions change quickly !) Café Costes, *in the* Place des Innocents *1st.*

THE CRAZY HORSE

What a bright idea to create a striptease with ı finesse that even the most bourgeois family man ›els respectable at the end of it. That's the for- that has kept the Crazy Horse in business for st 30 years. Fantastic lighting and stage effects the dancers at their aesthetic best... Of course, ct that they are all near-naked and perfectly pro- ned hasn't been too bad for business either. If ›ant to see for yourself, wander over to 12, av. ɜ-V, Paris 8th (tel. : 47.23.32.32.), between 8 p.m. '.30 a.m.

THE LIDO

Dinner and a show at the world's most famous ›t. You won't see many Parisians here, but, then, can you come to Paris and not see the glam- "Bluebell Girls" in their ornate feathers and sequins ategically placed to expose as much flesh as pos- ? 116 bis, av. des Champs-Elysées, Paris 8 th (tel. : .11.61).

MUSEUMS

Check the weekly Pariscope or l'Officiel des spec- for a complete list of museums in Paris and its ›ndings, with opening hours. All over France, Tues- s the usual closing day for museums, but some on Mondays instead, so if you plan carefully, you ›isit a museum every day of the week. Some ıms and art exhibitions stay open late one night ɜk (9 or 10 p.m. on Wednesdays or Thursdays).

SOPHIE SVP

A cultural and tourist information centre at the ‹ of rue Rambuteau and rue Pierre Lescot, above orum des Halles. A gold-mine of information.

RAILWAY STATIONS

Paris has six major railway stations, each one serving a specific part of the country (the Gare de Lyon for the southeast, the Gare d'Austerlitz for the south- west, the Gare Montparnasse for the northwest, etc.), so make sure you go to the right station!
Compostez votre billet : Even if you've just bought your train ticket, you still have to validate it before you get on the train. Punch it through the orange machines marked Compostez votre billet that are located near the platform.

AIRPORTS

Most French cities have only one airport, except for Paris, which has two: Orly for local flights, char- ters and some international flights and Charles-de-Gaulle for all other international flights.

METRO

There is the Formule 1, which offers a day's un- limited travel on second-class bus, metro and RER in central Paris and the suburbs. Also the Paris-Sesame ticket, which covers unlimited travel (first class) in Paris and its surroundings for two-, four- and seven-day periods. For longer stays, it's cheapest to get the monthly or weekly carte orange (the only disadvantage is that they are respectively valid from the 1st of the month or from Monday). If you opt for ordinary tick- ets, avoid buying them singly. They are much cheap- er in booklets of ten, and are on sale in all metro stations. Ordinary tickets and the carte orange may be used on buses as well as the metro. For further infor- mation, ask for the RATP brochure (available in English) at any metro station.

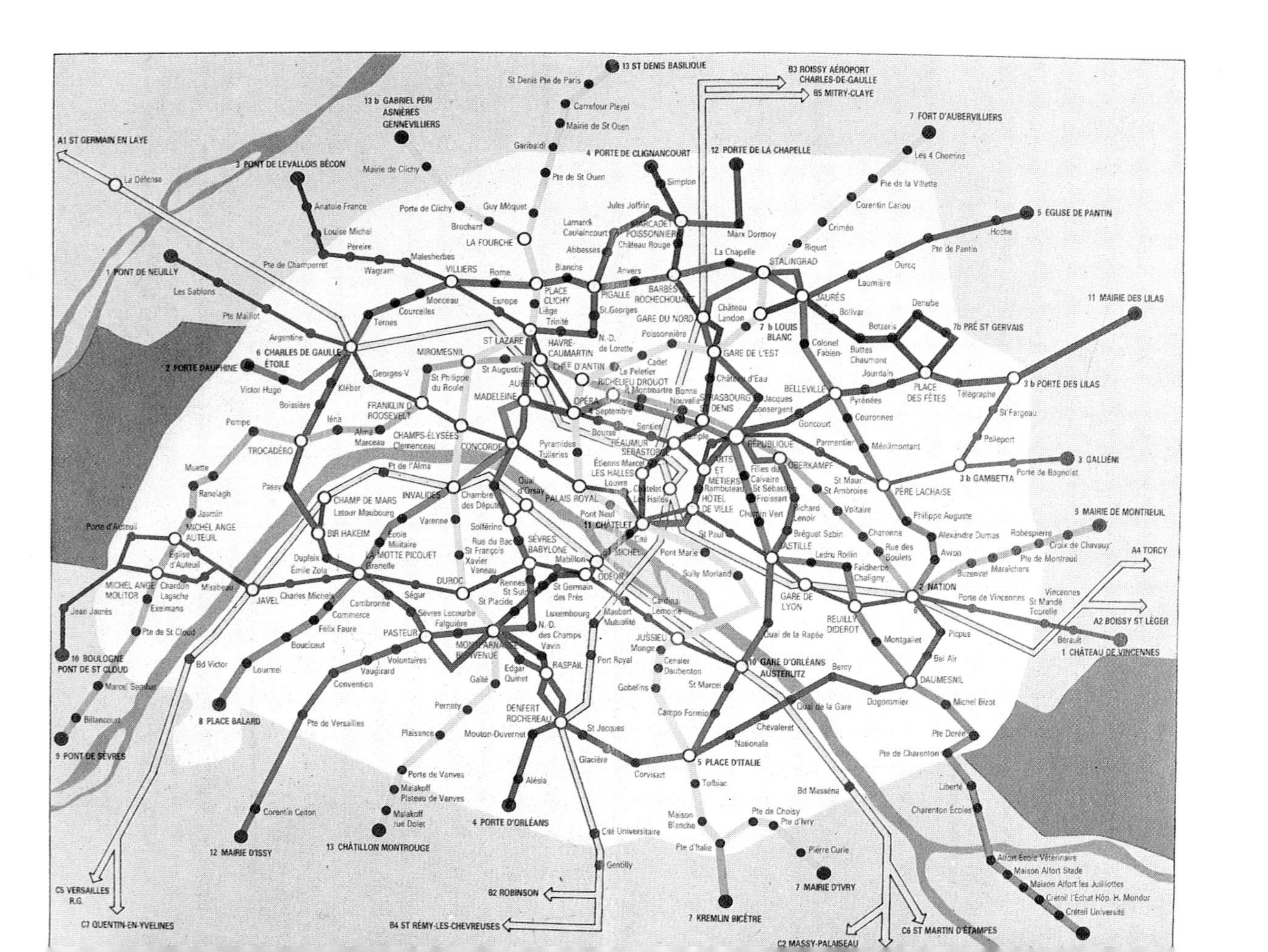

13 ST DENIS BASILIQUE
B3 ROISSY AÉROPORT CHARLES-DE-GAULLE
B5 MITRY-CLAYE
13 b GABRIEL PERI ASNIÈRES GENNEVILLIERS
7 FORT D'AUBERVILLIERS
A1 ST GERMAIN EN LAYE
3 PONT DE LEVALLOIS BÉCON
4 PORTE DE CLIGNANCOURT
12 PORTE DE LA CHAPELLE
5 EGLISE DE PANTIN
1 PONT DE NEUILLY
11 MAIRIE DES LILAS
6 CHARLES DE GAULLE ÉTOILE
2 PORTE DAUPHINE
7b PRÉ ST GERVAIS
3 b PORTE DES LILAS
3 GALLIÉNI
9 MAIRIE DE MONTREUIL
A4 TORCY
2 NATION
A2 BOISSY ST LÉGER
1 CHÂTEAU DE VINCENNES
10 BOULOGNE PONT DE ST CLOUD
8 PLACE BALARD
9 PONT DE SÈVRES
10 GARE D'ORLÉANS AUSTERLITZ
5 PLACE D'ITALIE
4 PORTE D'ORLÉANS
12 MAIRIE D'ISSY
13 CHÂTILLON MONTROUGE
7 MAIRIE D'IVRY
C5 VERSAILLES R.G.
C7 QUENTIN-EN-YVELINES
B2 ROBINSON
B4 ST RÉMY-LES-CHEVREUSES
7 KREMLIN BICÊTRE
C2 MASSY-PALAISEAU
C6 ST MARTIN D'ÉTAMPES

PRACTICAL INFORMATION

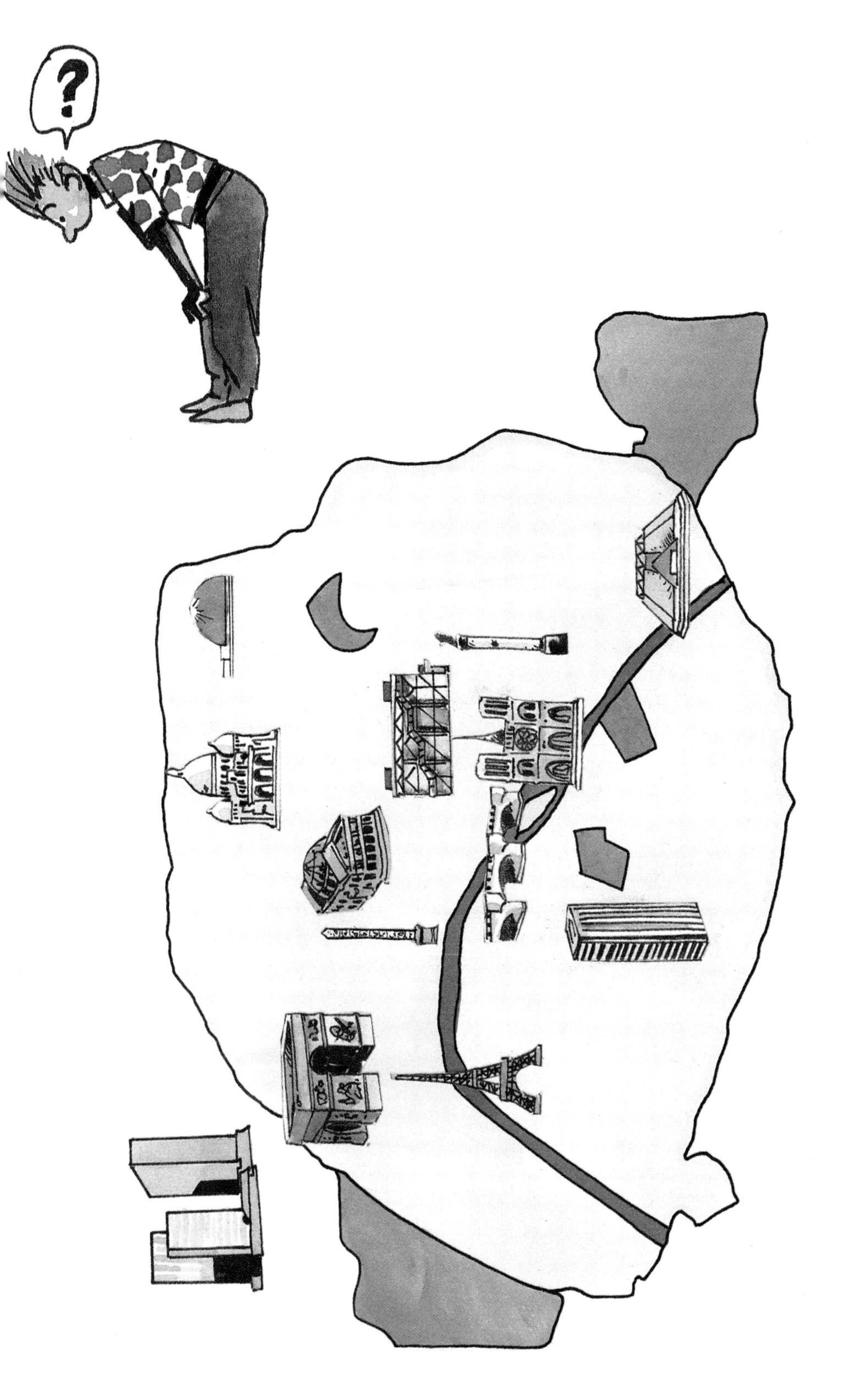

Buses are a great way to see Paris, but be careful: you have to pay two tickets for any trip covering more than two zones (check on the map inside the bus if in doubt). Remember to purchase your tickets in booklets of ten at metro stations, tickets are twice as expensive on buses. Good routes for sightseeing: the 73, which goes along the Champs-Elysées, the 72 (the banks of the Seine via Concorde and the Louvre), the 21 which crosses Paris north to south via the Opéra, the Ile de la Cité and the Boulevard St.-Michel. Get a bus map from the Paris Tourist Office, and you're on your way!

If you prefer taxis, you can chance your luck on the streets or at a taxi stand (marked station de taxi *blue and white sign) or call one at the following numbers: 47.39.33.33, 42.00.67.89, 45.83.16.05, 42.70.41.41, or look in the yellow pages phone directory. Tips are not compulsory, but it is usual to add 10-15 % to the fare. If a taxi is free the "taxi" light on top of the car is fully lit. If it isn't free, only a small light next to the "taxi" sign will be lit. For complaints, contact the* Service des Taxis de la Préfecture de Police, *36, rue des Morillons, 75015 Paris. Tel.: 45.31.14.80.*

ON THE ROAD

Car hire is easy enough at any of the known companies: Avis, Hertz, Europcar, etc. Cars with a chauffeur are available at Compagnie des Limousines *(tel. 47.89.43.08), Bernard Duran (tel.: 46.24.37.27) and Fast International (tel.: 42.25.77.15). For good, detailed road maps, get hold of the* Carte Touristique, *published by the Institut Géographique National. If driving around Paris, it's well worth investing in* Paris-Eclair, *which gives an index to all streets, one-way traffic systems, and car parks (parking can be horrific in the city centre). For information about itineraries, road conditions and traffic jams, telephone Inter Service Route: 48.58.33.33. To find out motorway tariffs, call S.V.P. Autoroute: 47.05.90.01.*

For travel within or outside France, ther of course, numerous travel agents (agents de v at your disposal. For bargain prices, try Inter Ch 9, boulevard des Capucines, 75002, tel.: 42.6 or Nouvelles Frontières, *74, rue de la Fédération, tel.: 42.73.25.25 (the latter deals in charter flig well as very out-of the ordinary group trips). F less penny-pinching, a fast, reliable service is at Wagon-lits Tourism, 142, boulevard du Montpa 75014 Paris, tel.: 43.20.07.17. For trips withir and France, contact France Tourisme, 3, rue c 75001, tel.: 42.61.85.50.*

Tours are organized (in English) by Cityrama Vision, etc. Brochures are often available in ho not, try any travel agent. Hotel bookings are h by the tour organizers for overnight trips. A m dependent (but also more expensive) way of tra is to rent a car. Here again your hotel or any travel agent can help you. The green Michelin Book offers cultural information, while the red Book lists hotels and restaurants.

Usual opening hours: 8.30 a.m. — 7.30 p. weekdays; 8.30 a.m. — 12.00 noon on Satu closed on Sundays. You can telephone long di from any post office (much cheaper than from hotel). Most post offices sell telephone cards, télé *which enable you to call anywhere in the worlc a street telephone box. You can also purchase* cartes *at some* tabacs.

BANKS

Jsual banking hours: 9.00 a.m. — 4.30 p.m., but
banks close at lunch-time and stay open till 5.30
Aost banks don't change money: so unless you're
ig bank on the Champs-Elysées, Opéra or Saint-
n districts, your chances of seeing a handed "No change" sign are high. But every bank
at least, be able to direct you to a bank that
change money.

For those who love prowling the big stores, the
ig grands magasins (open from 9.30 to 6.30 p.m.
0 p.m., with one late night), are a necessary
ition: Au Printemps, 64, bd Haussman, 75009
good for fashions, perfumes, toys, books and
s.

Galeries Lafayette, 40, bd Haussman, 75009, or
Maine-Montparnasse shopping centre : Good for
and ladies' fashions, shoes, perfume, china and
old goods.

Au Bon Marché, 38, rue de Sèvres, 75007 Paris:
for luxury foods, toys, antiques, perfume, fashions.

If you're feeling homesick after all this, there's
Marks and Spencer, at 35, bd Haussman ; no
tions necessary. Essential for those who can't sur-
vithout cottage cheese and muffins.

DRUGSTORES

Drugstores, which sell anything and everything are
av. Matignon 8th, 149 bd Saint-Germain 6th and
v. des Champs-Elysées 8th. They stock all French
any international newspapers and magazines, and
pen until 2 a.m.

GOURMET SHOPPING

Can't go home without your foie gras and petits fours ? First go to the bank, then to Fouquet's, 22 rue François-1er, 75008 Paris, or Fauchon, 26 pl. de la Madeleine, 75008 Paris. The array will make your mouth water: smoked salmon, patés, foie gras, Arabica coffee, and the best bonbons in the world. They're not cheap, but who ever said the best things in life were free ?

CHEMISTS AND MEDICAL HELP

Chemists open 24 hours a day, 365 days a year: Dhéry, Galerie Marchande, 84, av. des Champs-Elysées, 75008 Paris, tel. : 45.62.02.41. Telephone emergency services: SAMU (ambulance) : 45.67.50.50, SOS Médecins (doctors): 47.07.77.77, SOS Médecine douce (alternative medicine): 43.21.91.91, SOS dental emergencies: 43.37.51.00. Also most chemists have a list of pharmacies de garde (chemists open at special hours) posted on their doors.

TOBACCONISTS'

You'll find all sorts of things at cafés marked "tabacs", besides tobacco and cigarettes. They're usually well stocked with lighters, lottery tickets, telephone cards, télécartes, and all sorts of knick-knacks. Many stay open late.

METRIC MEASURES

Length

1 millimètre (mm) = 0.0394 in
1 centimètre (cm) = 0.3937 in
1 mètre (m) = 1.0936 yd
1 kilomètre (km) = 0.6214 mile

Area

1 sq cm (cm^2) = 0.1550 in^2
1 sq metre (m^2) = 1.1960 yd^2
1 sq km (km^2) = 0.3861 $mile^2$

Volume/capacity

1 cu cm (cm^3) = 0.0610 in^3
1 cu decimetre (dm^3) = 0.0353 ft^3
1 cu metre (m^3) = 1.3080 yd^3
1 litre (l) = 1.76 pt
= 2.113 US liq pt
= 21.998 gal
= 26.418 US gal

Mass (Weight)

1 milligram (mg) = 0.0154 grain
1 gram (g) = 0.0353 oz
1 metric carat = 3.0865 grains
1 kilogram (kg) = 2.2046 lb
1 tonne (t) = 1.1023 short ton

THE FRENCH PRESS

The French press is generally much less shy about editorializing and openly stating its political slant than the Anglo-Saxon press. Each newspaper or magazine tends to have its distinct readership among its own political family.

Some newspapers : Le Monde, Libération, Le Figaro.
Some weeklies : L'Express, Le Point, Le Nouvel Observateur.

Any news kiosk will stock all the newspapers and weeklies mentioned. Many also sell the International Herald Tribune, as well as the British Sunday papers, for those desperate to grab the latest news.

For classified ads, try Le Figaro, for general, the International Herald Tribune for English-speaking contacts and work. De particulier à particulier *(out every Thursday) for renting or buying property and* Libération *if you want to make contact with a French friend/lover/playmate.*

TV

The following films are often in English with French subtitles: FR3 Mondays at 10.30 p.m., Antenne 2 Fridays at 11.00 p.m. For a taste of a French talk show, try watching Bernard Pivot's highly popular programme on new books, Apostrophes, *every Friday at 9.30 p.m. on Antenne 2. It reputedly "makes" French best sellers, and publishers will do anything to have one of their authors on the programme.*

Radio

For the all-classical and jazz music station, tune to 97.8 FM (all over France). For the multitude of specialized music stations, just play with the FM dial. BBC4 can be heard on Long Wave 200 (northern France only). On the Cote d'Azur, Radio Coast (in English) rebroadcasts the BBC World Service on Medium Wave 104.

As all major cities, Paris has areas wh bustling business districts in the daytime, and lands at night. Here's a rapid run-down of Pari each district's main characteristics.

"Les Halles" and "Centre Beaubourg"

When the old Les Halles covered market w down, the surrounding district ceased being "th of Paris" as it had been since Zola's day to b a trendy neighbourhood of soaring property designer boutiques and art galleries.

The Pompidou Art Centre, with its contr bright blue factory-style architecture, transformed th acter of the district. In its wake came a host galleries, rapidly uprooted from the Saint-Germain bourhood. Today, the Pompidou Centre, or Bea as it is popularly known, houses an excellent r art museum, a library, a cinematheque and a of exhibition halls, which are always well att In the area where the covered market used to there is now a vast shopping centre, Le Forum *on three levels below the ground, and imme above the Les Halles metro station. The cheapest are on the lowest level, closest to the metro; shops are on the top level closest to the surface. major shops have an outlet at the Forum.*

*Although Les Halles has attracted countless food restaurants, the former "belly of Paris" is fa being a gastronomic wasteland. Many of the f restaurants from the covered market days are existence (*Le Pied de Cochon *for example) thoug clientele is much changed. The late-night cro tuxedos and mink coats no longer rubs shoulder bowls of steaming onion soup with butchers in stained white jackets. Today's clientele is alto more homogeneous...*

The Latin Quarter, "Saint-Germain", " parnasse"

Busy night life, lots of boutiques, cafés, fas and regular restaurants and cinemas. Although the Quarter is no longer the student centre that is to be, it still attracts many young people, from out of town.

The "Marais"

A beautiful area containing many palatial h now restored and converted into apartment bui A historical district worthy of a lengthy visit, e you don't have much time in Paris.

"L'île St-Louis" and "L'île de la Cité"

They say that Paris began here, on these two : in the middle of the Seine. Today, the neigh- ɔod still keeps a lot of its charm by outlawing ɔon signs and huge hoardings that disfigure much is. An expensive residential area dotted with tea restaurants and antique shops.

"Le Pont Neuf"

The Pont Neuf is the oldest and most beloved in Paris. It was built between 1578 et 1604 r years its graceful alcoves housed a ragged, lively of shops, minstrels, tooth-pullers, vendors, beg- and pickpockets. The bridge has gone through changes including being wrapped up in 40,000 metres of golden cloth by the artist Christo in but its basic construction has survived intact, the expression "se porter comme le Pont Neuf" ng to remain consistent in the face of adversity.

"Bateaux-mouches"

At the foot of the Pont Neuf are the Bateaux es, better known as the Bateaux Mouches, which ourists on multi-lingual river cruises of one hour. nds like a very clichéd thing to do, but the old gs on the Ile Saint-Louis, the shadows of the s, the ripples of the passing barges, and some most beautiful architecture in the world make ne-hour trip a worthy excursion.

Other bateaux-mouches organizations can be found "promenades" section of the weekly guide ɔpe.

The Eiffel Tower and Seventh Arrondissement

Besides being the home of the famous tower, eventh arrondissement is a quiet residential area gant apartment buildings and high rents. But it ns some excellent — and expensive — restaurants, g to the neighbourhood's discriminating residents.

"Montmartre" and "Pigalle"

Busy nightlife, some of it of the sleazy variety around Pigalle. If you walk away from the touristic Place du Tertre (that's where all the Sunday painters are) you'll discover another aspect of Montmartre : quiet, cobble-stoned streets, pleasant gardens, and even a vineyard ! If it weren't for the magnificent view of the rest of Paris, you'd think you were in a small provincial town.

"Opéra"

This is a banking and shopping area, so unless you're going to the Opera, there's not much to see here at night. At lunch-time, it's a hive of activity. All the major Paris department stores are here — including Marks and Spencer's.

From the "Champs-Élysées" to the "Louvre"

Paris in all its grandiose majesty — wide avenues, imposing façades, landscaped gardens. You'll find everything you need on the Champs-Elysées, until the small hours of the morning. Many of Paris' world famous hotels are here.

"Arc de Triomphe" and "Place de l'Etoile"

Napoleon ordered the construction of the Arc de Triomphe at the centre of twelve main avenues, in 1806, but the building was not completed until 1836. Now it is the site of the tombstone of the unknown soldier, where, every year on November 11th, hommage is paid to the millions of men who died in World War I. Visitors can go to the top of the Arc de Triomphe from 10.00 a.m. to 5.45 p.m. in summer, 4.15 p.m. in winter.

"La Défense"

A vast business and residential complex to the northwest of Paris, begun in 1964. About 30 tower blocks house more than one million square metres of office space and around 60,000 workers.

Look out for the Terrasse des Reflets, which offers a spectacular play of reflections from the green Tour Gan and the golden Tour Aurore. As much of La Défense is designated as a pedestrian zone, it's supposed to be pleasant for a nice stroll on a sunny day. How to get there: underground express train (RER) to La Défense (15 minutes from the centre of Paris) or on bus No. 173.

VOCABULARY

The glossary lists 1,500 words and idiomatic expressions used in the book. The entries are given in alphabetical order with English translations. Verbs are in the infinitive and adjectives in the masculine. For an explanation on how to form feminine adjectives, please consult the grammar section in the booklet.

VOCABULARY

abaisser — to lower
abbaye — abbey
absent — absent
accélérer — to accelerate
accepter — to accept
accident — accident
accompagner — to accompany
achat — a purchase
acheter — to buy, to purchase
acheteur — a buyer
acide — acid, bitter
à côté de — beside
acteur — actor
activité — activity
adapter — to adapt, to adjust
addition — bill, addition
à demain — see you tomorrow
à deux pas de — right next to
adjoint — assistant
admirer — to admire
adorer — to adore
adresse — address
adresser — to address
adresser (s') à — to speak to
à droite — on the right, right
aéroport — airport
affaire — a business deal, a case
afficher — to display
afficher (s') — to be displayed
affreux — awful, terrible
à gauche — on the left, left
âge — age
agence — agency, a branch
agence de presse — a press agency
agenda — appointments, diary
agir — to take action
agréable — pleasant, agreeable
agriculture — agriculture
agronome — agronomist
ah bon — you don't say
aider — to help, to assist
ailleurs — elsewhere
aimable — likeable
aimer — to like, to love
aimer mieux — to prefer, to like better
ainsi que — as well as
ajouter — to add
à la fin — in the end
à la mode — in fashion
Allemagne — Germany
Allemand — German
aller — to go, to feel (health)
aller (vêtements) — to fit, to go with, to match (clothes)
aller voir quelqu'un — to go and see someone
aller-retour — return, round-trip (ticket)
allô — Hello
allumé — lit, turned on (machine)
allumer — to light, to turn/switch on (a machine)
allumette — a match
allure — elegance
alors — so, well
ambassade — embassy
ambitieux — ambitious
ambition — ambition
Américain — American
ami — friend
amicalement — cordially
amitié — friendship
à mon avis — in my opinion
amusant — entertaining, amusing
an — year
ancien — old, former
Anglais — English
Angleterre — England
animer — to lead (a group)
année — year
annonce — advertisement
annuaire téléphonique — telephone directory
annuler — to cancel
à nouveau — again
antipathique — unpleasant, disagreeable
antique — ancient
août — August
à part — apart (from)
à partir de — from (date, location)
à peine — hardly, scarcely, barely
apéritif — drink before a meal
à peu près — around, about
à pied — on foot
à point — medium (steak, chops)
appareil — device, machine
appartement — apartment, flat
appartenir — to belong
appeler — to call
appeler(s') — to be called (name)
approcher(s') — to approach
appuyer — to press
après — after, afterwards
après-demain — the day after tomorrow
après-midi — afternoon
à propos — in regard to
à proximité de — near
argent — money, silver
argenté — silver-coloured, silver-plated
arme — a weapon
armoire — a wardrobe
arrêt — stop
arrêter(s') — to stop
arrivée — arrival
arriver — to arrive
arrondissement — a distric
arroser — to water
art — art
artiste — artist, performer
ascenseur — lift, elevator
aspirine — aspirin
asseoir(s') — to sit down
assez — enough
assis — seated
assistant — assistant
association — association
assurance — insurance, assu
attaché — attache, assistant
attaché de presse — press
attendre — to wait (for)
attention — be careful (impe
atterrir — to land
attirer — to attract
attraction — act (show)
au bord de — on the edge
au bout de — at the end
au bout du fil — on th (colloquial)
au cœur de — in the hear
au coin de — on the corne
au début — at first, at the b
au-dessous — under, below
au-dessus — above, over
au fait — by the way
au fond de — at the botto
au même moment — at t time
au milieu de — in the mi
au revoir — goodbye
audiovisuel — audiovisual
aujourd'hui — today
aussi — also, too
automatique — automatic
automne — autumn
automobiliste — driver (car
autorail — autorail
autorisé — authorized
autoroute — motorway
autre — other
autre chose — something e thing else
avancer — to go forward,
avant — before
avant-hier — the day before
avec — with
avec plaisir — with pleasur
avenue — avenue
avion — airplane, aeroplane
avoir — to have
avoir besoin de — to nee
avoir de la chance — to

de l'allure — to be striking,

du charme — to be charming
du feu — to have a light
du mal à — to have difficulty
g something
du succès — to be successful
envie de — to feel like
horreur de — to hate
l'air — to seem
le temps — to have time
l'heure — to have the time
l'intention de — to intend
mal à — to have an ache/pain
peur — to be afraid
raison — to be right
tort — to be wrong
e place — in your position
e service — at your service
— *April*

B

auréat — baccalauréat ('A' high school diploma)
e — luggage
tte — long French loaf
er (se) — to go swimming
oire — bath-tub
r — to lower
er (se) — to go for a stroll
— ballet
ue — suburb
e — bank
- bar, counter
- bottom, stockings
ı — boat
-mouche — ferry (on the Seine)
— to build
— beautiful, good-looking
oup — many, much, a lot
— beige
— Belgian
ue — Belgium
— stupid, an animal
e — butter
thèque — library
ette — bicycle
— well, good
sûr — of course
— good, fine
enue — welcome
— beer
ue — bilingual
— ticket

blanc — white
bleu — blue
blond — blond
bœuf — beef
boire — drink
bois — wood
boisson — to drink
boîte — box
boîte de nuit — night-club
bon — good
bon après-midi — have a good afternoon
bonjour — hello
bonne journée — have a nice day
bonne nuit — good night, sleep well
bonne soirée — have a nice evening
bonsoir — good evening, good night
bouchon — cork
bouillabaisse — fish soup
boulangerie — bakery
boulevard — boulevard
bouteille — bottle
boutique — shop
bouton — button
briquet — lighter
brochure — brochure
brosse à dents — toothbrush
brouillard — fog
bruit — noise
brume — haze, mist
brumeux — hazy, misty
brun — brown, dark
bruyant — noisy
bureau — office, desk
bureau de tabac — tobacconist's
bureau de poste — post office
bus — bus

cabaret — cabaret
cabine téléphonique — phone box
cachemire — cashmere
cachet — pill
cadeau — gift
cadre — medium or high-level employee
ça fait — that comes to (price)
café — coffee, coffee-shop
café crème — coffee with milk
caisse — cash-desk
calculatrice — pocket calculator
calendrier — calendar
calme — calm
campagne — countryside, campaign
Canada — Canada
Canadien — Canadian
canard — duck
candidat — candidate, applicant
candidature — application, candidacy
capable — able, capable
capitale — capital city
car — coach
carafe d'eau — jug of water
carnet de chèques — cheque book
carnet de timbres — booklet of stamps
carré — square
carrefour — cross-roads, intersection
carte — card, map
carte bleue — credit card (visa)
carte de crédit — credit card
carte d'identité — identity card
carte grise — registration papers (car)
carte postale — postcard
ça tombe bien — that's come just at the right time
ça va — that's fine, I'm fine
ceinture de sécurité — seat-belt
célèbre — famous
célibataire — single
ce n'est pas la peine — it's not worth the trouble
centime — centime (1/100 of a Franc)
centimètre — centimetre
centre — centre
c'est exact — that's correct
chaise — chair
chambre — bedroom
chambre double — double bedroom
chambre individuelle — single bedroom
changement — change
changer — to change, to exchange
chanter — to sing
chargé de mission — project manager
chariot — trolley
charmant — charming
charme — charm
châtain — someone with light brown hair
château — castle, chateau
chaud — hot
chèque — cheque, check
chéquier — cheque(check)-book
cher — expensive, dear
chercher — to look for
cheval — horse
cheveux — hair
chez — at someone's home
chiffre — figure (number)
choisir — to choose
chômage — unemployment
chose — thing

chrome — chrome
ci-joint — enclosed
ciel — sky
cigarette — cigarette
cinéma — cinema, movies
cinquième — fifth
circulation — traffic
citron — lemon
classe — class, classroom
classe préparatoire — preparatory course
classique — classical, traditionnal
clavier — keyboard
clé — key
clé de contact — ignition key
client — customer, client
climatisé — air conditioned
coffre — locker, metal box
collaborateur — colleague, fellow worker
collant — tights, panty-hose
collègue — colleague
combien — how much
combiné — number code
commander — to order, to command
comme — as, like
commencer — to start, begin
comment — how, pardon
commerce — trade, business, commerce
commercial — sales, commercial
communication — telephone call
complet — full (hotel)
compliqué — complicated
composer — to dial
composer (se) — to be made up of
composter — to punch (a ticket)
comprendre — to understand, to include (a price)
compris — included (service)
comptable — accountant
compter — to count
concentré — concentrated
concert — concert
conducteur — driver
conduire — to drive
conférence — a conference, a lecture
confier — to entrust (someone with)
confirmer — to confirm
confort — comfort
confortable — comfortable
congélateur — deep freezer
congrès — congress, convention
connaître — to know, to be acquainted with
conseiller — to advise
conserver — to keep
consigne — instruction, left-luggage
consommation — a drink
construire — to build, construct
consulat — consulate
consulter — to consult
contact — contact
contigu — adjacent
continuer — to continue
contrôle — to control
convenir — to suit
convoquer — to give an appointment to, to summon
coopérant — someone doing non-military national service
coquille Saint-Jacques — scallop
corps — body, a group of people
correctement — properly, correctly
correspondance (courrier) — correspondence (mail)
correspondance (train) — connecting line (in a metro or train station)
correspondant — correspondent
coucher (se) — to go to bed
couchette — berth (train)
couleur — colour
couloir — corridor
coupe de champagne — a glass of champagne
couper le contact — to switch
couramment — fluently
courant — fluent
courrier — post, mail
course — errand, race
court — short
couteau — knife
coûter — to cost
couvert — covered, cutlery
cravate — tie
crayon — pencil
créer — to create
crème — cream
crème à raser — shaving cream
croire — to believe
croque-monsieur — toasted ham and cheese sandwich
cru — raw
cuir — leather
cuisine — kitchen, cuisine
cuisinière — cook, cooker
cuit — cooked
curriculum vitae — curriculum vitae
cylindrique — cylindrical

d'abord — first
d'ailleurs — furthermore
dame — lady
dans — in
danser — to dance
danseur — dancer
date — date (calendar)
debout — standing
début — beginning
décalage — gap (time)
décembre — December
décorer — to decorate
découvrir — to discover
décrocher — to pick up (the t receiver)
dégivrage — defrost (a wind
déjà — already, yet
déjeuner — lunch, to have l
délicieux — delicious
demain — tomorrow
demande d'emploi — job ap
demander — to ask
démarrer — to start (car)
demi — half
demi (de bière) — a beer pint)
demi-pension — half board
dent — tooth
départ — departure
département — department
dépêcher (se) — to hurry
déplacement — trip, journey
dépliant — brochure
depuis — since, for
derrière — behind
désagréable — unpleasant, disa
descendre — to go down, to (a train, a bus)
désirer — to want, desire
désolé — very sorry
dessert — dessert
destination — destination
de temps en temps — from time, now and then
détester — to hate, detest
de toute façon — in an anyway
deux — two
deuxième — second
devant — in front of
développement — developm
devenir — to become
deviner — to guess
devoir — must, to have to
devoir à — to owe
diapositive — slide
différent — different
difficile — difficult
digérer — to digest
digestion — digestion
digital — digital
dimanche — Sunday

sion — dimension, measurement
— to dine, to have dinner
spectacle — dinner with show
ne — diploma, degree
né — graduate of
– to say, to tell
u revoir — to say goodbye
onjour — to say hello
— direct
ment — directly
ur — director, manager
ur du personnel — person-
nager
on — management, direction
ion générale — senior
ment
r — to manage
hèque — discotheque
er — to talk, to discuss
ible — available
ition — disposal
— record
uteur — distributor
e — divorce
ne — tenth
ent — document, paper
entation — documentation, prin-
ormation
r — to give
r sur — to look on to
— golden
r — to sleep
- back
— double
e — shower
— sweet, soft, mild
— flirtation
er — to flirt
— funny
— to last, to take (time)
nique — dynamic

E

- water
e cologne — eau de cologne
e toilette — toilet water
minérale — mineral water
ger — to exchange
— school
mique — economic, economical
r — to listen to
— screen
digital — digital display
— to write

effectivement — Quite! Indeed!
efficace — efficient, effective
efficacité — efficiency, effectiveness
église — church
électrique — electric
électronicien — electronics technician
élégant — elegant
élément — element
embarquement — boarding
embouteillage — traffic jam
embrasser — to kiss
emmener — to take (a person)
empêcher — to prevent
emploi — job
employé — employee, clerk
en bordure de — on the outskirts of
en cas de — in case of
en ce moment — at the moment
endormi — sleepy
en effet — Quite! you are right!
en face — opposite
enfant — child
enfin — at last
en fin de — at the end of
en fin de compte — when all is said and done
engager — to employ
en haut de — at the top of, on top of
en même temps — in the meantime
énorme — enormous
en panne — out of order
en plein — right in the middle
en plus — furthermore, as well
ensemble — together
ensoleillé — sunny
ensuite — next, then
entendu — certainly, agreed
entièrement — completely
entourer — to surround
entrée — entrance, entrance hall, first course (of a meal)
entreprise — business, company, firm
entrer — to enter, to come in
entrer en mémoire — to put into (a computer's memory)
entretien — maintenance
en vente — on sale
enveloppe — envelope
environ — about, approximately
envoyer — to send
épeler — to spell
épinard — spinach
équipe — team
équipement — equipment
Espagne — Spain
Espagnol — Spanish
espérer — to hope
essayer — to try, to try on

essence — petrol
essence ordinaire — standard grade petrol, gas
essence super — super grade petrol
essuie-glace — windscreen wiper
est — east
estomac — stomach
étagère — shelf
États-Unis — United States
étage — floor, storey
été — summer
éteindre — to extinguish, to turn out, to put out
et puis — and then
étranger — foreign
être — to be
être à l'heure — to be on time
être autorisé — to be authorised, to be allowed
être défendu — to be forbidden
être du quartier — to live in the area
être en avance — to be early
être en communication — to be on the line (telephone)
être en dérangement — to be out of order
être en ligne — to be on the phone
être en panne — to be out of order
être en retard — to be late
être en réunion — to be at a meeting
être en vacances — to be on holiday, vacation
être libre — to be free
être perdu — to be lost
être permis — to be allowed, permitted
être pressé — to be in a hurry
être pris — to be busy
être situé — to be situated
étroit — narrow, tight
étude — study
Européen — European
évident — obvious
exact — exact, right
exactement — exactly
excellent — excellent
exceptionnel — exceptional
exemplaire — copy
expérience — experience, experiment
expliquer — explain
export — export
exposant — exhibitor
exposé — presentation
exposer — to exhibit
exposition — exhibition
extérieur — outside, external
extra-professionnel — non-professional (activities)

fabriquer — to produce, manufacture
facilement — easily
facture — bill, invoice
facturer — to invoice, to charge
faire — to do, to make
faire de la natation — to go swimming
faire de la planche à voile — to go wind surfing
faire de la voile — to go sailing
faire demi-tour — to go back the way you came
faire des courses — to do the shopping
faire du... (taille) — to be size...
faire du bateau — to go boating
faire du cheval — to go horse-riding
faire du ski — to go skiing
faire du sport — to do sport
faire erreur — to make a mistake
faire la connaissance de — to meet
faire l'appoint — to give the exact amount
faire le plein (d'essence) — to fill up (with petrol, gas)
faire marche arrière — to reverse, to back up
faire un numéro de téléphone — to dial a number
faire un paquet-cadeau — to gift wrap
falloir — to be necessary
fameux — excellent, very good
famille — family
fauteuil — armchair
femme — woman, wife
fenêtre — *window*
fermer — to close
fermeture — closing, closing time
feu — fire, a light (cigarettes)
février — February
fiche — slip of paper, index card
filet — net
filiale — branch, subsidiary
fille — daughter, girl
fils — son
filtre — filter
fin — end
finalement — finally
financier — financier
finir — to finish
foire — trade fair
fois — time
fonction — duties, job
fonctionner — to be in working order
forêt — forest, woods
formation — training
formulaire — form
fort — strong
fou — mad, insane
foule — crowd
fragile — fragile
frais — cool, fresh
framboise — raspberry
Français — French
France — France
frein — brake
freiner — to brake
frère — brother
frite — chip
froid — cold
fromage — cheese
fruit — fruit
fumer — to smoke
fumeur — a smoker, smoking compartment
futur — future

garçon — boy, waiter
garder — to keep, to look after
gâteau — cake
gentil — kind
glace — ice, ice cream
gomme — eraser
gothique — Gothic
goûter — to taste
grand — big
Grande-Bretagne — Great Britain
grand magasin — department store
gratuit — free
gris — grey
gros — big, fat
guichet — ticket office
gymnastique — gymnastic

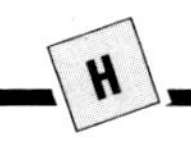

habillé — smart (clothes), dressed up
habiter — to live
hall — foyer, lobby, corridor
haut — high
hébergement — accommodation
heure — hour
heureux — happy
hier — yesterday
hiver — winter
homme — man
horodateur — parking ticket
hôtel — hotel, mansion
hôtesse — hostess
huile — oil
huitième — eighth
huître — oyster
humide — wet

ici — here
idéal — ideal
idée — idea
identité — identity
il fait beau — it is fine
il fait chaud — it is hot
il fait froid — it is cold
il fait jour — it is daylight
il fait nuit — it is dark
il paraît que — it seems th
il vaut mieux que — it w better to
il y a — there is, ago
il y a du vent — it is win
immédiat — immediate
immeuble — apartment, buil
important — important
imposer — to impose, prescr
imposer (s') — to assert on
impossible — impossible
impressionner — to make an sion on
inauguration — inauguration
incendie — fire
inclus — included, including
indicatif — dialling code, are
indiquer — to point to
industrie — industry
information — data processo
informatique — computing, c technology
ingénieur — engineer
insérer — to insert
instable — unstable
installer — to install
instant — moment
intelligent — intelligent
intéressant — interesting
intéresser(s') — to be intere
international — international
interrupteur — switch
intervenant — lecturer, spea

uire — to insert, to put in
le — durable
— to invite
— Italy
— Italian
ire — itinerary, route

J

r — January
— Japan
ais — Japanese
— garden
— yellow
— to throw
— Thursday
— young
femme — young woman
fille — young girl
gens — youth
homme — young man
is prie — please
- pretty
— to play
à — to play (sports)
de — to play (musical
ents)
— toy
— day
érie — holiday
l — newspaper
ée — day
— judge
— July
— June
e fruit — fruit juice
'à — until
— correct, accurate

K

— kilo
ètre — kilometre

L

there
— over there
atoire — laboratory
- lake
— ugly

laine — wool
laisser — to let, to allow, to leave
lait — milk
lame de rasoir — razor blade
langoustine — scampi
langue — tongue, language
langue étrangère — foreign language
large — wide
laver (se) — to wash
lent — slow
le plus — the most (superlatives)
léger — light
légume — vegetable
lettre — letter
lever (se) — to get up
levier — lever
librairie — bookshop
libre — free
lieu — place
ligne — line
lire — to read
lisible — legible
lit — bed
litre — litre
location — rental
loin de — far from
long — long, slow
longer — to walk along
louer — to rent, to hire
loup de mer — sea bass
lourd — heavy
lumière — light
lundi — Monday
lunettes — glasses, spectacles
luxueux — luxurious
lycée — high school

machine à écrire — typewriter
madame — Mrs., Madam
mademoiselle — Miss
magasin — shop
magazine — magazine
magique — magic
magnétophone — tape recorder
magnétoscope — video-cassette recorder (V.C.R.)
magnifique — magnificent
mai — May
maigre — thin, skinny
main — hand
maintenant — now
mais — but
maison — house
maître d'hôtel — headwaiter
malheureusement — unfortunately
manette — small lever, handle
manger — to eat
manquer de — to lack
manteau — coat
maquillage — make-up
marchand — shopkeeper
marcher (personne) — to walk (people)
marcher (machine) — to work (machines)
mardi — Tuesday
mari — husband
marié — married
marque — brand, mark
marron — brown
mars — March
massif — solid
matériel — hardware, equipment
matin — morning
matinée — morning
mauvais — bad
maximum — maximum
médecin — doctor
médicament — medicine
meilleur — better
mémoire — memory
menu — set meal
mer — sea
merci — thank you
mercredi — Wednesday
mère — mother
mesdames — ladies
mesdemoiselles — young ladies
message — message
messieurs — gentlemen
mesurer — to measure
métal — metal
mètre — metre
mètre carré — square metre
métro — metro, underground railway, subway
mettre — to put, to put on (clothes)
mettre (temps) — to take (time)
mettre en marche — to start (a machine)
mettre la radio — to turn on the radio
mettre le chauffage — to turn on the heating
mettre le contact — to start (a car)
mettre les essuie-glaces — to turn on the windscreen wipers
mettre un numéro en mémoire — to put a number into a (computer's) memory
meuble — piece of furniture
Mexicain — Mexican

micro — microphone
micro-ordinateur — micro-computer
midi — midday
mieux — better
millimètre — millimetre
mince — slim
mini-ordinateur — micro-computer
ministère — ministry
minuit — midnight
minute — minute
mobilier — furniture
mode — fashion
mode d'emploi — instructions
modèle — model
modèle réduit — scale model
moderne — modern
moderniser — to modernise
modifier — to modify, to change
moins — less
mois — month
monde — world
monnaie — change
monsieur — Mr., Sir, gentleman
monter — to go up, to get on
montrer — to show
monument — monument, historic building
mot — word
moteur — motor, engine
moutarde — mustard
musée — museum
musicien — musician
musique — music

naître — to be born
natation — swimming
nationalité — nationality
neige — snow
neiger — to snow
nettoyer — to clean
neuvième — ninth
Noël — Christmas
noir — black
noix — nut
nom — surname, name
nom de famille — surname, last name
nombreux — numerous
nord — north
notamment — notably
noter — to note, to write down
nouveau — new
novembre — November
nuageux — cloudy
nuit — night
nuit blanche — sleepless night
numéro — number
numéro de poste — extension number
numéroter — to number

obtenir — to get, to obtain
obtention — obtaining
occuper — to occupy
occuper (s') de — to take care of, to be in charge of
octobre — October
œil — eye
offre d'emploi — job offer
offrir — to give, to offer
olive — olive
omelette — omelet
on dirait... — it looks/feels/sounds/tastes like
opéra — opera
opérateur — operator
or — gold
orange — orange
orange pressée — fresh orange juice
orchestre — orchestra
ordinaire — ordinary
ordinateur — computer
organisateur — manager, organiser
organiser — to organise
oseille — sorrel
ou — or
où — where
oublier — to forget
ouest — west
oui — yes
ouvert — open
ouverture — opening, opening time
ouvrier — manual worker
ouvrir — to open
oval — oval

page — page
pain — bread
palais — palace
panne — breakdown
pantalon — trousers
papeterie — stationer's, station
papier — paper
papier à lettres — writing
papiers — papers
paquet — parcel
paquet-cadeau — gift-wrappe
par — by
par ailleurs — furthermore, e
parce que — because
parcmètre — parking metre
pardon — pardon
pare-brise — windscreen
parent — parent, relative
parfait — perfect
parfois — sometimes
parfum — perfume
parfumerie — perfume shop
parking — car park, parking
parler — to speak, to talk
partir — to leave
partout — everywhere
pas de panique — don't p
pas du tout — not at all
passeport — passport
passer — to spend, to walk
passer des vacances — to holiday, vacation
passer un appel — to transf
pastille — lozenge
patienter — to be patient
pâtisserie — cake shop
payant — not free
payer — to pay
pays — country, native region
paysage — countryside, londs
PDG (Président Directeur G — managing director, company p
pendant — during, while, for
pensée — thought
penser — to think
pension complète — full b
perdre — to lose
père — father
permettre — to allow, let, p
permis de conduire — dr cence
personnalité — personality
personne — a person, no one,
personnel — personnel, staff
peser — to weigh
petit — small
petit déjeuner — breakfast
peu — a bit, a little
phare — headlight
pharmaceutique — pharmac
pharmacie — pharmacy, che
pharmacien — pharmacist, c
photocopie — photocopy

:opier — to photocopy
:opieuse — photocopier
d'identité — passport (size)
ıph
ue — build, physical
— piano
— room
de théâtre — play
de monnaie — coin
– foot
— stone
— pedestrian
– worse
: — swimming pool
d — cupboard, closet
— space, room, seat
— beach
— to please
ıterie — joke
l'accès — street map
e à voile — wind surfboard
ue — plastic
(du jour) — dish (chef's
on)
ir — to rain
— pen, feather
– more
ırs — several
— rather
ux — rainy
— tyre
— pocket
n — fish
e — chest, bust
— pepper
— police
e — apple
e de terre — potato
à essence — petrol pump
er — fireman
ste — petrol, gas station
ıt
– bridge
— door, gate
euille — wallet
— to carry, to wear
e — door (car)
ler — to own, possess
— position, extension
(PTT) — post-office
— to post
: — powder
— chicken
ıoi — why
ıoi pas — why not
nt — however
er — to push, to grow
ir — to be able to
ıe — convenient, practical

pratiquer — to practise
précieux — precious
préférer — to prefer
premier — first
prendre — to take
prendre des vacances — to go on holiday, vacation
prendre rendez-vous — to make an appointment
prendre un jour de congé — to take a day off
prendre un verre — to have a drink
prénom — first name
préparation — preparation
préparer — to prepare
près de — near
présenter (se) — to introduce (oneself)
président directeur général (PDG) — managing director, company president
prêt — ready
prêt-à-porter — ready to wear
prier de — to ask
printemps — spring
prise — plug
privé — private
prix — price
probablement — probably
problème — problem
prochain — next
produit — product
professionnel — professional
profession — profession
profond — deep
programme — program
programmer — to program
projecteur — projector
projet — project, plan
promenade — walk
promener (se) — to go for a walk
proposition — proposal, offer
propre — clean
provençal — from Provence
province — provinces
public — public
publicité — advertising, publicity

Q

quai — platform, quay
qualité — quality
quand — *when*
quartier — district, neighbourhood
quatre étoiles — four stars
quatrième — fourth
quelle bonne surprise ! — what a nice surprise !
quelqu'un — someone, somebody
qu'est-ce que c'est ? — what is it ?
quitter — to leave

raccrocher — to hang up (phone)
race — race, breed
radio — radio
ralentir — to slow down
rapide — fast, quick
rapidement — fast, quickly
rappel — reminder
rappeler — to remind, to call back
rappeler (se) — to remember
rapporter — to bring back, to report
rasoir — razor
rater — to miss, to fail
rattraper — to catch up, to make up
ravi — delighted
ravissant — ravishing, beautiful
rayon — department
rayonnage — shelves
réception — reception
réceptionniste — receptionist
recevoir — to receive
recherche — research
recommander — to recommend
reconnaître — to recognize
rectangulaire — rectangular
reculer — to move back, to go backwards
réduit — reduced
réfléchir — to reflect, to think about
réfrigérateur — refrigerator
regarder — to look at
région — region, area
registre — register
réglable — adjustable
régler — to adjust, to pay
regretter — to miss, to regret
reine — queen
religieux — religious
remboursement — refund
rembourser — to refund
remercier — to thank
remonter — to go back up
remplir — to fill
rencontrer — to meet
rendez-vous — appointment, date
rendre — to give back
rendre (se) — to go to
rendre la monnaie — to give change
renseignement — information
renseigner — to give information

VOCABULARY

repartir — to leave again
repas — meal
répondre — to answer
réponse — answer
représentant — sales representative
représentation — performance
réservation — reservation, booking
réservé — reserved
réserver — to reserve, to book
réservoir — reservoir, tank, petrol, gas tank
responsable — responsible, department head
ressembler à — to look like, resemble
restaurant — restaurant
rester — to stay, to remain
retard — delay
retenir — to retain, to delay, to hold back
retirer — to withdraw
retour — return
retourner — to return
retrouver — to find again
réunion — meeting
revue — magazine
rez-de-chaussée — ground floor, first floor
rideau — curtain
rien — nothing
rire — to laugh
robe — dress
roi — king
rond — round
rose — pink, rose
rôti — roast
roue — wheel
roue de secours — spare wheel
rouge — red
rouge à lèvres — lipstick
rouler — to ride (car)
route — road, route
roux — red-haired
rue — street

sable — sand
sac — sack, bag
sachet — small bag
saignant — very rare (steak)
saison — season
salade — salad
sale — dirty
salle — room, hall
salle de bains — bathroom
salon — exhibition, lounge
samedi — Saturday
SAMU — emergency ambulance service
santé — health
savoir — to know
savon — soap
séance — session
sec — dry
second — second
seconde — a second
secrétaire — secretary
séduction — seduction
séjour — stay
sel — salt
semaine — week
sembler — to seem
s'en aller — to go away
Sénégal — Senegal
sénégalais — Senegalese
sentir — to smell, to feel
septembre — September
septième — seventh
série — series
sérieux — serious minded
service — department, section
service après-vente — after-sales service
service commercial — sales department
service des achats — purchasing department
service financier — finance department
servir — to serve
servir à — to be (used) for
session — session
seul — alone
seulement — only
si — if, yes
siège — seat
siège social — headquarters (of a company)
signaler — to point out, to inform
signer — to sign
s'il vous plaît — please
simple — simple, single, or one way, ticket
sirop — syrup
situation — situation
situer (se) — to be situated
sixième — sixth
ski — ski, skiing
société — company, firm
sœur — sister
soir — evening
soirée — evening
sole — sole
soleil — sun
solide — solid, sturdy
somme — sum, amount
sortie — exit
sortir — to go out
souhaiter — to wish
soulever — to lift, to bring
soumettre — to submit
souriant — cheerful
sous — under
sous-directeur — deputy dire
souvenir (se) — to remembe
souvent — often
spécialité — speciality
spectacle — show, performan
spectateur — viewer, spectat
sport — sport
stage — course, or on-the-job course
stagiaire — student, person course, trainee
stand — display stand
standard — switchboard, stan
standardiste — switchboard
station — station
stationnement — parking
sténodactylo — shorthand-typ
stylo — pen
succès — success
sucre — sugar
sud — south
Suisse — Switzerland
suisse — Swiss
suivre — to follow
superbe — superb
supérieure — superior
supermarché — supermarket
supplément — surcharge
supplémentaire — additional
supporter — to be able to stan put up with
supposer — to suppose
sur — on
sûr — sure
sur place — on the spot
surprise — surprise
sympathique — likeable, nice

table — table
taille — size
tant pis — too bad
taper à la machine — to
tard — late
tarif — price
tarte — tart, pie
taxe — tax
taxi — taxi
technique — technique, techr

ologie — technology
erie — dry cleaner's
te — phone card
nmunication — telecommunica-

one — telephone
oner — to telephone, to call
ion — television
— telex
— to telex
ent — so
rature — temperature
— time, weather
– to hold
— to be attached to, fond of
er — to finish
· head
tea
e — theatre
— ticket
de caisse — receipt
— stamp
— shy
- to pull
r — to fall
early
— button, key (keyboard)
er — to touch
rs — always, still
ne — tourism
r — to turn
sques (assurance) — comprehen-
er (insurance)
· all, the whole
fait — exactly
e suite — immediately
roit — straight ahead
– train
ille — quiet
rmer — to transform, to turn into
ettre — to pass on, to transmit
— work
ler — to work
leur — worker
ser — to cross
very
en — very good
e — triangle
me — third
er (se) — to make a mistake
l — tropical
— troupe
r — to find
r (se) — to be
r que — to find that
— truffle
- all taxes included
e dentifrice — a tube of toothpaste

uniquement — only
université — university
urgence — emergency
urgent — urgent
usine — factory
utiliser — to use

vacances — holidays, vacation
valoir — to be worth
variétés — variety show
veau — veal
véhicule — vehicle
veille — the eve, the day before
vélo — bicycle
vendeur — salesman
vendre — to sell
vendredi — Friday
venir — to come
vent — wind
vente — sale
verre — glass
vers — towards
verser des arrhes — to pay a deposit
vert — green
veste — jacket
vêtement — article of clothing
veuf — widower
viande — meat
viande à point — medium-cooked meat
viande bien cuite — well-cooked meat
viande bleue — extremely rare (blue) meat
viande saignante — very rare meat
violet — violet, purple
visiblement — visibly
visite — a visit
visiter — to visit
visiteur — visitor
vitesse — gear, speed
vitre — window, windowpane
vivre — to live
voici — here
voilà — there
voile — sail
voir — to see
voisin — neighbour
voiture — vehicle
vol — flight
volant — steering wheel
volet — cover, lid
volontiers — gladly
vouloir — to want
voyage — trip
voyage aller et retour — return, or round, trip
voyage organisé — package tour
voyager — to travel
voyageur — traveller
voyant — indicator light
vraiment — really
vue — view, vision

yeux — eyes
yoga — yoga

TABLE OF CONTENTS

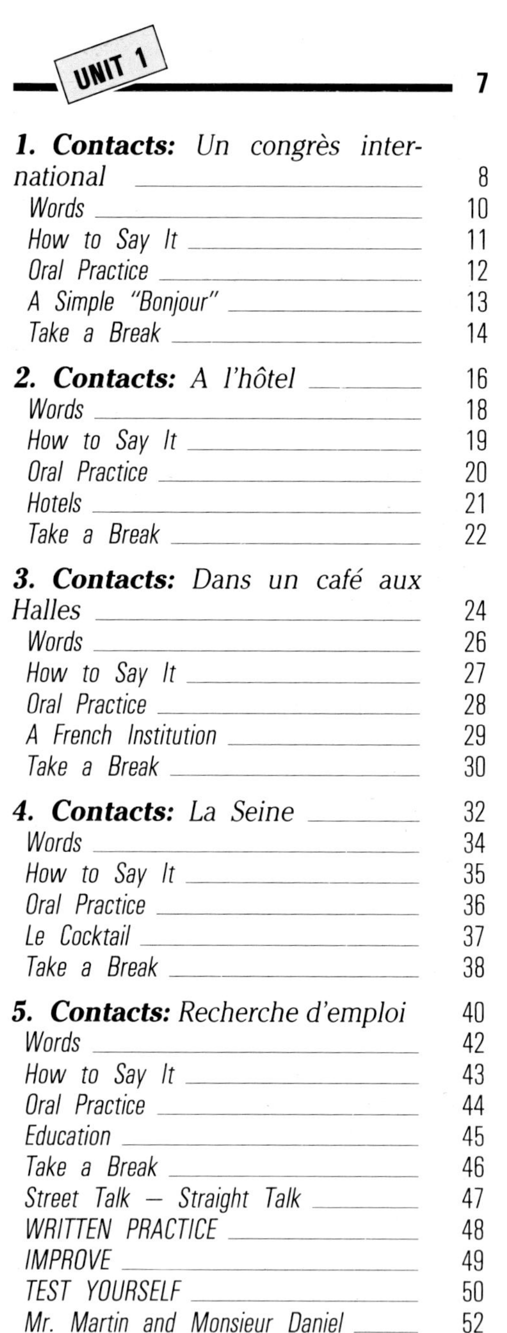

UNIT 1 — 7

UNIT 2

TABLE OF CONTENTS

SOURCES PHOTOGRAPHIQUES

p. 9 (1) : Explorer, Roux ; p. 9 (2) : Pix, Halary ; p. 17 (1) : Rapho, Halary ; p. 17 (2-3) : Lanceau ; p. 25 (1) : Rapho, d Sazo ; p. 25(2) : Rapho, Weiss ; p. 25 (3) : Rapho, Pupkewitz ; p. 25 (4) : Zefa, Damm ; p. 25 (5) : Explorer, Jalain ; p. 25 (6) Rapho, Clery ; p. 33 (1) : Explorer, Nacivet ; p. 33 (2) : Pix ; p. 40 (1) : Pix,Laubier ; p. 40 (2) : Pix, Cointe ; p. 40 (3) Zefa ; p. 40 (4) : Pix, Benazet ; p. 56 (1) : Pix, De Torquet ; p. 57 (2,4,5) : R.A.T.P. ; p. 57 (3) : Explorer, Clément ; p. 65(1) Pix, Dolmaire ; p. 65 (2) : Zefa, Bensent ; p. 65 (3) : Sygma, Rancinan ; p. 65 (4) : Zefa, Nicolas ; p. 73 (1) : Pix, D'Hérouville p. 73 (2) : Rapho, Rega : p. 73 (3) : Pix ; p. 73 (4) : Pix ; p. 73 (5) : Pix, Moes ; p. 81 (1) : Zefa ; p. 81 (2) : Pix, Torquat p. 81 (3) : Closerie des Lilas ; p. 88 (1-2) : Crazy Horse ; p. 89 (3) : Kairson ; p. 89 (4) : Lido ; p. 105b : Holger ; p. 113 (1) Peugeot ; p. 113 (2) : Pix, Meauxsoone ; p. 113 (3) : Pix, La Cigogne ; p. 113 (4) : Rapho, Charles ; p. 113 (5) : Ministèr des Transports ; p. 121(1-2) : Rapho, Clery ; p. 121 (3) : Gamma, Testelin ; p. 121 (4) : Pix ; p. 129 (1) : Pix, Chareton p. 129 (2) : AAA, Naud ; p. 129 (4) : Pix ; p. 129 (5) : Zelga, Halin ; p. 136 (2) : Explorer, Bohin ; p. 138 (3) : Pix, Torquat p. 137 (4) : Explorer, Duchemin ; p. 137 (5) : IC-PTT ; p. 153 (1) : Sopexa ; p. 153 (2) : Explorer, Jalain ; p. 153 (3) : Pix D'Hérouville ; p. 153 (5) : Explorer, Jalain ; p. 161 (1) : Pix, Schwartz ; p. 161 (2) : Pix, Benazet ; p. 161 (3) : Pix, Boeno p. 161 (4) : Pix, Benazet ; p. 161 (5) : Pix, Lancaster ; p. 169 (1) : Pix, Laubier ; p. 169 (2-3-4-6) : Lanceau ; p. 169 (5) Sipa-Presse, Pelletan ; p. 177 (1) : Pix, Chappe ; p. 177 (2) : Matra ; p. 184 (1) : Pix, Moes ; p. 184 (2) ; Scope, Sutres p. 185 (3) : Pix ; p. 185 (4) : Scope, Guillard ; p. 185 (5) : Pix ; p. 185 (6) : Scope, Guillard ; p. 185 (7) : Rapho, Tholy

PHOTO DE COUVERTURE : Jérôme BRÉSILLON. Recherche iconographique : Nicole LAGUILLER, Brigitte RICHO

N° d'éditeur CL 42849 I (P.F.C. VII) CI
imprimé en France. Mai 1987
par Mame Imprimeurs à Tours (n° 13229)